KEY
FREEDOM

A Psycho-Spiritual Approach
To Inner Child Healing

First published by O Books, 2008
O Books is an imprint of John Hunt Publishing Ltd., The Bothy, Deershot Lodge, Park Lane, Ropley,
Hants, SO24 0BE, UK
office1@o-books.net
www.o-books.net

Distribution in:	South Africa
	Alternative Books
UK and Europe	altbook@peterhyde.co.za
Orca Book Services	Tel: 021 555 4027 Fax: 021 447 1430
orders@orcabookservices.co.uk	
Tel: 01202 665432 Fax: 01202 666219	Text copyright Michelle Wolfe-Emery 2008
Int. code (44)	
	Design: Stuart Davies
USA and Canada	
NBN	ISBN: 978 1 84694 146 7
custserv@nbnbooks.com	
Tel: 1 800 462 6420 Fax: 1 800 338 4550	All rights reserved. Except for brief quotations
	in critical articles or reviews, no part of this
Australia and New Zealand	book may be reproduced in any manner without
Brumby Books	prior written permission from the publishers.
sales@brumbybooks.com.au	
Tel: 61 3 9761 5535 Fax: 61 3 9761 7095	The rights of Michelle Wolfe-Emery as author
	have been asserted in accordance with the
Far East (offices in Singapore, Thailand,	Copyright, Designs and Patents Act 1988.
Hong Kong, Taiwan)	
Pansing Distribution Pte Ltd	
kemal@pansing.com	A CIP catalogue record for this book is available
Tel: 65 6319 9939 Fax: 65 6462 5761	from the British Library.

Printed by Digital Book Print

KEYS TO FREEDOM

A Psycho-Spiritual Approach
To Inner Child Healing

Michelle Wolfe-Emery

BOOKS

Winchester, UK
Washington, USA

CONTENTS

Foreword   1

Acknowledgements   4

Introduction   6

Is this book for you?   10

Chapter 1
The perfect Childhood?   15
The real world   16
Denial   18
Rationalization   21
Repression   22
Natural forgetting   27
Erroneous Association   28
False memory syndrome   33
Therapy   37
Awakening   39
The right therapist   42
Your inner child   43
Connecting with your inner child (inner journey)   45

Chapter 2
The Womb   47
Connecting with your womb experience (inner journey)   50
Birth   51
Babyhood   54
Adoption   58
Sibling loss   60

Childhood:

   We are evolving   61

Adolescence   64

What's right?   68

Your childhood, how was it?   69

Chapter 3

Your mind is the source   73

A new perspective   75

Symptoms   79

Symptoms as messengers   81

Your treasure trove - The Unconscious Mind   84

Beliefs   88

Thoughts   91

What you can do now   92

The Ego   96

Victim consciousness   101

The 'better than' illusion   104

The people pleaser   106

The persecutor/controller   107

Why do we have an ego?   108

Our true self   110

We create it all - Judy's story   111

Chapter 4

How we create our reality   117

We co-create with spirit   120

Beliefs create experience   123

A scientific view   125

Our psychology: 126

Depression   126

Shop-a-holism   126

Jealousy   127

Alcohol and drug addiction   127

Food dependency 127
Illness 130
Stress/burnout 130
Anxiety/worry 130
Panic attacks 131
Loneliness/Intimacy problems 132
Homosexuality 132
Low confidence/Self esteem 134
Sexual problems 134
Self harm 135
Scarcity of love, money, friendships etc 135
Anger 136
Co-dependency 139
Co-dependency in dating 140

Chapter 5
Inner child healing 143
Working with your inner child (with inner journey) 147
Problems relating to your inner child 150
Overcoming blocks on your road to recovery: 153
The fear of facing the past and dealing with the
    emotions/thoughts therein 154
The fear of recovering from the past and becoming
    a healthier and happier person 156
Other blocks:
Victim Consciousness 158
Exercise to overcome an inner block (inner journey) 159
Letter writing 161
Letter writing to a parent/carer/teacher etc 165

Chapter 6
The Gold Counselling (TM) Technique 172
Constructing a map from your list: 177
Working with the map stage 1 182

Working with the map stage 2   184
Working with the map stage 3   185
Working with the map stage 4   187
Working with your list and map: 189
Working with your map stage 1   190
Working with your map stage 2   194
Working with your map stage 3   197
Working with your map stage 4   200

Chapter 7

Who is responsible for your childhood?   208
Self Blame   211
So Are you responsible for anything?   212
Confronting parents/carers   214
Arranging a meeting   217
The meeting itself   218
Writing a letter   222
Prepare for change   225
Other family members/friends and entrenchment   227
Dealing with elderly, sick, disabled, deceased parents 229
A happy future with your parents?   231
Forgiveness - Yes or No?   233
Giving up the need for revenge   235

Chapter 8

Grief   238
Loving yourself: 239
Hush your ego's negativity   240
Be kind to yourself   242
Forgive yourself   243
Take care of your body   246
Simplify your life   248
Have fun and nourish your soul   249
Take responsibility   250

Understand the messages	251
Give your problems to spirit	253
Follow your dreams	254
Appendixes I	
Directory of common physical ailments and their	
emotional link	257
Appendixes II	
Sexual Abuse	266
Further Reading	269
Resources	271

For Aisling

FOREWORD

In Michelle Wolfe-Emery's outstandingly riveting book, *Keys to Freedom: A Psycho-Spiritual Approach to Inner Child Healing*, you will be invited to respond to your personal wake-up call as a means of gaining enlightenment, inner wisdom and spiritual transformation on your voyage of self-growth.

Wide ranging in scope and backed up by sturdy research, *Keys to Freedom*, points out that our thoughts, feelings and motivations are driven by a sub-surface force. Your healing journey, thus, will entail opening up your awareness of the hidden depths of your soul but this will certainly be well worth the effort you expend. Throughout the book, you will be introduced, in an understandable and palatable form, to the ways in which your mind holds its secrets and then reveals them as a means of creating our own personal life-logic and everyday reality. Much has been written about the inner child but, in this work, the subject is dealt with more lucidly and comprehensively than elsewhere because of Michelle's depth of understanding and her supreme gift in conveying this message. If you are determined, therefore, and have reached the point of wishing to take the blindness from your eyes because "hiding the truth is no longer viable", then this book will be a must for you.

Keys to Freedom will undoubtedly help you to gain a wealth of knowledge and insight which you will be unlikely to discover in the normal course of events. Packed with real-live case-study material and numerous examples of her work, Michelle demystifies the psycho-babble by adopting an effortless, step-by-step approach which tells it like it is and leaves no area for uncertainty in your mind. Michelle's book, for instance, explains the purpose of tracing your experiences back to the womb, infancy, childhood, adolescence and formative years while, simultaneously, expelling those common myths and misconceptions about the role of therapy. Discover for yourself how current-day effects, symptoms and hardships can be viewed as useful mind-messengers which can point the way for you towards freedom from the myriad of symptoms and effects of emotional unease, physical malaise, life tragedy, relationship trauma and your own perceived lack of fortune. Decipher the way in which your mind can work to your detriment but can be untangled to your advantage by investigative therapy and self-aid. Learn how to deal effectively with those demons of denial, repression, resistance, rationalisation and justification which could prevent you from altering erroneous beliefs, negative thoughts and unhelpful yet repetitive patterns. For the non-faint-hearted, moreover, *Keys to Freedom* unashamedly exposes the truth about childhood abandonment, violence and abuse supported by startling statistics. Controversial issues, such as confronting others, the retrieval of damaged relationships, when possible, and self-forgiveness are also successfully discussed.

Michelle is a consummate expert in her field and you will find her book a veritable treasure-trove of wisdom and revelation and I would encourage you to take up this never-to-be-missed opportunity to learn about yourself. This book is more than just a cursory glimpse into the real, gold-backed worth of therapeutic investigation and self-help. In *Keys to Freedom*, Michelle explains the domain of her work as a psychotherapist, hypnotherapist and metaphysical philosopher and, through numerous invaluable and creative self-help assignments, you will be assisted to unleash the power of your inner mind which might have hitherto been hindering your personal level of contentment. We all have an inbuilt need to take responsibility for ourselves and for life's so-called misfortunes and disaster-areas. With *Keys to Freedom* in your pocket, you will no longer have to suffer the meaningless, surface-level aspects of life relieved only by illusionary indulgences and ineffective stop-gap measures. Learn now to create your own destiny, carve out a viable reality and exercise your personal power and choice about your own future.

Keys to Freedom is an essential read for all therapeutic practitioners and their clients both past, present and future. I am convinced that this work should become a best-seller and that the universe will benefit from Michelle's wisdom, insight and foresight. Look forward to your future with excitement and anticipation which with *Keys to Freedom* should guarantee you a fulfilling, self-caring, discerning and nourishing lifestyle.

Jacquelyne Morison
Author of *Analytical Hypnotherapy* and *The Truly Dynamic Therapist*
October 2007

ACKNOWLEDGMENTS

My acknowledgments go to all those who have believed in, and supported me through the writing of this book

John Hunt and all the staff at O Books publishers.

Kathy Hadley for her hours spent reading and editing of the manuscript, and her continued encouragement and support. Thank you Kath very very much!

Jacquelyne Morison for her years of friendship and her valued contribution to this book.

Julia McCutchen for her wise counsel and expertise in the field of publishing.

My friends and mentors over the years whose wisdom and teachings have allowed me to create this book, Georges and Lyn Philips, Terry Watts, Vera Peiffer and Susan Hill.

Past clients who helped with their individual case studies; Ginny, Paul, Stephanie, Alan, Rhia and Chris. And the amazing Butler family - my dear friends and colleagues Leah and Robert, and Louise, Rebecca and Rowenna.

All of my clients over the past 14 years you have taught me so much and your faith has allowed me to become the healer I always hoped to be.

Eternal gratitude to my unseen friends and guides, Orin and Daben. Tabrina, Zandra, Jed, Tula, Peter and my power animal Zor. And special loving thanks to my inner child little Michelle.

For all the inner children out there waiting to be heard

All the authors, therapists, teachers and lightworkers out there doing their fantastic work to help heal humanity and the planet. Your teachings, determination and incredible visions have been an inspiration to me.

And not forgetting my constant companions throughout the writing process, Bobby and Jenny.

'The time came when the
risk to remain tight in a
bud was more painful
than the risk it took to
blossom'
Anais Nin

INTRODUCTION

'For any speculation which does not at first look crazy,
there is no hope'
Freeman Dyson

May 1988....... Wake Up Call

No one had noticed the bruising on my forehead as I left the ward
that afternoon. I had deliberately hair sprayed my fringe in place
to hide the evidence of an encounter with my husband's fist the
day before. The rain poured down outside as I pushed the crash
helmet forcefully over my head, and started up my 49cc moped.
As I proceeded on my journey home against the harsh weather, I
wondered what awaited me in my house that day. I was taken
back to an afternoon in the week when I was gazing out of my
bedroom window in my very ordinary house, in my very ordinary
street. Some part of me longed to be free of this place, of this life.
Some part of me knew that life could be so much greater than
this........and a big part of me knew that I deserved that greatness.

As I opened the front door Dave, my then husband,
approached me holding a newspaper, at least he isn't drunk I
thought. His expression was fraught with worry, and his eyes
were tinged with guilt. As they always were when he had
completed his drinking binge cycle and abuse of me. "Look there's
something in here which I think you'll find interesting," he said,
avoiding the real issue. The advert read 'Hypnotherapy Training -
Study At Home!' The advert was talking about a self-study course
which involved various days in-college training, but no overnight
stay would be necessary.

For some time I had been telling Dave how I wanted to do
some further training or study in a different field. I had concluded
my nurse training some months before and was becoming bored.
Dave who was more worried that I might be becoming bored with
him took it upon himself to find something for me to 'do'. But my

thing to 'do' needed to be carefully controlled by him, and had to be confined to certain parameters which meant I wasn't out of the house for more than 12 hours at a time. It wasn't essentially Dave's fault that he was so insecure, that, coupled with his aggression, was the result of his mother's beatings. Although now as an adult it was certainly up to him to do something about his 'problems'.

Ironically though on this day standing in the hall way of my Surrey home Dave was in fact presenting me with my doorway to freedom, my ultimate escape from his stifling grip. I didn't know it then but I was on the verge of my own personal 'wake up' call.

In 1989 I completed the first level of the Hypnotherapy training. By 1990 I had left Dave and begun a new life. It was a precursor of the course to go into therapy yourself, as I did I began to unravel the darkness of my past and the reason for my subsequent low self worth, and problems accompanied. It was as if I had been hiding in a shell for a very long time, but my emergence was due. It was time for me to 'wake-up' and walk the path of greater understanding. As I did I found my inner strength, and being with men who abused, hurt and controlled me was now becoming a thing of the past.

2006 +

In recent years I have been amazed to discover how many people in the past 18 years and earlier have been receiving a similar 'wake-up' call. That is to heal themselves within and move up to a new level of consciousness. Whether this be as a result of personal tragedy, suffering, a decision to make changes, therapy or through spiritual teaching.

Not everyone is ready, but more and more of us are. And those who answer to the call of inner transformation help others to achieve it too. Its like a impetus begins and the 'collective consciousness' responds. Going into therapy or reading a book like this can signify the beginnings of transcendence from suffering. Many of those who experience loss, hardship, tragedy or pain are now using their experiences to 'grow' too. That is to see the reason for the situation and to use it as a pathway for overall healing.

We are now part of an expansive process which is shifting faster than it ever has, humans are facing an evolutionary leap. They are evolving into a wiser more aware species. We are expanding into a race which longs to shift from a 3rd dimensional perspective (to live in 3d is to live in a reality of struggle, drivenness, tiredness, guilt, anxiety, shame, self-pity, melodrama, numbness, loneliness, depression, obligation, burnout, frustration, lack of control, feeling trapped, hopelessness, concern with status, racialism, criticism, feeling undeserving, feeling unsafe and much more) To a 4th or 5th dimensional perspective, which is to exist in a reality of feeling happy and fulfilled, peaceful and harmonious, to love ourselves, to feel joy, play and relax, to be creative, feel energized, have clarity of higher purpose, solve problems with ease, find spiritual awareness, a balanced life, live our dreams, have reverence for nature and all living things. To radiate love and light.

It may be that you have been on a path of growth for a long time now, or maybe not. Whatever, everyone is going to have the opportunity to go even higher now. For a while it will seem, or even now may seem, as if you are living in two different realities. Some days you might feel lost in 3d feeling stressed, fearful, depressed or burdened. Other days may feel more like 4d as things go swimmingly and you feel joyous and energized. Or maybe you feel your on the humdrum treadmill of 3d days constantly! The 4d days are the natural state we are all attaining to now. The 3d days are just showing us what needs to be healed. Some 3d days may seem overwhelming and hopeless, as if we are never going to be free of our self made traps and problems. It's those days that this book is for.

Aspects of your life that are not working are really going to shout at you now. You can't just ignore your problems anymore. You are going to have stronger and stronger urges and messages to sort out what isn't working. Whether this be in relationships, work, health, money, where you live or how you feel about yourself. This has to be transformed. Because if it doesn't it will just become more uncomfortable.

So much of what is around us in our current lives is holding us in the past. You may live with a partner who represents your father, or use clutter as security, you may struggle with money to punish your parents, or never go for promotion because you feel you are worthless. You may put on weight to protect yourself from intimacy, or smoke 40 a day to destroy or punish yourself due to guilt. You may drive recklessly because of anger, or take drugs to cover your feelings. You may live a meaningless life because you feel undeserving, sabotage relationships because you are scared, manifest stress because you are resentful, or have a long term illness due to repressed grief. The list is a long one!

Whatever is not working for you, seems to be a problem or is a pattern which keeps reoccurring, is an issue from the past - from childhood. This book will show you how to address these issues now no matter how hopeless it may seem.

You have the ability and the power within you to change any aspect of your life and any aspect of you. As you make these changes from within your outer world will naturally change for the better. As you work through these issues which no longer serve you, you clear the path to be your true self. You will discover your unique reason for being on the earth and what you have come to do, whether it's to look after children, do voluntary work or run your own business. You have a contribution to make. You are needed. It's time now for you to prepare for this 'Golden Age' of higher consciousness, to join the millions of others hearing the call to grow.

Michelle Wolfe-Emery

'All that man can choose to change is consciousness,
but to change this is too change all'
Rodney Collin

IS THIS BOOK FOR YOU?

If you want to enhance your life, understand and solve the problems that are affecting it, this book is for you. Maybe (like many of us) you are putting the blame elsewhere; "But its my husband who makes me feel worthless," "Its my job that stresses me," "Its my kids who make me angry," "Its my metabolism that keeps me fat," "Its my illness (or lack of money) that holds me back" and so on. We live in a society where blaming someone or something else is second nature. But what if the source of all your problems come from within You. So instead of thinking "My husband makes me feel worthless," you could instead say, "Why am I with a man who creates feelings of worthlessness in me? What can I really learn from this situation? Where do these feelings originally come from?" Or, "Its the lack of money that keeps me miserable" could be rephrased as "Why am I always broke? Why do I feel undeserving of abundance? Am I gaining something by playing the victim?"

When you begin to question the underlying reasons for a situation or feelings, you find that everything is being created for a reason. Nothing happens to you by 'accident'. Everything that is happening to you now is meant to be happening to you Now. There are no exceptions to this even if you'd still like to protest "But it's him, it's her, it's that" etc. The bottom line is this; it really has nothing to do with what is going on 'out there' but everything to do with what is happening inside of you. Everything out there is merely a reflection of your inner world. The more undeserving you feel the more you will see this in your external circumstances. In a monetary sense poor people feel undeserving, rich people feel deserving - even if both examples are completely unaware of their beliefs.

Your life and those in it can show you the myriad of complex feelings, beliefs and attitudes you have about yourself and the world. When you are ready to explore this you begin to unravel your amazing complexity which has been shaped by your past. Its only by going back to the past that you find the tools within to re-invent yourself and your life.

This book is for those who desire to do this, who have a desire to change.

If you have a strong enough longing to work through your issues or be released from pain, then the keys to freedom you have been searching for are within your reach. When you decide to take responsibility for yourself you reclaim your power and hold these keys within your grasp, it is then up to you to open the necessary doors to take back your freedom. Freedom is your birthright, it is the birthright of everyone.

All symptoms and areas of your life which are not working usually have connections to infancy, and contained in these writings are exercises which will help you begin to make those connections, and work through what is troubling you or stopping you from reaching your potential. We will look at many aspects of childhood, from the relatively ordinary to the most abusive. If you come from an abusive background you may find it valuable to read other books in this area (see further reading). The subject of maltreatment and its long-term impact is relatively extensive, and would be too broad an area to cover comprehensively in these writings. Still even if your upbringing was difficult or traumatic there is plenty here to aid the healing process, whether you are new to inner change work or have been doing it for many years.

So IMAGINE a life free from 'addictions' like shopping, food, alcohol, smoking, work, drama, stress, sex, drugs, caffeine and more. Imagine feeling so much peace within, you don't need the 'buzz', 'high' or distraction.

IMAGINE letting go of struggle, fear, driven-ness, guilt, shame, depression, pain, illness, anger, fatigue, powerlessness, obstacles, feeling trapped, low self worth and much more........

IMAGINE feeling happy, fulfilled, positive, strong, focused, in control, relaxed, energized, abundant, loving (to yourself and others), free, healthy and well, safe, valuable, independent, blissful, and having time to do those things that bring you joy and make your heart sing.

Now these things are not reserved for the 'lucky', rich or famous (not assuming they have all these things of course) you are an unlimited being and everything mentioned above is waiting for you. It is how you are supposed to be living. Even if right now you feel undeserving or not good enough, or maybe you feel skeptical and believe it's not possible. That's ok, that's your ego talking - your limited self (more about your ego later). As Orin says 'All negative thoughts are an illusion. Higher positive thoughts speak the truth'.

As we grow as a nation, apart from reaching for a higher quality of life, we are being encouraged to administrate our own healing. That is to seek outside help if we need to, but in the long term become our own 'therapists'. Ultimately we are responsible for our own inner transformation.

When working through this text you may find looking at your childhood perplexing, confusing, upsetting, hopeless or easy to manage and liberating from the onset. Parts of you may resist the process and make excuses to not do the exercises or see the book through. If your past was abusive then naturally I would urge you to seek further assistance. Even if it wasn't, the task of unravelling the causes of your current problems may seem daunting. If so working with a therapist alongside reading this material would be of great benefit. We all need help sometimes; we can't always be strong or resilient. Especially when aspects of our past are creeping up and sending us into panic, turmoil or any other 3rd dimensional state. For this purpose please refer to chapter one which gives helpful hints on finding the right therapist.

In retrospect you'd be amazed at how much you can actually do for yourself. In society we are generally taught to listen to professionals and not trust in ourselves, unless we've had extensive training in counselling, healing and the like. Yet really the answers you seek are all within you. No one knows you or will ever know you like you do. Other sources can be of enormous help, but you are your greatest source. When you begin to walk the path of awakening it is also a great asset to learn to do it independently. So seeking therapy can be an essential requirement, but only in the short term. Your therapist will show you how to heal yourself and assist you in the process. Your therapist is your teacher and someone to learn from, but they cannot be there for you throughout your life or provide you with all the answers. When you are on the path of personal evolution you may meet many teachers and mentors, those who come into your life at the perfect time and show you the way. This though is a transient time. Your greatest teacher is you, and your greatest source for unlocking that magnificent part is through connecting with spirit and healing the past.

Included in these writings are plenty of factual case studies, although some names have been changed for privacy reasons. All the stories mentioned had a positive outcome as childhood issues were resolved, and the ensuing adults moved away from their difficulties. These illustrations reveal to us that self help and inner child healing can have remarkable and life changing effects. Also outlined are many individual problems like addiction, depression, panic attacks etc although covering them extensively is not possible. When we begin a journey of healing usually one book cannot cover it so I would strongly advise seeking out as much information as possible regarding your particular problems to gain the most benefit. So if your ready it is now time to begin this transformational process for yourself, please enjoy the adventure as you embark on Your journey to freedom.

'When survival is threatened by seemingly insurmountable problems, an individual human- or species-will die or become extinct or rise above the limitations of their condition through an evolutionary leap. This is the state of humanity now, and this is its challenge'
Eckhart Tolle. A New Earth

1

'A journey of a thousand miles must begin with one
single step'
Lao-tze Tao Te Ching

Why are you unhappy, stressed, out-of-sorts or confused? Any
problem you have probably has links to your childhood. We recreate patterns or past events in our adult lives because they need
to be healed. It takes a complex and amazing organism to do this,
we do it perfectly! So let's begin to fathom our stunning psyche,
as well as the limited parts of ourselves, those parts who want to
cloud our judgment, and put on a smiley face about the effects
our upbringing has had upon us.

The perfect childhood?

For any of us to have experienced a 'perfect' childhood it would
have to have gone pretty much like this:

We always had our own way. We had lots of friends and felt
liked. We had lots of love, attention and affection. We felt safe and
secure at all times. We felt liked/loved by our parents and other
caregivers, relatives and teachers. We did well at school. We were
good at lots of things. We had enough stimulation and learning
experiences, ones that made us happy. We were the center of our
parents' world, who stayed together and loved each other. We
had all our needs met on every level. We never felt sad, hurt,
angry, in pain, embarrassed, ashamed, frustrated or afraid. Now
if your saying, "Yes this is me!" then your the first, and pretty
much in denial I would imagine! And is this the perfect childhood
anyway? From an adult perspective we can see that this kind of
upbringing would in fact stunt a child's emotional growth and
ability to be in the world, yet from a child's perspective it is
perfect. This is what a child longs for every minute of everyday
(read the above again and you'll see what I mean). But no child

ever has this completely.

The real world

In the real world the concept of a perfect childhood is a myth. This is because in the real world we were raised by human beings. People with their beliefs and ideas about life (usually limiting), their problems and issues, their own emotions and upbringing influencing them. Whether this is within the family structure, with partners, with work, with money, with sex, with their own self image and so on it would have influenced us to a lesser or greater degree.

For example Laura came to see me after experiencing panic attacks when driving. She discovered repressed (forgotten) memories of her mother also panicking at the wheel. Laura never knew why her mum had reacted so fearfully when driving, however Laura did learn that driving was frightening and unsafe. She then brought these false beliefs into her own adult encounters with driving. All in all Laura did in fact have an ok childhood, and was upset when I suggested her phobia probably came from the past. Yet she was also equally surprised when we discovered it did come from there. Ruth had a relatively stable childhood but she often witnessed her father mulling and fretting over household bills. This lead to Ruth having money problems later as she learnt to believe 'there is never enough money' and 'there's always something to pay'. Roy talked of a 'great childhood' being brought up in India. With his parents being teachers his life was materially secure and his parents were apparently loving. He had many friends and enjoyed school life. As an adult though he had a disabling fear of public speaking. He 'coincidently' worked for a large corporate firm where presentations were given by the managers regularly. As Roy was a manager he had to face his fear many times, but the intensity of his nerves never lessened. Roy discovered that his fear came from an incident where he gave a talk to the whole school. As he was only 12 at the time the anxiety he experienced in the days leading up to the talk left a negative impression in his mind. When he was faced with the same situation years later his body responded with a dry mouth, shaking and sweating. His emotions responded with fear, trepidation and distress. His mind said, 'I can't do this, I'll get it wrong, I'm out of my depth'. This response mirrored his childhood reaction with spot on precision.

Now the reason I'm emphasizing these areas is because so many clients come to me saying they have a problem, but their childhood was fine. I see them wincing at the thought that mum or dad (or someone else) might be responsible for something. It is true to say some of us were fortunate enough to have had a good deal as a child, but whatever problems you are facing now could still be linked to that time. I tell people not to worry, if there's something upsetting that needs to be remembered that was inflicted by those who were meant to be caring for us -then that will come up. And in contrast if there's nothing 'terrible' to remember, nothing will come. Only the incident/s that happened and need to be recalled to be healed will be remembered.

So yes some childhoods can be fairly stable, but never perfect. No matter how 'sunny' it was we still leave home with blocks, limitations, negative beliefs, doubts, self-criticism, stuckness and false thoughts about the world, ourselves and how we should live. We have all been affected by our past. We have all experienced disappointment, sadness, hurt, fear, anger and loss. This is all part of the human experience, the challenge of being a child. These experiences in some senses can be good for us as they create empathy, determination, problem solving skills, self-control and other qualities that need to be developed if we are to function as an adult. Yet on the other hand they can be damaging, purely because as children we don't have the adult reasoning to work stuff out, and also because as children we feel emotions more passionately and with a greater intensity than adults.

Yet for the 10% of those who had a comparatively happy youth there is the other 90% whose circumstances were not so fortuitous. You may be well aware yourself that your past was difficult, traumatic, sad, lonely, or maybe even abusive. If you are conscious of this and are looking to change then great. You have now reached a point in your life were things are going to begin to shift, but first lets look at another area. Over the years I have observed many clients coming with some or multiple problems, and they had a 'blessed' childhood too. The only difference between these individuals and those whose infancy was well founded, was that their's wasn't. They still say, "But my past has nothing to do with this, everything was fine, my parents were great." Hundreds of people tell themselves this everyday, some of us wish to ignore the truth. We adopt denial, who then becomes a long term if not life long companion.

'All that I ask of you is to make room for the truth'
The Book of Miracles

Denial
Denial is a powerful defence mechanism, and it allows us to form a make believe reality about our past or minimize the impact it had upon us.

Steve was suffering from depression after his relationship ended. He was on the verge of suicide, and I could see was in a classic state of denial. In therapy he recalled his mother's mental health problems which lead to her admittance to hospital on numerous occasions. During these times he was either cared for by his father who was distant and difficult to approach, or other relatives. Steve often said, "I don't know why we're looking at this, my parents did their best, I can't see the connection." After some time Steve began to see his infancy from the perspective of his child self. It was then his long suppressed hurt and despair began to surface. Even though his mother was ill she also made Steve feel in the way, unwanted and a burden. From this 'awakening' Steve was finally able to comprehend why he felt compelled to please women, why he was so needy, and why he attracted rejection. Steve confronted his past and faced his denial, in doing so he broke free from a 'protective' shell. An encasement of denial which no longer served a purpose. He was then able to heal his past hurts and move on.

Steve now leads a fuller life, he has transformed into a self-confident and self-assured man. He doesn't need anyone to validate him or help him feel special, he is doing that for himself. Steve won't forget his past, but on yielding to the truth about his upbringing he began to disengage himself from it.

Many people in therapy say their past was fine, great, no problems. Then they discover this wasn't the case. At first this can be quite shattering. They've been telling themselves for years that it really was all ok, mum and dad were great, they wanted for nothing, all was fine. Then they realize, with a sudden sinking feeling, that it wasn't. Now it seems to me that things are shattered for a reason, worlds are crushed, lives are shaken and things can never be the same again. From this comes the process of rebuilding, of starting over, of re-birth. Instead of it being a terrible realization it is now the opportunity to grow. Once you break free of this cocoon you discover your true self, and that self has pure potential. It takes courage to break free from our self-made cocoons, because they allow us to feel safe. Yet they are also restrictive, false and stifling. This can show up in our lives as boredom, settling for less, fulfilling obligations, being someone we're not, pleasing others, frustration, hopelessness, depression etc. And then telling ourselves it's not that bad, we should be grateful, we expect too much or we're not deserving.

Denial develops in childhood. As children we are young, defenceless and helpless. Our parents are everything to us. They ensure our survival and provide food, housing, love, care and protection (that's what we expect anyway). We inherently know they could, if they chose to, abandon us. *This is our greatest fear.*

To avoid this terrifying concept we decide they do love us, are in control and are always right. So long as we believe this we feel safe, wanted and protected. Now it doesn't mean this isn't necessarily true, but sometimes things happen to make the child question the 'love us, in control and always right' beliefs, which is frightening. And if we think our parents are not doing their job properly we feel insecure, we fear for our own survival.

Children feel powerless in the world and parents are their shield. What then if our parents say we're no good, not wanted, less than or a failure? What if they hurt or abuse us? In this sense to keep the notion we are loved and therefore safe, we deny that the problem lies within our parents. We instead blame ourselves. We learn to believe *we* must try harder, are failing our parents or letting them down. Have you ever heard someone say, "Its a shame he's really letting his parents down" or "They expected better of him" or "His parents tried so hard why'd he have to go and hurt them like that." Often these comments are expressed when the child has matured and is suddenly not conforming to their parents or others expectations. The parents are seen as all knowing, always right and above the child. When someone drops out of college and seems to be 'wasting' his life, does anyone think this might be to do with the parents? No not usually! The child is generally blamed, everyone says "Tut tut letting the family down" etc etc, without even questioning the parents behavior. Well it was nothing to do with them, no of course not!

No wonder as adults we adopt denial, we're not supposed to speak ill of our parents. Instead we must 'respect' our parents and find fault with ourselves.

So denial is utilized for four reasons 1) We don't want to face what our parents are doing because this may imply they don't like or love us - which may lead to abandonment. 2) Society tends to naturally blame the child for 'bad' behavior, and the parents bear little responsibility. 3) It may turn out that we truly are not good enough, bad, worthless or a failure. 4) The memory is just too painful to acknowledge.

These reasons keep denial alive (by the way reason 3 is false), also that same denial keeps with us long into our adult years.

Now I'm not an advocate for ultimately blaming parents, but I do feel if they messed up they should be held accountable. This means to take responsibility for what they did, understand why they did it and grow from that. Everyone makes mistakes and parenting is challenging. When parents 'get it wrong' it is usually as a result of their own upbringing, beliefs and experiences - but this doesn't always make it ok. Also some parents can be blatantly cruel, abusive and neglectful knowing full well they are harming the child. And until recent years nothing that may be damaging to the child was ever questioned, or even thought to have a consequence.

Denial says, "I am wrong, you are right (parents), I will sabotage my life, live with my panic attacks, keep taking pills, stay with the wrong man, never succeed, maintain my eating disorder, have sleepless nights -so you (my parents) can always feel okay and not get upset." Do you really want to go on ruining your life or not reaching for more to protect your parents, or whoever it was that hurt you? Do you really want to keep wearing those rose tinted specs? Is it honestly worth it? Nothing awful is going to happen to Ma or Pa, or that horrible teacher if you face the past. Equally nothing is going to change for you, or get better, if you don't. In the words of Sufi Aphorism, "When the heart weeps for what it has lost, the spirit weeps for what it has found."

Rationalization

Rationalization is another form of denial, but instead of pretending our past was rosy, we make excuses for other people's behavior or diminish the impact it had upon us. What follows are some common rationalizations.

"My dad had to work all hours 'cos we were poor, I know we

never saw him but we did ok. What else could he do?"

"Sure we used to get smacked a lot but it never did me any harm"

"My mum drank because she was unhappy, it wasn't her fault she couldn't take care of us"

"My uncle sexually abused me because I let him. I was stupid and weak it was my own fault"

"My mother only screamed at us because she felt trapped and frustrated. We should have behaved better"

"My dad only left and never saw us because my mum always picked a fight with him, he moved far away I don't blame him"

"Yeh my parents would criticize me a lot, but it made me try harder"

Sandra was in her mid thirties and had consistently experienced volatile relationships with her boyfriends. She would often fly into a rage if they looked at or talked to other women. As a child Sandra's mother would cry on her shoulder whilst her father was out with other women. Sandra would rationalize this by saying, "Well I couldn't blame him really my mother was like a mouse and never took care of herself. He had no respect for her." But Sandra was soon to learn that her insecurities, hurt and anger had been suppressed in relation to her father's behavior. These feelings were now being expressed toward the men in her life as violence and fear.

'There is no coming to consciousness without pain'
CG Jung

Repression

With denial and rationalization we choose to put a different face on our childhood, or tell ourselves it wasn't so bad. With repression we completely blank out, that is to forget, incidences or whole areas of our childhood. We push these events into our unconscious mind and have absolutely no recollection of them.

This is because the incident or period in the child's life at that time was too traumatic to bear, cope with or live with.

Amanda was a 32-year-old nurse who had a fear of buttons. She would laugh about the fear as it seemed so absurd. She was ok with buttons until she was up close to them on clothing; this then incited feelings of fear and panic in Amanda. When I saw Amanda she had also been suffering with bouts of depression and a lack of interest in sex. After some searching under hypnosis Amanda recalled that her button fear was in fact related to sexual abuse. Amanda previously had no recollection of the abuse, but painfully described to me how her father would get her to seductively strip and then undress him. This often meant undoing buttons on her own clothing and then on his, all the time experiencing distress, guilt and fear. As we worked through other related repressed memories Amanda's button fear began to diminish. As did her depression and sexual problems.

Harry had a fear of flying. We discovered though it wasn't flying he was ultimately afraid of, it was being trapped, "Especially in warm suffocating places," he said. To heal this claustrophobic problem Harry needed to relive a repressed memory. As he did his face turned red and he felt he couldn't breath, terror pulsated through his body as he began to recall his nanny holding him down with a pillow over his face, he writhed about in the chair just as he had at that time in his cot. Harry was only six weeks old when his nanny deliberately held the pillow over his face to stop him crying.

Lucy came to see me with a fear of frogs. Unfortunately for Lucy she had an abundance of frogs in her garden (this often happens with fears as we attract what we are afraid of). Lucy's mother also had a fear of frogs, and her brother would delight in bringing home frogs to make his mother scream. Lucy witnessed her mother become a terror-stricken nervous wreck at the sight of these frogs. Sadly this proved to be traumatizing for Lucy who repressed the memories and later developed her own phobia.

The number one killer in the world today is not cancer or heart disease, it is repression'
Dr A Janov

Repressed memories always present us with symptoms later in life. Cause and effect. These symptoms have clues to their origins. Some easier to work out than others. Symptoms can show up as fears, feelings, experiences, behaviors, attitudes, reactions, circumstances, illness, physical problems, beliefs and thoughts. They are evident in anything that feels uncomfortable or not right in your life. They are expressed in anger, jealousy, hurt, sadness, guilt, numbness, fear, pain or feelings of inadequacy. Like John who would fly in to a raging temper just as his father had when under stress. Or Andrea who experienced a mental block when doing math's in her head - just as she had as a child when the math's teacher would shout at, and humiliate the children. Both John and Andrea repressed these past upsets.

Sometimes events can be remembered but emotions repressed. Some clients may say, "Yes I think I know where this comes from, but for some reason that incident didn't effect me as much as it would have someone else. I don't remember getting very emotional at all." Only on visiting that past event again and reliving it as a child, can they begin to remember just how painful the episode was. Like repression this happens because the event would have caused too many disturbing feelings for the child to cope with at the time. So the feelings are repressed, and the carers in that situation may remark at just how well the child coped. Not realizing that the numbing of feelings in children is a natural defense mechanism.

Often repressed memories will begin to surface when we are facing a life crisis. The reason for this is two-fold. Firstly it takes a considerable amount of energy to keep memories repressed (this being a very common cause of lethargy). If we are going through a bad patch our energy has to be temporarily diverted, allowing memories to surface. Secondly the current trauma or crisis probably has a direct link to the memory surfacing.

It is quite common for repressed memories to begin to materialize when we begin self help or therapy and when we are focusing on a completely different issue. So we may be looking at our nail biting problem, and stumble upon the day our granddad died. Which may not be related to us nibbling our nails at all. So often I find the unconscious will 'lead' us into therapy or self-help on the pretence that we are working on something else. This is because it knows we have other troubles that need attention, and it will as if by magic lead you to the right person or help to recall these.

It is possible to repress memories when we are adults, but far less likely. It would take one heck of an incident to cause this, however it does happen. Have you ever been involved in an accident, say a car accident, and have no recollection of what happened? Individuals who have been the victims of crime often can't remember what the perpetrator looked like, or forget much of what happened. These are all forms of repression, if the event is traumatic enough we use repression as a way to cope. Mothers who experience agonizing and drawn out labours often remark on suffering from post amnesia. That is they 'forget' the pain and the long hours in labour. This kind of oblivion though is more likely to be a trick of nature - if we lose sight of how painful it was we are far more likely to do it again!

A good example of repression in adulthood is that of helicopter pilot Hugh Thompson in Vietnam. On March 16th 1968 he was flying his helicopter around a town called Pinkville. He was helping wounded civilians shot down, or injured by American soldiers. Everywhere he looked though he saw bodies, bodies of dead children, men, women and the elderly. He became desperate in his need to help and finally found a wounded child amongst many bodies in a ditch. The child was the same age as his own son, who they flew to a local hospital. Naturally the whole incident was very traumatic for Hugh Thompson.

Two years later when interviewed by army investigators, it was discovered he had forgotten everything. He knew he had been in Vietnam that day, and although his heroic actions were documented in the army's report, any details of the My Lai Massacre had been completely repressed, he could not recall a thing.

Post Traumatic Stress Syndrome is now a widely accepted condition, and also recognizes that adult repression is utilized as a way of coping. This, along with recalled events, result in symptoms such as nightmares, sleeplessness, weight loss, stress, anxiety, depression and much more. The truth is the post traumatic stress is not the only issue which requires healing here. If we ask the question why these individuals 'created' this trauma in their adult experience, we would need to go back further into their childhood aswell to find the answers.

So if adults repress incidences that are harrowing enough, it has to be acknowledged that children do too. Also upsetting or painful experiences are more intensely felt when we are children. This means that something as common as parents divorcing or a one off incident of humiliation can be repressed just as easily as abuse can be.

Not all memories are repressed, and some individuals remember past abuse or trauma. Some recall parts and forget parts. In a National survey it was revealed that 20% of severe trauma survivors forget the whole experience, and a further 20% forget certain details. Repression doesn't only occur when the incident is traumatic, but painful enough for the child to want to forget it. Like a client of mine who had an allergic reaction to a bee sting. The incident resulted in a small amount of treatment in hospital and wasn't considered serious. Still as an adult the girl concerned developed a fear of injections as she completely repressed the whole bee sting episode. To someone else this may have been a relatively insignificant event. We are all different and what may disturb one person may seem insignificant to another.

Also repressed memories do not always have to surface in therapy, as a rule many of them don't. These memories can begin to transpire gradually or more suddenly through triggers. These triggers may take the form of news stories, conversations, similar events happening again, relationships, certain smells or places, during sex, when seeing someone from the past, hearing stories of trauma survivors or stories similar to your repressed material, in dreams, tragedies, around children, on a birthday, a certain name, when in pain or when ill, when stressed or overwhelmed. There are thousands of examples, yet these memories will only be triggered when it is the right time to remember. So you may have been fine with dogs before but suddenly one growls at you and a phobia erupts, you slowly recollect being afraid of dogs as a child. Then you have glimpses or flashes of being attacked by a dog. It is time to remember.

This is why I believe when working with a book like this reading all the chapters is essential. It is often tempting to skip some areas because you assume they don't relate to you, yet it may well relate and only needs a little nudging or 'reminding' to bring something light.

Natural forgetting

It is of course natural for us to 'forget' some of our childhood, especially the very early years, and this must not be confused with repression or denial. Childhood lasts a long time and we will not retain everything that went on. Many memories will naturally fade as the day-to-day things we did as a child drift deep into our unconscious filing cabinets. This is natural forgetting. Denial and repression are always linked to experiences that are too painful for the child to feel or know about. They are applied when a child is powerless to change a situation or deal with it. Repression forces the memory into the unconscious, and denial allows the child and then adult to minimize the effects of situations. This does not mean the child always denies their plight. They may be well aware their mother gives a sibling more attention than them, or that their father is strewn out drunk again on the sofa. In this case the denial may be adopted later as the adult tries to cover up the pain of his past.

Repression can occur as early as being in the womb to as late as adolescence, and in some cases later. Denial can occur as soon as the child is aware something is wrong and maintains itself throughout the rest of that person's life. Natural forgetting is a part of life, and will include happy, sad and neutral experiences. It begins from the womb and can get worse as we get older (but only to those who believe it!).

> 'The real voyage of discovery consists not in seeking
> new landscapes but in having new eyes'
> Marcel Proust

Erroneous Association

Erroneous association is a common 'red herring' when seeking the true cause of a problem. Many people may say, "Yes I know where this comes from, its obvious. I have a fear of birds because when I fed them in Trafalgar Square, London, they flew at me, and I was frightened." Or some may know what happened to trigger the problem and put it down to that, but are still confused. Often we will recall when a phobia or problem started in our life, but this isn't usually the initial cause. So many of us would 'like' the problem to be from that time in adulthood, but the truth is it came from childhood. Erroneous (meaning incorrect) association is also a form of denial, which allows us to avoid painful truths or upsetting past occurrences. It stops us from exploring the problem further. If you think your phobias, fears, triggers, depression or hang ups come from a time in your adult life, then it's time to think again.

Paula had a fear of trains. She didn't like stations or anything associated with trains. She said, "When I was eighteen I traveled home late one night. There was a man sitting near me who made me feel uncomfortable. He kept staring and smiling at me. As I got off at my stop he got off too. The platform was very quiet, as I walked down the stairway he grabbed me. I was very frightened but managed to struggle free. I ran out to the street where people were walking. As I looked back he was nowhere in sight. Its because of this time I now have a fear of trains." It understandable that Paula would have associated this time with her train fear, especially as the phobia began after this incident, and we will get back to Paula shortly. In the meantime there are some crucial points you must understand if you are to get to the root of our problems and they are:

1. Our symptoms come from childhood
2. As we become adults things will 'happen' to begin the emergence of past repressed/denied feelings. Our minds and bodies want us to remember what we need to know in order to heal, to do this it will recreate events in our adulthood to mirror past problems, traumas or upsets from childhood.
3. It takes an awful lot of emotion or continued conditioned thinking (in childhood not adulthood) to create problems for us as adults. For example, a fear of enclosed spaces would be the result of something very frightening happening to us when little to result in a phobia later. Or being told we are worthless constantly would condition us to believe it. Very little in our adult life would create enough emotion or have a marked effect for it to become a neurosis.

So it may seem that your husband neglecting you, or you getting trapped in a lift for two hours is the cause of your problems. This though is erroneous. They are just circumstances created to tell us something deeper, and further back in the past needs to be resolved.

I had a friend whose husband's constant flirting and straying triggered jealousy and insecurity in her, so much so it became pathological. After leaving him her other relationships were dogged with jealous outbursts and fear of abandonment on her part. She constantly blamed her first husband for her problems, but on exploring her childhood we discovered that her father was also a constant flirt, had affairs, paid attention to other children and not her, and eventually walked out of her life. That time for her as a child was devastating. Remarkably life had attracted to her a man who would bring out these long repressed feelings, someone who personified her father. This was all amazingly designed, as it is for everyone, by some greater intelligence to help my friend heal her past.

Getting back to Paula, her fear of trains came from a time when she witnessed someone jumping on the track and getting killed. She was only eight at this time. Paula had no recollection of this incident until she came into therapy. She was also molested by an uncle when she was ten. The man who followed her at the station, and then attacked her brought on those past feelings her uncle created in her, fear and powerlessness. The incident at the train station when Paula was eighteen had served to 'remind' her of two very disturbing times from her past. This is often the case when 'bad' things happen to us as adults, it can usually relate to more than one repressed or denied memory.

In hindsight though erroneous memories can be potentially helpful when actioning detective work on the riddles of your afflictions. Like Harry who developed a fear of flying due to an asphyxiation trauma as a baby, recalling the erroneous memory allowed us to eventually find the cause. If you have an issue or problem where you believe you know the cause comes from (or think you know) explore that memory. Especially write down all the feelings and thoughts that come up from that time. Plus any triggers that create those feelings and thoughts. For example, if you suffered from agoraphobia and feared leaving your house you'd note down the feelings of maybe panic, trepidation, like something bad is going to happen. You feel you may even die. You may remember the agoraphobia starting when you had your first child. In this scenario you may need to explore further your experiences and beliefs about childbirth, maybe it was a difficult birth and unconsciously reminded you of your own painful entrance into the world. On exploring further you actually nearly died when being born, and the feelings of panic and terror you felt as a newborn coincidently reflect perfectly how you feel now when leaving the house. So what's happened here is this; the difficult birthing of your first child triggered agoraphobia but you don't know why (erroneous association but a great clue). Your own near death experience as a baby created fears of being born or leaving the comfort of the womb. Your house as an adult depicts the womb. These past fears, now at the surface, mean you're afraid to leave your house because you actually believe you might die. The act of stepping out the front door is like re-enacting your own birth, and leaving the womb. No wonder you're scared!

Let me give you a simpler example. Craig has a fear of going to the dentist. Not only is he afraid but as soon as those silver contraptions enter his mouth he is heaving. Craig has a clear memory of going to the dentist as a teenager, the tooth extraction was particularly painful and the blood and bits and pieces from his broken tooth made him gag until he almost vomited. Since this time Craig has had a phobia. He describes his feelings of going to the dentist as this, "Terror, choking, can't breath, panic, confusion, nausea, distress." The past dental memory is erroneous, all it did was trigger repressed feelings associated to a memory that Craig's mind wants him to remember. The evidence is in his above listed feelings. When we took 'Terror, choking, can't breath, panic, confusion, nausea and distress' back to its original cause Craig said this;

"I'm sitting at the dinner table, my mum and dad and sister are there. We are all eating. The sun is streaming through the window and I'm chatting about my triumphant football game. I excitedly describe how I put the ball into the net when......oh hold on.....I can't breath (holding his neck and starts coughing), I'm getting up, help, panic.....please help me....mum help me...... I can't breath........I'm choking...there's something stuck....oh God I'm so frightened........it really hurts.........I fall down......feeling confused.....I hear my mum shouting...someone's grabbed me their banging my back....I still can't breath....terror oh God please help me. I want to run about but I'm over a chair now.....their thumping my back.....I feel sick, think I'm going to be sick... (suddenly breathes very quickly).......its come out.......its come out I'm breathing again. I'm crying my mums holding me. I'm so relieved...crying."

Craig choked on a very hard pea at the age of ten. The tooth pieces that kept getting lodged in his throat during his tooth extraction triggered this repressed memory at a feeling level, but not a memory level. So each time Craig visited the dentist his fear was relived. I'm happy to say Craig completely recovered from his experience within minutes and a week later rang to tell me he went to the dentist for the first time in years. All his negative symptoms completely disappeared, he was over the moon.

Just to say when repressed memories are recalled they don't have to be as dramatic as Craig's experience. Many people recall events with much less intensity because not all memories have to be so harrowing to cause problems later. But if you were to relive a near death experience then go with it. Nothing awful is going to happen, in fact something fantastic will probably arise from it. That is freedom from your symptom. So be assured you didn't die then, so its not going to happen now!

In relation to the above examples there could be a thousand other reasons why we fear the dentist or open spaces. The mind is complex and intriguing. We may have the same symptoms as our friend but the causes of those symptoms will be altogether different, because we are unique. Our experiences, perception, ways of thinking and background are like no one else's. Who we are and where we come from is inimitable to anyone else. Even if it appears we have ended up in the same place.

Sadly in the modern world we are generally oblivious or do not question the effects our childhood may have had upon us. We seek easy answers like, "Oh its the kid's" or "Its just me" to short term comforts like shopping or alcohol to cope. We are told, "Not to open that can of worms" or 'What good can it bring to think about that again." Yet 'opening that can of worms' and 'thinking about that again' is imperative if we are to resolve our past, and find inner peace. Our formative years, without question, influence our waking minutes in the grown-up world. Which is why so many of us struggle to live healthily and happily as adults for any length of time.

> 'The ordinary response to atrocities is to banish them from consciousness'
> Judith Herman M.D

False Memory Syndrome

False memory syndrome has become a widespread fear in recent years and false memories can occur, but only under certain circumstances. If a therapist was to suggest to you they believed the cause of your problems resulted from abuse before you had discovered this for yourself, or said they thought the culprit might be Uncle Fred this could result in the creation of false memories. Sadly, but very rarely (and often without intention) some therapists do this. When most people visit a therapist, the therapist can become a parent-like or all knowing figure, so how can they be wrong? If you take on their diagnosis, it is then possible to weave a tapestry of make believe happenings. Or you may just say, "Sorry that doesn't feel right" and never return.

There are many excellent therapists about who realize the pitfalls to this risky and short cut approach, and will gently guide you to discover the truth for yourself - without suggestion or second guessing. The problem is these aware therapists can sometimes be accused of helping their clients concoct false memories.

In all my years as a psychotherapist I have helped countless clients recover memories of trauma or abuse. They were completely unaware of these memories, but when retrieved they began to get well. That is over time their relationships changed or improved, they began to like themselves, irrational fears dissolved, their perception, attitudes and beliefs altered for the better. On the whole their lives progressed, usually dramatically. They also remarked on how things began to 'fit' into place like, "Now I know why he gives me the creeps" or "That explains why I'm so angry with my mum" or "No wonder I have anxiety problems." Its like a giant piece of an elusive puzzle has been missing for many years, and once that piece is recovered and put in place, the whole picture can then be viewed. And that picture reveals the reasons behind the current state of that person's mind and life. It literally is like a big "Aha!" then everything falls into place. None of my clients have ever said to me "I don't think that's true." They may say at first, "God did that really happen?" and then on reflection they intuitively sense a change within themselves. It seems the only people who are saying these memories are false are the perpetrators of the crime, or guilty parents who didn't protect the child at the time.

Many individuals who confront their parents or the perpetrator are met with denial or disbelief. Some may use guilt by saying, "We did so much for you, sacrificed everything and you chuck this in our face." Some may become angry or blame the injured party for what happened. Some may be sorry or remorseful. Others may go into victim mode by having a panic attack or becoming ill, then ensuring others make you feel bad for it. Then some might say the memories are false, and equally convince the victim of the same because they said so "I should know I'm your mother, this could never have happened without my knowledge" or "Your imagining it sweetheart I would never do anything like that to you, not your Dad I love you." These remarks can cause a blow to the individual's sense of truth, and is a way to ensure the parent doesn't have to feel ashamed, inadequate or take responsibility.

Clara recovered memories of physical abuse. She had chosen to 'forget' her father's regular beatings after her mother died. It only went on for a short period, but Clara could not accept what her father was doing and so repressed it. As an adult Clara had a poor self-image, blamed herself for almost everything, and attracted relationships that were volatile. When she uncovered these past episodes of abuse she was in shock. She was still living with her dad at the time, and after a drunken night out on the town with her friends she confronted him. He denied the attacks, said she was dreaming and told her to stop the therapy. But she didn't. During the recollection of similar assaults Clara cried in anguish became angry and felt utterly broken, but it was also at this stage she began to repair. As she worked through the pain of losing her mum and then having to deal with her father's violence, her life began to change. She felt more peaceful and in control. She moved out of her father's house and her self-confidence grew. Two years later she met a man who provided her with a loving relationship, something she hadn't experienced as an adult before. She wrote to me and said, "My father still insists he didn't take his grief out on me, but I know he did. I don't really see him now because he brings me down. I mean how could it not be true? Ever since I remembered that time my life has improved beyond recognition, and so have I. The harm he inflicted on me did instil feelings of worthlessness and attracted violent men. The more I think about it the more true it seems. It just makes complete sense." So many clients say the same thing to me.

I have personally only heard of one case where the memories recovered were initially considered 'false'. My colleague in Exeter, UK saw a client who recalled a terrifying memory which involved witnessing a murder and multiple rape. As the sessions proceeded though her client began to unravel fact from fiction. She began to recall sexual abuse by a close relative. She realised her initial memory was an exaggeration of this. The 'murder' was the feeling that her own inner child was being killed, and the 'multiple rape' represented the years of abuse she endured. Now if after the first session (where she recalled the murder and rape) she went to explore the likelyhood of the happenings she may well have found out there was no murder in her village, and her friends had not been raped. She would have then concluded the memory must be false. But because she continued the therapy she was able to understand that the memory was not 'false' exactly but grossly exaggerated. Her unconscious was so full of trauma it divulged everything at once, and it poured it out as a nightmare recollection. There is of course no smoke without fire and with the professional help of my perceptive colleague together they worked out what the 'false' memory was trying to tell them.

I recently read in the paper a case where the NHS were being sued. It seems a women in the inpatient psychiatric unit had recovered memories of abuse which involved her father, a paodophile ring and the killing of a child. Now in this case it was concluded the memories were false because the lady in question was on presribed drugs, and of course naturally drugs which are mind-altering could certainly account for false memories. Now I may be putting myself out on a limb here but I would still say there is no smoke without fire, and any traumatic memory recovered has some truth to reveal.

We are coming into a time in human civilization where hiding the truth is no longer viable. This is because to heal the conflicts within us and then that of the world, we need to face our own truth. Generations before us have learnt to suffer in silence, because it was disrespectful to question our upbringing, or 'weak' to admit to our limitations. We are changing though, and the adults and children of today either are or will see the benefit of self-analysis and freedom from denial. In opening up and healing old emotional wounds we clear our bodies of pain, illness and heartache. Learning from and letting go of the past is not the easy option, in fact it is the most challenging, but it also brings the greatest rewards. Because it brings growth, joy, purpose and freedom, something we are all striving to find.

'A life which is unexamined is not worth living'
Plato

Therapy

Even today in our society seeking therapy or other help can be a sign of instability or weakness. Yet in reality it is a sign of strength. Facing your ghosts or inner turmoil takes courage, those who avoid therapy or avoid dealing with the real issues are the ones who are scared. At times looking inward is painful, disillusioning and frightening. Its like slaying a dragon, when you've killed the first one you become stronger and more courageous, you have the initial tantalizing glimpses of self control and power. You are then ready for the next. During the battle the dust may become unsettled, you may get tired and doubt your abilities. You may have to put all your strength into it whilst dodging flames, and being thrown about. As well as this you may have 'concerned' others attempting to pull you from the battle field, or telling you to give up. Yet if you don't rid yourself of this dragon it will end up chasing you about for the rest of your life.

Of course therapy doesn't have to be this dramatic, but any self scrutiny brings its own test. What you have to ask yourself is whether you want happiness, truth and liberation enough - to accept the challenges ahead.

These days there are therapists and therapies to suit just about everyone. To work through your childhood or current day issues psychotherapy with hypnotherapy is one of the most effective forms of discovering causes and creating an everlasting release. Hypnotherapy itself is a wonderful tool which allows you to relax and access childhood memories, and is especially effective with repressed memories. This happens because when under hypnosis or in a relaxed state you can bypass your conscious mind. This part deals with all your day to day thinking, decision making and rational thought. It needs to be bypassed to access your unconscious mind, so if it is encouraged to relax this is then achievable. The unconscious mind has within it stored every memory, every feeling, every event, every thought, in short everything that has ever happened to you. Yes it is the most amazing computer on earth, and it's right there in your head!

Many people fear hypnosis because of the media distortions it has had to endure. Like it renders you unconscious so you have no control, or it can reveal all your secrets, or worse still it can turn you into a different person and your past identity is wiped out! All of these are old age myths kept alive by the seemingly all powerful stage hypnotist of today. Anyone though who experiences hypnosis is aware of what is going on, unless it is suggested to them they will experience some amnesia after the event. If so this is short lived. With a stage show the hypnotist will sift through his audience to discover the more relaxed and fun individuals, or the more suggestible. Together with alcohol and the relaxation hypnosis brings the subjects become much less inhibited. With self-conscious feelings eliminated running around like a chicken or doing a pretend strip is just all part of the fun!

Hypnosis is really a form of deep relaxation with no swinging watches to bring it on (not in recent years anyway). Your body feels relaxed and your mind becomes focused inward. You do not lose conscious control as you are aware of everything you are saying, and remember all that's been said after the session. When using hypnosis or relaxation (I say relaxation because they are one and the same only varying in intensity and depth) alongside thinking about childhood memories an energy or void is created which allows significant memories to surface and be released. It is often possible and beneficial to think about thoughts or feelings from present day issues to trigger memories to the surface. When these recollections are felt and talked through the healing that takes place can be profound. This healing can be so extensive that whole areas of life can begin to shift because our attitude and feelings toward them have changed. Fears can be eradicated, beliefs updated, relationships harmonized, illness remedied, problems resolved and negative thoughts dissolved. You can find greater inner peace, release from limitations and obstacles, as well as fulfillment, abundance and contentment. All you need do is to be willing to liberate yourself from the past, your conditioned thinking and fears. To learn from your personal history and grow, and to become your true self. The magnificent being you were born to be.

'Do not believe anything because it is said by an authority,
or if it is said to come from angels, or from Gods,
or from an inspired source
Believe it only if you have explored it in your own heart
and mind and body,
and found it to be true
Work out your own path through diligence'
Guatama Budda

Awakening

So what is awakening? Well awakening is so named because it literally is a time where you begin to 'wake up'. It is not a singular event, and you may not even realize it has begun until some years later. Awakening is a process in which a new state of consciousness begins to ease its way into a person's awareness. It is the shift which causes us to question our current state of being and the way our lives are running (consciously or unconsciously). It may mean we examine how things are and decide we want change, or we just 'happen' upon a chance meeting or encounter and the process begins.

Often a desire to change may come because things seem to be worsening in our life or a symptom is getting out of control. The increased disruption becomes a burden and living with 'it', ourselves, or someone else is no longer an option. We begin to perceive that maybe the problem or unhappy scenario is not about who we truly are and we act on this instinct. But what we're seeking is not a resolution through drugs, finding love or going on holiday. What we want now is a deeper understanding of the issues and a way to say goodbye to suffering - for good. It's as if something abstruse within is pushing us to find answers, not quick fixes. This gnawing growing urge is both exciting and confusing. It's as if a life force is welling up inside, an energy growing in momentum, albeit subtly. Sometimes though it can become so strong and urgent you want to scream in your desire for knowingness. For others this inner nudging may be more sedate, but no less life changing. It may come as a thought, a feeling or a happening which begins the process of unfoldment. It may be the gentle prodding of a friend to seek help, a distant memory which visits our dreams or words from a book which capture our willingness to know more. All of this is the beginning of awakening.

Awakening cannot be made to happen nor does it follow any set route by the conscious mind. Awakening is orchestrated by a universal intelligence and begins with our time of readiness. The very fact that you are reading this book signifies your own awakening process, which may have only just begun or have been in action for some time now. Your ripeness to awaken comes when you are prepared to honestly face your issues and problems, and want to be free of the chained conditioning of your mind. When you want to feel happy, peaceful, loving, joyful, creative, energized, balanced and healthy all the time. And will do whatever it takes to achieve this. It often comes with the need for inner expansion and to be doing something meaningful. To want freedom on all levels.

The awakening process is by no means a straightforward route, although it is a forward route. If we have to recall frightening memories of abuse to find inner peace, then that is what we have to do. If we have to leave our spouse to grow and change, then that is what we have to do. As we walk the path of awakening we will know what we have to do to continue to grow. That doesn't mean the choices will be easy or that we will be willing to make those choices. Resistance and fear are just two of the obstacles we will need to grapple with, and these alone may make us hold out until the next step is imperative. So staying in the same place until our time is long overdue is not uncommon for even awakened souls. Yet the urge to move on and change will become so strong that in the end remaining static will be unbearable. As the earlier quote so eloquently describes, 'The time came when the risk it took to remain tight in a bud was more painful than the risk it took to blossom.'

Many metaphysical teachings state we don't need to grow through suffering, we can infact grow through joy. I agree with them but.......how can we grow through joy if we are suffering! Growing through joy is a wonderful concept, but in reality you need to be further along the path of enlightenment to experience this truth. It is something to reach for, something to experience at the right time, but only when suffering has been put to rest. To put suffering to rest we must feel it, it is only in feeling it, understanding it, and working through it can we truly be healed from it. Pain, anguish and hurt are not emotions that can just be switched off. This process itself will bring about unprecedented growth and awakening. It may be that you will suffer very little to achieve growth. For most though this is not the case. Many individuals try to grow through joy but a nagging voice inside says, "But I'm still in pain". This voice needs attention, it needs to heal. Following this comes the light of joy which takes us to a new level of awareness. Suffering is part of human life. Often those who suffered much as a child become the most motivated and compassionate of people. This doesn't mean that if you suffered at the hands of mum or dad or Grandpa Joe that's ok, no it isn't. But we can learn from our suffering and become better people for it.

Dr Scott-Peck author of *The Road Less Travelled* likens awakening to a voyage through a desert. He says, "If we are to grow up we can only go forward in the desert of life. Making our way painfully over parched and barren ground into increasing levels of consciousness, but that journey can be hard and consciousness painful. So most people stop their journey as quickly as they can. They find what looks like a safe place, burrow in the sand and stay there. Those who don't choose psycho-spiritual growth stop learning early in their lives and become fixed. Often they lapse into their 2nd childhood walking about as emotional children in adults clothing. Those who come to psychotherapy with genuine intent to grow are those relative few who are called out of immaturity. They proceed into the desert and meet suffering head on. They learn to accept the fact that everything that happens to them is for their own spiritual growth, everything that happens teaches them what they need to know on their journey. Consciousness brings pain but it also brings joy, and the further into the desert you are prepared to go the more joy you will find".

The right therapist
If you decide to seek the additional help of a therapist your initial call to make an appointment may give you a 'good' or 'bad' vibe about them. Listen to your intuition. If you feel comfortable with a particular therapist on the phone then the next step you need to take is to arrange a consultation appointment, most therapists will

offer a free initial consultation. Meeting a therapist one on one allows you to see how comfortable you feel with them, and if you actually like them. It is true to say that not all clients and therapists resonate with each other, and this is a recommended ingredient. Of course you may feel nervous initially and it takes time to develop trust. So what you really need to ask yourself is: Do I like this therapist? Do they do inner child work? Can I talk to them? Do they seem sincere? Could I open up to them in time?

If possible arrange consultations with other therapists in your area. It is wise to look around and find the right person for you. Working through current issues and childhood memories is a very personal affair so your therapist needs to feel like a 'friend' although in a professional capacity.

A 'good' therapist is hard to define, as so many therapists have different skills, and what suits one person may not suit another. Preferably seek someone who is experienced and open-minded, who won't push you to uncover memories or work too quickly. Someone who seems self-assured, and who has gone through their own analysis (therapy). Therapists who have had no therapy themselves make limited therapists, so it is okay to ask this. It is also okay to ask about qualifications and background, a genuine qualified therapist will be happy to answer these questions. If you know you have been sexually abused as a child then it may be a good idea to seek someone trained in this area.

'The child is the father of the man'
William Wordsworth

Your Inner Child

"Hello little girl in my thoughts, you beautiful image of innocence. Your long brown hair, your happy smile, your sparkling eyes, the skip in your walk, your eternal energy. So full of love, so close to God, so shining an example. Thankyou for teaching me so much, thankyou for helping me, thankyou for showing me the way. I'm so proud of your courage, astonished by your loyalty, blown away by you perseverance and ability to survive. Nothing on this world can compare to the strength and endurance of the inner child, the love and the wisdom, the heroism and valour. You my child are my inner light, the love I shall never need to seek, you are the beat of my heart, the strength in my soul. I will love you eternally. Thank you for everything" Lisa, June 1998.

Within all of us is a small child. The child we once were. This inner child is waiting and hoping that someday someone will come and take care of them. Until that happens we remain tied to the past. It is our inner child who holds onto hurt, sadness, fear, shame, guilt, anger, resentment and inadequacy. Our inner child will repeat 'scripts' from the past in the hope of making every-thing alright this time around. Like someone who repeatedly dates men who hurt them. The inner child here is trying to repair the past. It thinks, "Lets find a man like daddy, lets please him, look after him, be perfect for him. That way maybe daddy won't leave me again, if I'm better and do what he wants then he'll stay, and I'll have the happy ending I always dream of." Ever wondered why some women are attracted to the 'bad' guys. Ask about their fathers!

The inner child lives by childhood beliefs and images. It feels powerless and vulnerable and it is up to us to go back and help the child inside. If we don't our inner child ends up running the show, which is destructive to our lives. This child doesn't have the reasoning or ability to decipher what's good for us as adults. It may still be clinging to thoughts such as "I'm not good enough, I'm not deserving or happiness never lasts." If you can't commit to relationships because your mother couldn't, are afraid of meeting strangers, starve yourself to stay slim or work with animals to avoid humans your inner child is dictating this. And these are just a few examples. The inner child needs to feel safe and so keeps within the confines of the familiar or limited, even if it does us no good. The inner child is the part of you that went through your childhood, all the hurts and disappointments that you experienced at that time are still being lived out by your inner child. This part of you has not grown up, it is still living and seeing its world as a child does. The sooner you connect to this part of you and nurture it, the better you and your life will run.

In reality your inner child does not enjoy painful, difficult, debilitating, confusing or out of control feelings. This may just be the norm for your child. It may also believe it doesn't deserve any better or that life is full of suffering. There is though another aspect to your inner child, the side which allows you to feel happy, carefree, playful, spontaneous, in wonder, alive, energized, trusting, affectionate, joyful, excited and loving. This is who your inner child really is, this is also who you really are. All you need to do is give your child the unconditional love it longs for and to become the parent it now needs.

Throughout this book we will be discovering ways to connect with and heal the inner child. That is to heal painful emotions and memories, change limiting beliefs, let go of victim consciousness, heal illness, transform relationships, let go of fears and struggle, work through blocks, re-programme 'old' scripts. To do this you need to learn to love your inner child, let go of the past and work toward the life you desire, not the one you think you should have. The child within you can be your greatest ally when creating the life you want, but if it goes ignored or denied it can also become your greatest block and sabotaging influence.

Connecting with your inner child

Take a couple of deep breaths and begin to relax, close your eyes.............allow your breathing to become calm and gentle..........Make sure you are comfortable and allow your shoulders to become limp, letting go of tension. Imagine your scalp and forehead relaxing. Your face and neck relaxing.................let your arms and hands become heavy............breath away tension and tightness..........let your mind become quiet and focused...........relax your back and chest..................feeling relaxed more and more.................let your tummy loosen and relax your legs all the way down to your feet........just let go..............................Now allow an image to come to your mind without trying.............think of a place from your childhood...somewhere you are likely to find yourself as a child, maybe your bedroom at home, or in the garden, out on the street, or maybe at school. Just allow an image to come to mind now, seeing it as clearly as you can. When you find yourself somewhere begin to look for your child self...................when you see them approach them telling them who you are, for example 'I am your adult self, your future self and I have come to help you'................don't worry if it isn't clear you may just get a sense of being there...............see how your inner child responds to you........they may be overjoyed or hesitant.........reassure them if you need to.............ask them what they are doing and show an interest in them................they may have questions for you or may want to tell you things..........spend some time getting to know them again..............................this is your inner child, the part who longs for your love and acceptance..........................your inner child may want a hug or to be picked up, do whatever feels natural and right.....................you may want to tell your inner child you love them and are now here to take care of them..............say whatever feels ok at this time. Be cautious if you need to, some inner children lack trust so it may take time, others come running brimming with excitement....you know what to do.................Now if possible hold the child close to you and hug them, as you do let them merge with you. Taking there place inside of you, all safe and protected. If this is not possible ask the child to take your hand and come back to the present time with you. If the child does not want to say goodbye for now letting them know you will be back soon........now return to the room you are in.

Please repeat this exercise as often as you need to.

2

People travel to wonder at the height of mountains, at the huge
waves of the sea, at the long courses of rivers, at the vast
compass of the ocean, at the circular motion of the stars;
and they pass by themselves without wondering
St Augustine

The Womb

Julian came to see me having suffered with anxiety for almost all
his life, the anxiety wasn't something that was triggered by
outside stimuli, it was a feeling within him that he lived with day
and night that sometimes abated when Julian was particularly
happy in his life. He described it as a fear that was intangible, a
feeling he couldn't really grasp, it was just 'there' a gnawing
doubt, a free floating apprehension, a quiet dread. This
uneasiness put Julian on edge at all times, he could never feel 100
per cent safe in the world, he found it hard to trust and decisions
were difficult to make as any option had a sense of danger
attached.

After some searching under hypnosis Julian found himself in
a dark place, an enclosed space, he felt very small, he felt his life
was just starting.... he was in the womb. He was aware of his
mother's heartbeat and the faint inaudible sounds coming from
his mother's world, but he also had a strong sense of discord.
Even though Julian was possibly only 14-16 weeks old he was
already aware of the conflicts going on with his parents. He was
picking up on fear, sadness, trauma and distress. He was learning
that his world 'out there' was not a safe place to be in, he was
concluding that the environment he was to be born into did not
seem secure, and he was also absorbing his mother's fear and
anguish.

Julian quickly realized his current emotional state as an adult
was exactly like this, as it was when he was in the womb. To come

to an awareness like this can often create a great healing shift, which it did for Julian. Once he realized it was his mother and his immediate surroundings as a fetus that didn't feel safe, and not his current world Julian was able to restore his natural feelings of safety and heal his deep seated apprehension. It transformed his whole life.

Julian asked his mother about her pregnancy with him and she confirmed that there were multiple problems going on at this time. Julian's father had left his life soon after his birth, during the pregnancy Julian's mother was aware that the relationship was breaking down and felt very insecure and vulnerable, she already had two children and was fearful that she wouldn't be able to cope with another baby as a single parent. Julian's mother said during the pregnancy her relationship with his father had become very volatile and explosive. We can't underestimate the affect our womb experiences can have on us.

As a society we tend to think that life begins when we are born, and then we go on to ignore the impact our baby and childhood years has on us. So what of the womb? If we are ignorant about the significance our childhood has on our lives then we are far less likely to honor our womb experiences too, yet these episodes can often have the greatest influence's if they upset you enough at this tender time. The need to recall a womb experience often comes about when there is high anxiety being presented, fears of death or change, stuckness, feeling unworthy or not feeling wanted in the world. Which can later manifest as low confidence, anxiety, panic attacks and phobias, depression, poor self esteem, submissiveness, feeling undeserving, agoraphobia and more. If you were to administer childhood regression and your problems stemmed from the womb you would at some point be guided back there by your unconscious, if they did not initiate there it is unlikely you would visit this time unless you made a conscious decision to do so. This means you would only need to explore the womb if some trauma or upset had occurred, and if your problems do come from this period then discovering this can be the most liberating and releasing of experiences.

David Chamberlain wrote an article entitled *What Is Early Parenting?* In it he states, "As it is with the establishment of physical settings in utero, the emotional system is also organizing itself in relation to the types of experiences encountered. A baby surrounded with anxiety, fear, and anger will adjust itself to the world and carry out those settings into life. Patterns of fearful reaction already visible via ultrasound before birth are replicated after birth.........although apparently safe in the womb, the baby can be having emotional disturbances, can feel rejected, and can arrive in the world carrying unconscious baggage of anxiety and uncertainty about it's identity and connections."

Psychologist Eric Erikson, in his child development scale, uses trust or mistrust as the first building block of personality he wrote, "The one which is chosen is the result of our first learned experience and that first experience is in the womb, during birth, or in that critical period immediately after birth. Early messages create life long patterns of trust or mistrust." Even Sigmund Freud wrote that traumas in the womb or in birth be the "seat of all anxieties."

Scientists are now making discoveries about the womb period which is having enormous implications on how we view this time in our lives. They are now aware that the mother does pass on information content to the fetus during pregnancy. This is telling the fetus how the environment is, the mother's attitudes about life and her emotions such as fear, anger, love, hope among others, and it can alter the genetic expression of the child. The body releases these 'signals' into the blood through molecules which travel through the placenta and affect cells in the fetus, and although the growing child may not be fully aware of the details - it will pick up on the emotions and feelings. The prenate is also able to judge its world by intuition and 'gut feelings'.

'A woman may become pregnant in order to be babied-
which is what she has actually needed to be all her life'
Dr A Janov

Some pregnant clients I have seen have had problems bonding
with the new life growing inside them and usually find it is their
own womb experience that is causing them to feel detached. They
are reacting to their own relationship with their mother. After
regressing back to their time in the womb we often find that these
mums-to-be have picked up on their mother's own difficulty in
forming an attachment with them. This is so often the case when
we have children, as soon as we are a parent, from the moment of
conception, we are getting signals about our own childhood.
These signals may be positive or negative, they may cause us to
feel happy or uncomfortable, tearful or joyful. If you are a parent
and find you are reacting negatively to your children, in some
situations or many situations, or if you find it hard to bond with
one of your babies, then this has something to do with your own
past. Our children are like little mirrors, constantly reflecting back
to us the inner feelings, disappointments, upsets, difficulties,
fears, hurts, as well as the love, affection, happiness, excitement
and wonder of our inner child.

Like the mums-to-be who felt detached from their babies, all
that was needed was some inner healing. When we understand
where our 'problems' are coming from, then the process of healing
naturally begins to take place. Analyzing our emotions, restoring
these and then replacing those feelings with pure maternal love
can really help the child develop. It can also help to avoid post
natal depression, which usually occurs because we did not
successfully bond with our own mother after birth.

Connecting with your womb experience
Close your eyes and begin to relax, take two deep breaths and
breath away tension.......................... Feel yourself relaxing more

and more. Let your shoulders loosen and undo any tight clothing........................... Feel your eyes, mouth and jaw relax. ....Allow your breathing to become slow and rhythmic, feeling calmer and calmer...................... Feel any tension in your body drain away....................... Now allow yourself to drift back through time, in your imagination feel yourself being pulled back through time. ....Imagine yourself drifting back and as you do you become younger and smaller.............................. younger and smaller. Imagine your legs and arms, body and head becoming smaller.. Becoming very small within yourself, becoming very childlike and then smaller still............................ Imagine within yourself you are becoming as small as a toddler............................ and then smaller still.............................. time is ticking backwards and you are as small as a baby.............................. Now smaller still, going back now until you sense you are as small as a fetus surrounded by water.......................................surrounded by darkness that feels safe and natural...feeling completely immersed in this safe bubble of life...feeling warm and secure in your mother's womb......................Maybe you hear or sense muffled sounds............................your mother's heartbeat..............................see your tiny arms and legs maybe the umbilical cord too. Just enjoy bathing and feeling suspended in the womb.......................................there is nowhere you have to be nothing you have to do, you are happy to just 'be'..... enjoy this time now............................ begin to allow yourself to come back to the room you are in now, leaving your womb time behind. Come back and slowly open your eyes.

Birth

The journey from womb to birth could be seen as a journey of initiation, a rite of passage. It is the journey we all must take to begin our voyage on the earth plane. Yet like many rites of passage the birth experience is not always an easy one, and could be seen as the first doorway were we have to push ourselves to reach the next phase of our lives. Birth is a very natural and beautiful thing and the initial challenge of moving through the pelvic bone and the walls of the uterus can only be good for us. It sets us up to deal with challenges later on our life journey, and prepares us to move through these times with fortitude and ease. Yet what if the birth experience is beset with problems or steers away from 'naturalness?' If this occurs, as many psychologists and scientists have discovered, then some long term effects could be inevitable.

From Birth Trauma: The Psychological Effects of Obstetrical Interventions William Emerson writes, "While the goal of pain reduction is a noble objective there are also negative aspects that should be considered. Some anesthetic babies have difficulty bonding and later have problems with substance abuse.........these infants who were dosed may sometimes find later many 'feelingful' events of their lives such as sex feel dulled, or they may go numb when a transition or task is required of them. The administration of drugs such as Oxytocin and Pitocin can also make the fetus feel overpowered and controlled, and this too has been noted to link with substance abuse later as well as feelings of poor control or of being controlled. The use of forceps and vacuum extractors has been discovered to create a defence around babies when they are older, this is because many adults who had this encounter as a baby felt invaded and subjected to violence. Often this results in not wanting to be touched or held, and a lack of trust in others."

Caesarean surgery is becoming more common these days but can have many negative effects on the infant as well as long term effects on the adult. Infants born via Caesarean section have been found to cry more, have feeding difficulties, digestive problems and colic as well as an increased chance of developing asthma as children . Also the shock of being taken from the womb in such a hurried fashion has been noted to prevent them from taking 'big' steps later in life, and causes them to look to others for solutions and the hope of rescue.

Near death experiences during the birthing process also cause untold trauma and distress as the infant is a truly conscious being when traveling down the birth canal. As we know the baby is very aware in the womb, and it's senses will be even more heightened at the time of birth. If problems occur and the infant becomes stuck or nearly dies it may later develop irrational fears, claustrophobia, panic attacks, be hyper-sensitive to its surroundings or feel unsafe in the world.

The above birthing experiences and short and long term effects have been researched by professionals and doctors, but may only be indicative to some of the population. And of course all the procedures are necessary for the safe delivery of so many babies. You may have had a forceps delivery yourself or been anaesthetized at birth but do not recognize the long term effects as relating to you. For some though the birth experience and subsequent traumas are relevant, and may need to be addressed if the individual is to move on. I have often found that many people who feel 'stuck' or unable to move forward in their lives relate this to being stuck within the canal walls leading up to birth, and once this is resolved they miraculously move on as adults. Then for some just the bright lights, noises, being moved across the theatre upside-down, intruded on by strangers and the clinical handling of birth in modern hospitals can cause distress. So as with the womb experience we really can't underestimate the impact our birth experience may have had upon us. If the natural process of birth cannot be carried out then some effects of this will understandably have to be expected, even if it is not in all cases.

'After all, what is God? An eternal child playing an eternal game in the eternal garden'
Sri Aurobino

Babyhood

Tony Robbins is a well-loved and hugely successful life coach in America and states, "Relationships are the most important part of your life because they can bring you the greatest amount of love, joy and ecstasy that you could ever imagine. Yet this is also the place of pain, where people can feel devastation, where for many life can lose its meaning"

The human being is a very social creature, and longs for love and acceptance, even if many say they don't need others. It is true that we can spend long periods of time in isolation and be fine, in fact sometimes it is necessary for our personal growth. Deep inside though we love to be with others, especially if they resonate with us and love us. When you think of your happiest occasions you may well find it's with others, if we have happy news we are bursting to tell someone else, because in sharing it we heighten it. If we have problems its nice to share it because it lessens it, someone has heard us, sympathized and shown care for us, so we immediately feel better.

Our need for others doesn't develop as we grow, it is a part of our desire as soon as we are born. Babies come into the world affectionate, loving and warm, no matter if they are healthy, premature or handicapped. And to develop these attributes naturally they need to be cuddled, loved, interacted with, played with and held. They need human contact right from the word go.

It has only been in the last decade that psychologists have discovered the importance of this, until then babies were often left to cry for hours in case they were 'spoilt' by getting their own way. Jan Parker from *Raising Happy Children* writes, "Ignore anyone who bleats about making a rod for your own back. Young babies are not 'naughty' or 'manipulative', 'wilful' or 'trying to wrap you around their little finger' - they simply get hungry, hot, cold, windy, wet, frightened, tired, uncomfortable, lonely and need you to do something about it"

Babies are extremely sensitive to their parents and others

around them, they look to their carers reactions and responses to them, and this will have a profound influence. A good example would be of Michael who was a workaholic and spent hours on his business, he was a perfectionist and every moment was spent at work. Michael could never take a holiday as he feared his staff couldn't manage without him. Michael came to see me suffering from depression and was at the first stages of 'burn out', his wife was on the verge of leaving him and his relationship with his children was suffering. Michael could not have been more surprised when he found his problems stemmed from his time as a baby.

Michael's mother was unable to show love and he spent long periods alone in his cot. When he was fed, washed or changed it was a quick if not difficult affair for his mother. She couldn't wait to get the process over with and put Michael down. Worse still Michael's father believed he didn't need to interact with his son as it wasn't the man's place. As a young baby Michael felt isolated, abnormal, hurt and desperate. If he cried he was either shouted at or ignored, he quickly became a 'good baby' as this would pacify his mother, so when she did pick him up she wasn't rough or angry. Even though Michael was only a baby he 'knew' something was wrong, as we all come into the world needing love and if it is absent there feels as if something's missing. Michael decided there must have been something wrong with him, babies naturally think this.

Now it may seem amazing to you that a baby can have all this going on in their awareness at such a young age, and yet they do. This is why healing our babyhood if it was difficult, lonely or traumatizing is essential if we are to overcome adulthood obstacles to happiness. Michael's obstacles were always having to be busy, having to prove something and avoidance of intimacy. Deep down Michael feared the rejection he experienced as a baby so to counteract this he didn't get close to others, not even his wife, that way he was less likely to get hurt. He went out of his way to create a successful life, because he believed he if did that his parents might finally love and accept him. All this created a life style where Michael was constantly trying to achieve. This meant painful childhood feelings never had the chance to emerge, and realizations of adult loneliness could never surface. It took time for Michael to work through it and it was very painful. Accepting that your parents were unable to show you love can at first be devastating, because we have to re-experience how that was for us as an infant. For Michael the pain was so intense that as a baby he often just wanted to die. Some psychotherapists have suggested that this kind of reaction may be linked to cot death, and although not conclusive, it is possible to conceive that if a child feels so unwanted they could in fact bring on their own death.

So from the moment we are born we are learning how to interact with others and decide how we fit in the world, and all this is crucial to our development. Until recently neither psychology or medicine has given adequate attention to very early development, in the false belief that babies could not feel, remember, learn or be influenced by experiences. Barbara Findeisen, Director of *The Star Foundation* in America which researches early experiences in childhood, said in an interview for a magazine called Touch The Future, "In the case of birth or early childhood experiences nobody thinks early wounds make any difference, most people don't believe babies really have feelings, they are not conscious, sensing, human beings. Wait two or three years until the baby can talk then maybe it will matter they say. But just because you don't have the vocabulary doesn't mean you are not having the experience and are not recording it, which in fact, you are!"

Babies have feelings and take in everything around them, and as Barbara Findeisen states above, it is all being recorded. At an unconscious level everything is being recorded through perception, which will determine how the baby feels about himself, how he will develop relationships later and how he will fair in life as he grows up. Everything is relevant from love to trauma, acceptance to rejection, safety to fear and so on, the growing baby is aware of it all and it is shaping his self esteem and ability to love. Even premature babies who have to spend a certain amount of time in an incubator, experience feelings of isolation and maybe rejection.

Connie came to see me for a consultation when I lived in Devon in the UK, and I was about to witness the most rapid therapy ever. Connie never came back to start therapy, she didn't need to, something I said to her in the initial consultation sparked a change which resulted in Connie losing two stone in weight. When talking to Connie about why some people experience weight problems I touch on babyhood. I said that sometimes babies are fed and then not cuddled or interacted with afterwards, but just put down. And if that feeding time is the only time the baby experiences intimacy and closeness, then pretty soon the baby associates intimacy and love with food. Especially sweet food. The baby later on uses food to replace the love it never had, or is not getting as an adult. The only way it has learnt to find love and comfort is through food, so food becomes the pinnacle for that person's world, everything revolves around it. When there is a trauma - reach for food, when there is pain - reach for food, when there is a challenge - reach for food, when there is change- reach for food, even when there is happiness -reach for food. Food becomes a companion of comfort and safety in all situations that induce stress. Connie nodded at what I was saying and left the consulting room saying she would be in touch and how interesting it all was etc etc. I didn't hear from Connie for four months until I bumped into her in a book store in Barnstaple, I didn't recognize her though because of all the weight she'd lost. I saw this very trim woman running up to me excitedly saying, "Michelle I've been meaning to call you, after our consultation something clicked inside me. I don't know what it was, it was as if the baby inside me had finally been acknowledged and understood. It was then I began to lose weight. I realize that what you had talked about when I came to see you was so relevant to me thank you so much." Wow! I thought. Wouldn't it be nice if everyone could lose weight this easily! Connie's story is an amazing one, but I think it shows us just how much of an influence our babyhood can have upon us. Babies feel, experience and are affected just as we are even if it's not evident at first.

"I didn't even know how much I missed my mum until I remembered the day she let me go"
Christina 1995

Adoption

Adoption or fostering at any age is always an upsetting and perplexing time for a child. There are always necessary reasons as to why children have to be cared for by others who are not their parents. Yet whatever the age children will find this time difficult, even babies.

Robert is a colleague of mine who works as a hypnotherapist in Harley Street, London. Before he completed his exams to practice he came to see me to work through some issues that had been bothering him. During the sessions one issue came up which would be directly related to Robert's adoption as a baby, and he was very surprised when it did. He had been having some complex feelings toward his wife Leah and didn't know if he was imagining the problem or if it was for real. He said he had been feeling rejected by his partner and left out of her life. Yet he also realized she was going through a busy and trying time, taking care of the family and practicing as a therapist herself. Robert thought he must be over reacting. Often though with unresolved childhood issues we are sensitive to what can remind us (unconsciously) of those issues, so if Leah goes through times of being a bit evasive Robert will feel 'rejected' as he has unresolved feelings of rejection to heal. As described earlier we also unconsciously create situations that bring up our unexamined hurts and conflicts, as the mind and body are always looking to heal. So maybe at this time Leah had her own agenda to deal with and wasn't necessarily 'rejecting' Robert. Whatever brought it up doesn't really matter so much, what matters is Robert's reaction to this. When the reaction is addressed and the emotions are healed, this paves the way for the 'problem' to be transformed. This means Robert's perception of the issue will change, which will either transform the situation and/or transform him. Either way Robert wanted to feel ok about himself and happier in his world. I asked Robert to write down his feelings, he put, 'Unloved, Rejected, Left out, Upset, Sad, Lonely'. When Robert was relaxed I repeated the words over and over as he traveled back into the past, then I waited. Robert was quiet for a while then he whispered, "My mum.......it was when I was a baby....I see cream walls and a bed with spindles....mums sitting there, sitting up... I think she's sad...... I see her dark hair I can see her face. She's holding me and crying, now she's letting me go....... I feel so empty, like a hollow feeling, I don't understand. She's being strong and accepting it...................(goes back to the day previous)........... feel like I'm being cuddled and held by my mum, it's a warm and lovely feeling, but something is wrong...............(returns to present thought).... Its not fair, feel so confused, something's happening.......I'm being taken away..........a nurse is holding me and putting me in a cot. I'm in a different room, just looking up, feeling sad and lonely. Feel rejected.... I know this is it......I won't see her again........feel terrible and so alone."

Robert was only six weeks old when he was adopted, his mother was seventeen and unable to look after him. Robert hasn't seen his mum since that day. Who would not be moved by this story? It is a sad and painful situation for babies to be in and makes us understand how aware and perceptive they really are.

Freud and many other psychotherapists have always taught and maintained that the first stage of psychological growth includes the development of trust, as a foundation for secure relationships with others. Many adoptees find it hard to love and trust, as they can fear being abandoned again. And from that abandonment many people feel betrayed, angry, hurt and confused, even if they intellectually know why they were adopted. This can then influence their self image, self esteem, family life, relationships and maybe even money and career at some point. Even if the child had a loving and secure upbringing since the adoption, there will still be some grief and feelings of betrayal felt toward the original birth mother. You can't have a nine month relationship with someone (albeit from the womb) then be separated and feel nothing, it is not possible.

Sibling Loss

Another sense of loss that a baby will feel, and which again goes unrecognized as a problem for the infant, is the loss of a sibling or twin. This loss may be in the womb, during birth or soon after. Whenever it was the baby will be significantly affected by the loss. A psychologist in America was fascinated by twins, he took pictures of them, studied them and interviewed them. Ironically a philosophical friend posed the question on whether he lost a twin as a baby. The psychologist asked his mother, who said he had. He had a twin brother who died at birth. This amazing story is not uncommon, as studies have shown that infants who lose a twin often have a fascination for them, or feel there is something missing in their lives. Even if they are not aware of the death of their brother or sister.

Some of my own clients have needed to go back and address the loss of a sibling in early childhood, as it seems the time in utero with another child is a time of great bonding and companionship, and the loss of this can be felt for decades.

Chapter 2

'An infant is pure spiritual gold'
Deepak Chopra

Childhood:
We are evolving

As I outlined in chapter one, no one really has the perfect childhood. It doesn't exist. How can it? How can our needs be meet all the time? How can we have our own way all the time? How can we be sure we are loved all the time? When we live with adults we basically have to live in the world they are creating, adapt to the responses they are giving us and deal with the way they treat us. Some get it good, some get it ok, some get it bad and some get it awful. Yet whatever bracket you come under your childhood will be influencing you in some way. Especially if parts of your life are not working, or you have a lot of issues to deal with.

As discussed previously consciousness is rising, that means as people we are evolving. People who choose to have children now are more likely to want a happier relationship with them, as well as understand and give them a healthy and balanced life, emotionally and physically. People are more willing to address their own problems, and there is also more support available. This doesn't mean the world is any less stressful, because in fact it seems more so. Parents though do seem much more aware of their children's needs, despite the added stresses of life. And I'm sure we will see the benefits of this approach as we move into the new age of consciousness that is coming.

This doesn't mean children are not being abused, hurt or damaged at this moment. This is occurring even as you read these words. In fact abuse seems more prevalent and widespread, which is a paradox considering what I've just said. So what is really happening?

Well let's go back a bit in time............. if we look at the sixties and before children were seen and not heard. It was the general consensus that children didn't really have feelings or thoughts of any value. Parents didn't have to be kind, just or even right. In fact they could be downright irrational, critical, unpredictable and beat you with a belt if they so pleased. Even teachers and other carers had this right. The adults did have a responsibility to lead their children and create boundaries, but many of them abused this responsibility and exploited their parental power.

Susan Forward of *Toxic Parents.* states;

Children from these generations were more likely to be taught;

- I am wrong my parents are right
- I am weak my parents are strong
- I am bad my parents are good

Of course many parents are still utilizing their Godlike powers even today to create these beliefs in their children, but thankfully this is lessening. People are learning that children are people too. They have their own thoughts, feelings, interests and personality. And of course I don't advocate children ruling the roost! Children are children after all. They need role models, the security of boundaries and effective guidance. I do believe children need to be cared for in ways that enhance their individuality, promote their self-esteem, regard their thoughts and feelings, and respect the way they view the world. The saying, "The hand that rocks the cradle rules the world" couldn't be truer. If we want to heal the world then children require happier childhoods. This doesn't mean divorce won't happen, a parent won't die or issues won't come up to affect the whole family. What I mean by a 'happier' childhood is one where individual thoughts, feelings and experiences are seen as important. Where children are supported through stress and bad times, as well as loved and acknowledged through good times. Where children are allowed to be themselves and not what their parents expect them to be.

So getting back to this parallel. Why so much abuse now and

yet parenting is improving? Abuse, in fact, has not increased - we are just becoming more aware of it. Nothing can be healed unless it is brought to the light of conscious awareness, so abuse is surfacing and being faced so it can be healed. As we move with evolution we grow and become better people, so as we see the new concepts of positive parenting being implemented life has to naturally move with this change. This means everything that doesn't fit this 'new age' concept must now be exposed and dealt with. As a race we are expanding, old ideals, beliefs and ways of being don't fit anymore. We are undergoing a transformation, an evolutionary leap. We are becoming more connected, loving and at one. We may not be seeing this in our everyday world or the world of others at the moment, but this time is coming, and is being introduced now. This means the mistreatment of children has to be acknowledged, learnt from, healed and removed. Its time has come.

If you are a parent and throughout this chapter have been berating yourself for your 'failings' please stop now! It's time to take a different stance. You are the result of our own upbringing. This doesn't mean you don't have to take responsibility, what it means is you have to acknowledge you learnt to parent from your parents. Even if you decided to do things differently, how often do you find yourself doing the same things. You are also prone to stress, have your 'hot buttons', find it more difficult to cope some days, go through bad times or say and do things in the heat of the moment you later regret. Yes we've all been there! This all adds up to making parenting more challenging, but there is hope. The very fact that you are reading this book means you want change, you have acknowledged to some extent that something needs to change in you. These two steps have taken you further than most, so don't beat yourself up. Yes things have happened in the past, but you want to progress from that now. You want to take control of yourself, your emotions and your life. In doing this you will become a 'better' parent, but you can never be a super, flawless, supreme parent, only better. Maybe the best parent you can be, and that's good enough. There is alot of pressure in society to be a 'good' parent, but in doing that you can sacrifice too much of yourself, you need to find the balance. This means taking care of yourself and your kids, but not trying to be perfect or super-human. You'll find the more freed up you are from the past, the happier you'll be, and then parenting becomes much easier anyway. So pat yourself on the back you are taking a big step. It is a trick of the ego (more in Chapter 3) to dwell on your 'mistakes' and to put yourself down. It keeps you stuck in antiquity and doesn't allow you to move on. If you dwell upon your own misgivings as a parent, you stop focusing on your present day issues and what you need to heal. It becomes a distraction to resolving your own 'stuff'. Its time to focus on you now, because when you do your children will benefit more than you could ever imagine.

'There are two lasting bequests we can hope to give our children. One of these is roots; the other, wings
Hodding Cart

Adolescence

Adolescence is for many an ambiguous time. Physical, cognitive, psychological and social changes are occurring. The child is moving from the infant phase to the adult phase in a period of only five years (approx). Many adolescents may have an intact family life and proceed through this time with the normal anxieties and changes included (i.e. changing school, puberty etc). They may look back and find their teenage years easy, usual, best time of their life, or maybe, uneventful. For millions more this is not the case. In psychotherapy we have to remember the impact of adolescence. We may focus much on our inner child to the expense of our inner teen, who is in just as much need and care as the child is.

Entering adolescence can be a time of complex feelings. Perhaps an assortment of independence, powerlessness, fear of change or rebellion. And if you come from a childhood which is traumatic, difficult or problem-filled you may be ill prepared for adult life. This is because security or validation may have been absent which can make the world, in your perception, a challenging place. Due to this many people get 'stuck' in juvenescence because it is safer to do so. They see taking responsibility and being 'grown up' too burdensome or frightening. Or they are reluctant to let go of their childhood because they felt they never had one. Most of us can detect our inner adolescent through our thinking or behavior from time to time. Here are a few questions that will help you discover if you are in any way cemented in your teenage self.

1. Do you; Need to be in control all the time and hate others taking the lead? Have 'control' over your emotions - this can show up as fearing intimacy, running away from commitments, withholding affection, rejecting before you are rejected, minimizing your feelings (or those of others) by saying, "Don't be silly, he's not worth it" or "I'm being so daft now, can't let that affect me." Or are you 'addicted' to soaps, tabloids, traumatic stories and gossip to get your emotional - yet safe - expression.

2. Do you; Find it hard to take responsibility for your life? Tend to blame others or feel secretly angry with them? Manipulate your relationships by making others feel guilty or sorry for you? Judge others? Expect close friends and family to know what you are thinking or feeling? Become self-absorbed with your own problems, often ignoring the needs of others to put yourself first? Self harm to get help or gain attention? Rebel against authority or rules? Feel dependent on friends, family or partner to meet your emotional needs?

3. Are you; Concerned with appearances? Is it important to impress others, or to have material items for show - like designer clothes, a nice car or good looking girlfriend? Do you; Idolize pop stars, actors or people in the media wishing you could be or live just like them? Constantly worry about your weight or how you look? Get a sense of never being your true self and are always performing? Worry about others seeing your vulnerabilities or 'faults'?

4. Do you; Easily get 'hooked' on outside pleasures to help you feel happy, or to avoid emotions? This may be shopping, work, sex, drink, drugs, nights out, gambling, food etc. Take risks with drinking and driving, or drive fast to get a thrill? Are you 'addicted' to falling in love, or do you get a 'high' from drama in your relationships?

Many of us will see traits within us when reading the above. If you find yourself relating to much of it parts of you may well be hovering in adolescence, although really the problems originate from childhood. For example rebelling in adolescence my represent suppressed childhood anger or worry over appearances comes from low self worth. In this case healing the inner adolescent and then tracing the true problems back to infancy is crucial. When you discover what's making you tick from this angle you allow these parts to conciliate and grow, from this comes the liberating unshacklement into adulthood.

The commonly known midlife crisis which 25 per cent of Americans and 20 per cent of the UK population say they have been through, can be linked to the unresolved turmoil of the inner adolescence and parts of the self being fixed at this period. This 'phase' occurs between the ages of 39 and 50 and often arises when an individual realizes that life does not go on forever. Yet this crisis of confidence and self image does not have to be negative or discomforting it can in fact bring about reformation and transformation as independence, relationships, life, sexuality and "What now?" are explored. In our 20's and 30's we tend to conform to what society expects, but in our 40's we question this and ask, "What about me? What do I want? What am I going to do now?" Much soul searching takes place with a chance to start over. Around 70 per cent of my clients are aged between 40-50 years. They are not necessarily in a middle age dilemma but want a deeper understanding of their past and what it means, they want answers and seek guidance for their future. Something inexplicable is tapping them on the shoulder and saying, "Hey there's more to discover you know." So I prefer to call this time midlife metamorphosis, if we choose to learn and grow from it.

Getting back to the main theme, for many teens adolescence can be a time of trauma, difficulties, confusion or fear. Even though the teenager is growing up, if physical, emotional or sexual abuse has happened to them in infancy this can carry on well into the teenage years and often into adulthood. Or some teenagers become pregnant and find themselves in the role of the parent very young. Others may have the responsibility of taking care of younger siblings (or parents) if parents are sick, working, needy or neglectful. Many parents at this time are divorcing as the children are becoming independent. A high percentage of teenagers are bullied at school, it is thought in western societies every seven minutes a child is being bullied in high school. 1 in 4 children/teenagers are bullied regularly. Bullying is damaging to self-esteem and confidence. Often those who are subject to abuse of this kind already have low self worth which makes them an easy target for bullies. Yet bullies themselves have deep seated feelings of imperfection and weakness, and will use their victims to gain control or power. The bully and the bullied often have to look at their home life to understand the set up that has caused them to be either.

Problems in adolescence need to be healed just as much as in childhood. You don't magically cope better when you reach your teens. Just because you're six feet tall doesn't mean your a man, just as wearing a 34B bra doesn't make you a woman! Yes your periods may have started or you may need a Remington Titanium beard shaver but you are probably still not ready to tackle what most adults would find stressful. Not alone anyway. So be aware of yourself at this time, think about your teenage years and note the issues you may have had to deal with. Relive your emotions, thoughts, feelings, and memories. Maybe jot down your life story from twelve to eighteen. Look for patterns, 'bad' behavior, negative times and feelings.

What's right?

So the perfect childhood/adolescence doesn't exist, and that's ok because children don't necessarily require their parents to be perfect, only to be responsive and loving most of the time. Children need to be brought up in an environment where people are basically 'people', this teaches them to live in the real world and adjust adequately to whatever comes along. It is how we are with them that matters. It depends on how much we show them we love them, how much we are there for them and how valuable we make them feel. Children also need to be accepted as unique individuals rather than reflections of parental wishes and aspirations. This involves tolerating and appreciating the differences between you.

"If we show our children that we love them unconditionally, that they and their feelings and wishes matter and that we value, acknowledge and care for them, we will boost their sense of self worth. From this will spring the confidence and security they need to understand their feelings and manage their behavior, to get along with others, to grow in independence, to seek assistance when they need it, to cope with life's knocks and imperfections, and to love. In other words it sets them up for life," Jan Parker, *Raising Happy Children*. Jan goes onto say; "A happy childhood is not about doing just as the child pleases or creating a child who behaves impeccably. A happy childhood is when you have the following; Loved for who you are; Appreciate your worth and the worth of others; Your feelings, needs and development are understood; You are shown how to be caring and considerate; Given affection, love and security; Your needs are met; Given time and stimulation; Encouraged to develop your confidence and make the best of yourself; Learn to deal with problems and to love life."

So did you have all this? Yes it's an ideal and most children don't have it all the time, and many children wouldn't have a clue as to what Jan Parker's talking about. It's true what people say, "Children don't come with instruction manuals!" No they don't, but on the other hand with a little bit of thought, some common sense, education, listening, sensing, communicating, reflecting on what you would have liked as a child, and self healing- things could be different.

Your childhood, how was it?

We have all come from different backgrounds, and often I find the more severe the problems we have as adults, or the more frequent, the more likely we were to have had a unhappy, unsettling or difficult childhood. This is not always the case though, some people can go through life with a surface reality that reflects happiness and fulfillment. Only to find later something occurs to shake their world, and their past problems begin to break through the illusion as the inner truth transpires.

For example, Joyce was a 44-year-old lady whose children had left home. She explained that her life had been happy, she felt content, and couldn't have wanted for much more. When her children left though her world fell apart. She felt depressed, worthless and directionless. When we explored these feelings further Joyce realized she had been hiding within her family life. She had been avoiding contact with her true inner self, the self that had been ignored as a child, the self that was lonely and sad.

She had been keeping so well occupied over the years tending to her children, that she was able to ignore her quiet despair.

And Ian a successful business man who believed he had it all. Lovely home, lovely wife, great kids and financial freedom. Until his business partner stole thousands from the company, meaning Ian had to sell his home to make ends meet. During this time Ian became depressed and felt betrayed, this then allowed repressed memories of being abandoned by his mother to surface. Ian always new something was 'wrong' as he had a drinking problem which was gradually increasing. He ignored his inner urges to get help though and finally life presented him with a problem which ensured he sorted things out.

Sometimes if we walk about pretending everything is 'ok' (denial), in time life can have this habit of turning things upside down, to show us it is not! In metaphysics they say, "Listen to the whispers so the Angels don't have to shout!." So be honest with yourself, how are you? How's your life? And how was the past really? Maybe you are not sure, maybe you are worried about being over sensitive, maybe you are hesitant about facing it. This is a normal reaction, facing the possibility that all may not have been well in our distant past, or that our current problems are a result of our past, does take time to get to grips with. The following questions may help:

1. Did one or both parents treat you differently to other siblings or ignore you, make you feel you were in the way, or treat you as if they didn't really like you?
2. Were you ever told you had been an accident or were unwanted, and were a burden?
3. Were you criticized, or called names, put down, humiliated, laughed at, or made to feel bad or worthless. Even if not all the time?
4. Did the family home break up? Did you see one parent inter- mittently? Or did one parent leave your life and never

return?

5. Did you lose a parent or sibling, or other close relative/friend through death?

6. Did you move house at any time and find it particularly traumatic?

7. Did you find one or both parents unloving and unable to give affection?

8. Did you find starting and settling into school difficult, were you bullied or a loner?

9. Were one or both parents over protective, controlling, dominating or interfering?

10. Was one or both parents passive and ineffective, allowing you to do just as you wanted?

11. Were you disciplined physically? Were you ever hit with belts, whips, fists, or other objects, or kicked, shaken, burnt, or smacked frequently?

12. Were one or more parents suffering with mental illness, alcoholism, drug abuse, depression or other physical or mental health problems which made them unavailable for you? Did you ever have to take care of your parents or other siblings because of this?

13. Were you adopted or put into foster care at any time?

14. Were you neglected? Did you have to take care of yourself most of the time i.e. washing, dressing and feeding yourself?

15. Did one or both parents, or anyone else, do anything to you that you had to keep a secret? Did you suffer any form of sexual abuse?

16. Did your parents fight frequently, that you were aware of?

17. Were you frightened of one or both parents most of the time?

18. Did you feel secure?

19. Have you blanked out long periods of your childhood?

20. Did you experience any upsetting, traumatic or difficult times in your childhood which you're not sure if you've come to terms with?

21. Did anything ever happen that made you feel confused, guilty, ashamed, uncomfortable, hurt or frightened?

If you answered 'yes' to any of these questions then you probably have issues to work on. If you can't remember or feel none of the above relate to you but you're having problems or worries in your adult life then I suggest you read on. These issues are in some way linked to the past and it's time to find out what that link is.

'The miracle is not to fly in the air or to walk on the water
but to walk on the earth'
Chinese proverb

Your mind is the source

In my early 20's I began my hypnotherapy/psychotherapy
training, whereupon I discovered how influential the past can be
on our state of health as an adult. Alongside the course I was
working in a psychiatric hospital in the UK, and had recently
completed my nursing studies. I was nursing patients who had
suffered long-term psychiatric problems and were not deemed
able to take care of themselves in the community.

It was at this point in my life that I began to really understand
'cause and effect', how the causes of childhood can affect us as
adults. Here's some examples; Schizophrenia and long-term
psychosis - these people have lost touch with their essence, their
true selves, due to mental limitations being reached. Most had a
difficult relationship with either both or one parent (usually the
opposite sex), or their reality as a child was too painful to deal
with. As adults a 'make-believe' reality is utilized to cope. Manic
depressives, or sufferers of severe depression - these adults
usually endured a huge depth of emotional wounding at some
stage of their infancy due to fear, rejection, abandonment, humiliation or betrayal. High anxiety, obsessive compulsive and
hypochondriacs -these are very sensitive individuals and usually
suffered a severe lack of attention in their past or felt out of
control of their surroundings.

These conclusions, although documented, were not always
recognized as relevant in psychiatric care. This was mainly due to
the lack of psychotherapeutic 'thinking' at the time. Yet as an
eager therapist (or hyno-anorak as I used to be called!) I wanted
to know more, and do more. My hypno-training was teaching me

that adult 'ills' could be treated and relieved by child regression therapy under hypnosis, so it was natural to conclude that all adult afflictions came from the past.

At the latter stages of my nursing career I was based on a short stay acute ward. I was still caring for psychotic, high anxiety and depressive clients, but was also seeing a wealth of suicidal people, bulimics and anorexics and extremely stressed individuals who had just lost the ability to cope with their day-to-day lives. On further exploration I discovered that most of the suicidal patients felt they were not taken adequate care of as children, or had suffered some form of abuse. As we all know most attempts of suicide, or self- harm, are cries for help and these people were no exception. The bulimics often had issues with their mothers and feared being abandoned. The anorexic clients had lost the desire to live and so rejected food, this bore its roots with either parent often due to abuse. They were also renouncing their own femininity and feared growing up. The highly stressed clients who felt they were heading for a 'break down' often came from a multitude of upbringings most of these emanating from perfectionism, a fear of failing, and/or trying hard to please one or both parents, or over control. Or for some it was a source of stimulation, which acted as a distraction from the difficulties of their past.

These findings are in no way conclusive and only give us the most common causes of emotional/mental illness. Everyone is individual and the mainspring of their psychosis or neurosis is unique to them. Yet we do know that it all comes from the past.

I've talked about the more extreme instances of mental health, but really there is a very thin line between these in care cases and those individuals walking about with psychological/emotional issues in society today. The thin line really is in the extremeness of it, the ability to cope and the support structure that you have within, and without. People who necessitate psychiatric input are really no different to you or me their symptoms have just become exaggerated to the point that they require intervention and care.

So whatever your issue/instability/affliction it will be coming from your past at some level. Everything that ails you is created by your own mind. Everything! From panic attacks to bed-wetting to toothache. Your mind and body are trying to tell you that an area is out of balance or not healed, something needs to be addressed. Even physical illness has its roots in emotional imbalance. There is a wound inside of you which causes illness or problems in your current life. The wound seeks to communicate, it wants to get well. It talks to you through your present circum-stances, although it relates directly to your past.

A new perspective

Gill was a client of mine who was dealing with feelings of inferi-ority at work, although she had a senior position in an advertising company in London, she felt like a fraud. Gill was highly ambitious, but when she reached another height on the executive scale she felt inadequate for the job. She then spent the whole day fretting about whether she was good enough, what mistakes she'd made and whether anyone liked her at all!. Gill thought her problems stemmed from working in a highly competitive environment with 'high flyers' who gave great presentations and generally stole the show. Yet when we took Gill's feelings of inadequacy back to her childhood we discovered her inner child, and this child felt insignificant and valueless. Not surprising when we uncovered her father's constant criticism and berating. Gill's father was very driven, he wanted his children to be the best and to achieve the highest accolades, yet his ideas about how to do this proved to be more destructive than constructive. Gill's father, and many before and after him, believed criticism was the key to making your children work harder and achieve more, yet constant criticism is the surest way to slowly break your children down. Later this will either be expressed by children who flunk school/university/good jobs and 'let the family down', or like Gill go on to do what their fathers wanted but deep inside are convinced they're not making the grade or in anyway reaching the standard required. This is because they grow up believing they are defective, inapt or incomplete.

So think about your feelings/issues/agendas/difficulties at the moment, and write them down. Maybe your feeling depressed regularly, have to deal with fears, feel stressed, lonely, overwhelmed, panicky, unloved, unimportant or worthless, restless, are arguing with your partner, have anger issues, are dealing with pain, hate your job, have money worries, have food issues or weight problems, or have a multitude of things going on in your life. Whatever the issue/s or feeling/s just take one and put it as a main heading for example, Panicky. Now under your heading list all your feelings, thoughts, emotions, how it affects you, any physical feelings like tension or nausea, how you behave, your beliefs about the issue or anything that relates to that area. In other words what are you going through or thinking when the problem is present or when you're focused on it. So going with my example Panicky may bring up the following thoughts, feelings, beliefs and behaviors when experienced:

Panicky
Fear
want to run
sweat
heart beats
hands tremble
feel tense
feel sick
feel dizzy
help
can't cope
feel a failure
feel stupid

feel weak

OR (another example)

Arguing
Fight
distress
angry
going round in circles
shout
cry
throw things
exciting

OR

Food
eat loads
love it
hate it
need it
guilty
comfort
get angry with myself
despair
hate myself
get fat
self loathing

Now these are just examples and your lists will be unique to you, with your own personal feelings and thoughts. It's best to have more than five items on your list, and make it like a shopping list with short snappy definite descriptions of what your experience is (if you haven't got a piece of paper and pen yet because a part of you thinks 'we'll just skip this bit and come back to it' then don't listen to that part! nine times out of ten you won't return to it. Its your resistance that orchestrates this. (If you want to overcome your problems you need to overcome resistance from the onset)............................ Now look at your list. Somewhere at some point in your past (childhood or adolescence) within this list are feelings, thoughts, beliefs and experiences you have had before. Now it may be easier to assume that it is your present day predicament that is causing the discomfort or episode within you, but in fact this bone of contention has only arisen because of unresolved matters from your past. Now you may say "But how can fighting with my husband be something I did as a child!", well naturally that can't be possible. Yet what is possible is at the core of this situation are feelings, thoughts and behaviors which have been experienced before but under similar or different circumstances, at a different time in your life. The circumstances are different (or similar) but the triggers and the subsequent feelings, beliefs and thoughts match. So if fighting with your husband brings on fear, insecurity or anger this may relate to you witnessing your parents fighting, and fear, insecurity or anger were how you felt as a child when witnessing those clashes. Or if it feels more like rebel, hate, trapped you may be re-enacting your teenage years when fighting with your dad. Its all relative and shouldn't be underestimated.

Please keep your list as I will be explaining further, and showing you how to work with this and other lists in Chapter 6. This technique is called *Gold Counselling (TM)* and is one of the surest ways to get to the root of present day problems and concerns.

'One must have chaos in oneself in order to give birth to a
dancing star'
Friedrich Nietzsche

Symptoms

Symptoms (or effects) are created by the mind to let us know something is wrong, or out of balance, and needs healing. Symptoms can range from headaches to rejection, from skin rashes to car accidents. Symptoms may present themselves as troublesome feelings, unwelcome emotions, unpleasant thoughts, detrimental beliefs or recurring physical ailments. Or symptoms may be expressed outwardly, have you ever had a bad day? Have you ever had one of those days when everything goes wrong? I have had numerous days like that! Not so much these days thankfully. I remember a particular day when; the car wouldn't start, my skirt got ripped, I had a letter to say a cheque had bounced, my dog was sick on my new carpet, the power went off, the front door lock broke. Yes these things can happen all in one day!! as many of you may well know.

So why is it when things go wrong sometimes it tends to happen as a succession of events? Well I believe this is a symptom being expressed outwardly, your mind is trying to tell you something needs healing, your mind is shouting at you to address an area, and these 'days' will come again and again until you get the message! (isolated, upsetting or trying events are also just as important, and will carry their own message).

I have many examples of how this has affected me in my own life, and the lessons I have learnt, but instead of me writing reams on that alone let me just give you one further example. I woke up one morning feeling a bit tense, when I got up I found my dog Jenny had urinated all over the lounge floor, the toilet was blocked (both of these are signs of needing to release something), when I had dropped my daughter off at school a woman pulled out of her drive too quickly and nearly hit me then she went on to stick two fingers up at me and mouth a swear word, I was very annoyed! I later took my dogs to the park and Jenny got into a fight, I went into town and couldn't get any money out of the bank and had to embarrassingly tell the car park attendant the same, when I got home I had a letter telling me the rent was going up, and then my back fence blew over. At this point I began to cry I'd had enough!, I felt like life was punishing me and singling me out, that 'God up there' was laughing at me, I felt victimized. With this a growing anger began to rise within me, at that point I had a phone call from my ex-husband to say he wouldn't be able to look after our little girl when I had clients that evening. I thought ,"Why is life throwing all this at me, what have I done?" Then I realized I was creating it myself, it occurred to me that life was trying to make me angry and it was doing a good job!!. When I worked on it I discovered I needed to release some festering anger that had its roots in my childhood. When I eventually let the anger out about the 'right thing' i.e. the past issue, my day began to go swimmingly. My sister popped round and said she could baby sit that evening and lent me $10, my neighbor's fence had also blown over so he very kindly agreed to repair mine too. Suddenly the sun was shining on my world again! Yet in reality it wasn't anything 'out there' that had changed, I had changed. And changing something within me caused the 'out there' to change too. I felt better so everything around me 'got better' too. Have you ever noticed that on those days you feel good things tend to go well? This isn't just a coincidence, we have the ability to create our own reality depending on what's going on within us at any given time. Depending on our thoughts, feelings and beliefs. If we feel bad- things go wrong, if we feel good- things go right. It's a universal law. Learn this law, resolve to live by it and...hey presto your in control.

The reason there is so much chaos in the world is not because God is punishing us, it's because we have not learnt to understand ourselves, once we heal the chaos within each of us then the world will be at peace. This may be a profound statement but it is one hundred per cent true! Once we all find peace within ourselves the world will be in harmony, because the world mirrors us. What we need to do is devote time to looking at our symptoms, whether they be from our emotions or bodies, or projected out as experiences or situations, we owe it to ourselves to become whole. If we make a conscious decision to grow and change this will have a knock on effect. We are coming into an age where the consciousness of human beings is rising to a higher vibration, this means we are all being moved to heal ourselves, because in healing ourselves we heal the world. It is no coincidence you are reading this book, at some level you have been guided to do this. At some level you are being shown how to heal because it is time, so feel thankful that spirit has chosen you as one of the people deemed capable of taking on this quest. As time moves on you will realize what part you will play in this unfoldment of the new age, because you have a part (a very important part) and the journey toward this will become more apparent as you harmonize, heal and balance the inner you.

Symptoms as messengers

Below I have included a brief list of what some symptoms (internal and external) can mean. This small catalogue of signs is merely for general reference and has been included to give you some idea as to how manifested problems have their links in the past, or are trying to give us a signal about something that needs to be addressed in the present that is in some way related to the past. Please read all of them to get a full appreciation as to how our bodies and the universe wants to communicate with us about unresolved issues. For a more condensed listing and description please see Lise Bourbeau's excellent book *'Your Body's Telling You To Love Yourself'* and *'Sign Posts'* by Denise Linn.

Accidents: Feeling like a victim of some change, feeling powerless or being urged to change. Unresolved anger or poor self worth.

Acne: Dislike self and are very sensitive. A sign of struggling to please one or both parents. Repressed hurts festering.

Agoraphobia: Usually dependent on mother as a child and felt responsible for her happiness. May also come from an early isolated incident in childhood, or from wanting to protect self or others.

Aggression: Seeing aggression around you is a sign of unresolved anger within yourself.

Aids: Have deep seated low self worth related to emotional or physical rejection as a child.

Appendicitis: Repressed anger, often to do with an authority figure in life who unconsciously reminds you of a parent. May feel trapped and ready to burst.

Arguments: If recurring in your life signals unresolved conflicts within yourself, usually from the past.

Asthma: You take on too much. Want to seem strong to others to gain love. Suffocating yourself with obligations, and tried hard to please one or both parents as a child to gain acceptance. Also suppressed grief.

Bad breath: Tremendous internal pain, thoughts of hatred, vengeance or extreme anger that seethe below the surface, with roots in childhood.

Bed wetting: Repressed fear of one's father, or main carer, fears displeasing this parent and not living up to his expectations. Pent up emotions related to this are released at night.

Being Chased (in dreams): What are you running from? What are you afraid to face in your life? Also fear of abuse as a child.

Blocked sink or toilet: Blocked emotions that need to be released. What are you holding onto?

Breaking things by accident: Time to take a break, get out of a situation or resolve something, to break free or time to break up with someone.

Bronchitis: Results from a family crisis or constant quarrelling. Wanting to branch out and have own life but may be too young or feel guilty.

Cancer: Significant emotional wounding as a child usually linked to rejection, abandonment, humiliation, betrayal and/or injustice. This results in anger toward one or both parents, and with other emotions repressed this creates a growing wound - the cancer.

Cysts: Manifestations of unresolved issues, usually linked to sadness or sorrow from the past

Epilepsy: A result of self criticism and self loathing, blaming self and turning anger and violence inward. This self dislike comes from childhood, and if children suffer from it this is usually to distract problems between two parents so they will come together to care for the child

Flood (in your environment): Overwhelming emotions that haven't been addressed.

High blood pressure: Unconsciously harboring unhealed and unresolved emotional wounds from the past. Anger.

Insomnia - Underlying anxiety which has its roots in the past.

Knee problems - Unresolved hurt and resentment from childhood.

Mumps: As a child felt criticized or ignored causing accumulated resentment to swell up.

Obesity: Usually related to feeling humiliated or ashamed as a child. Often related to abuse and other childhood trauma which would necessitate weight being used later on as protection. Need to feel big in the world to be safe or keep others away.

Tooth problems: Right side indicates unresolved issues with father, left side with mother.

and the list goes on...

"Whatever you send out is what you draw back in. Take responsibility for the thoughts and emotions you send out, for they go into the universe and create the events and circumstances that come back to you"
Orin

Your Treasure Trove- The Unconscious Mind

Vera Peiffer author of *Positive Thinking* accurately likens the mind to an iceberg, and it is the closest representation I have found. The mind like the iceberg consists of two parts. The conscious mind is the tip of the iceberg and this part helps us to deal with day to day life, it gets us up, washed and dressed in the morning, it enables us to tell the time, make decisions through the day, have conversations, type on the computer, organize other people, organize the children, make phone calls, hoover the floor, go shopping and so on. It is our rational part. The unconscious mind however is quite different and far more complex, and can be compared with the submerged part of the iceberg, and this part in recent years has only begun to be properly understood.

The unconscious mind has many amazing functions, as well as

gifts, and I'm not sure that even in this great century of technology and advancement we will still fully appreciate the power and potential the unconscious mind holds for us. One of the better known functions of the unconscious is that it stores repetitious behavior. If we learn to drive a car at first we are doing it consciously, but then as it is repeated again and again we begin to store the experience of driving as memory- within our unconscious. When this happens we don't need to consciously think about driving, it becomes automatic. It becomes unconscious. The same applies when we do a long journey a few times, after a while we don't need to consciously think about the route, it becomes automatic, or when learning a new dance, after some practice our bodies just do the steps without us even having to think about them. Our unconscious takes over.

However the conscious and unconscious mind work very closely together, the conscious mind is continuously filtering information from the external (environment) and internal (thoughts) world to the unconscious, and all this information is stored. The unconscious has the most amazing filing system known to man, more amazing than a computer. Your unconscious is a true treasure house, because within it are all your memories (and the feelings associated with these memories), and you can access those memories.

Thinking back to my client who had been stung by a bee as a child and then had an allergic reaction to the sting. The incident then went on to be stored in her unconscious mind, and this 'memory' then gave her an automatic reaction each time she saw a bee thereafter. She felt fear, distress, panic and completely over-reacted each time she saw a bee, or anything that represented the bee sting, for her it was injections.

This also happens with repressed memories as discussed in Chapter 1 if the memory is too traumatizing for us to cope with as children it is filtered through our conscious as experience, and then stored in our unconscious as memory - not to be remembered, until it can be revealed at a later date. But with cause there is effect (symptoms), so if we were sexually abused as a child (cause) we may go onto have weight problems (effect, symptom) as adults, to protect ourselves from sexual advances.

Our conscious mind will also filter through how we view ourselves in the world, as well as absorb things that were said to us. So if either one of our parents was regularly absent we may filter from our conscious mind to our unconscious that we are unlovable or not good enough, and later as an effect of this we may harbor deep seated feelings of insecurity about our worthiness.

Or you may have been repeatedly told you were stupid, or useless. Over time this message would become imbedded in your unconscious mind as a truth. Then as an adult you will have a deep-seated belief that you are useless and stupid, and beliefs have to full fill themselves. As a consequence you will later (in adulthood) enter into a situation (unconsciously) where eventually you will be made to feel stupid or useless. This may be a work situation where your boss is very critical or the workload is overwhelming, this is what's known as a self fulfilling prophecy. So this is where a cycle begins, you believe deep down that you are stupid and look here your boss says the same, so it must be true! But it isn't! It was your dad's decision to tell you were stupid (probably a message given to him as a child) and that doesn't make him right.

Your unconscious mind is suggestible when you are growing up and it will readily accept whatever messages are being filtered through, it is like a clean slate waiting to be drawn upon. So if your dad tells you your stupid then this becomes a sentence on your slate, and a sentence in your life!

Have you ever met those people who say, "See I told you something would go wrong" or "I said happiness never lasts look at me now!" or "I knew it would be bad luck to walk under that ladder I've just lost 20 dollars." What's happening here is at some point these individuals have taken on the belief that happiness never lasts, or whatever other negative belief that has become their truth, and because they believe it they will attract situations or people to fulfill the belief. Making them believe in the belief even more!

The good news is that the unconscious also stores positive beliefs and memories. So if you felt loved as a child no matter what, you will learn that its ok for you to make mistakes as an adult without it affecting your self esteem. You will view mistakes as a learning curve and not bully yourself about them. You will find relationships easier because you like yourself and know you deserve love, respect and care. Generally all aspects of your life will be easier due to your childhood messages being of a positive and loving nature. Even if you only have a few happy memories, your unconscious would have learnt pleasurable feelings to accompany these times, and each time you're in a similar situation you will experience these feelings again. Like my sister Abbi who has happy memories of caravan holidays as a child, and now relives those feelings each time she goes to a caravan park.

So to fully heal ourselves we must understand what is happening within our unconscious mind, and to do this we must explore our symptoms and our beliefs. When our perception is constructive, when we see the truth, when the thoughts and awareness being filtered through is harmonious, life-enhancing, positive, radiant and peaceful, our unconscious responds. It is then we truly understand and witness the treasure house within all of us, it is then the unconscious can show its infinite magic.

When you begin to undo the negative thinking and resolve the past hurts your unconscious will help transform your life. Your relationships will become more fulfilling, you will find work you love, money will no longer be an issue, it will be easier to let go of 'addictions' such as smoking, food or sex, you will feel balanced, clearheaded and strong. You will gain a new perspective on life as if you have just 'woken up', you will have more energy, feel in touch with yourself and in control (plus more besides).

Life expanding riches are within you, you have the power to turn your life around, you have the power to live joyously and abundantly. There is no magic formula 'out there', there is in fact nothing 'out there' that can keep you consistently happy if you are not happy 'within'. To be truly happy we must sort out our inner garden, we must pull up the old weeds, get rid of the rubbish, create a space and plant new seeds. We must then tend those seeds, water them, feed them and bath them in sunlight. These roots will grow strong and our new plants will flourish, and we will have a new healthy, alive, colorful, vibrant, abundant garden. Our unconscious mind will become the floral delight it was meant to be before all the weeds and rubbish came to prevent positive natural growth.

Beliefs

At 17 years old Bethany had just married a man who was an alcoholic, and when he drank he became violent and abusive. Although she 'loved' him, she realized she was with him because she didn't believe anyone else would want her, Bethany's self esteem and feelings of self worth were at zero level. Unconsciously Andy personified her father. At a young age Bethany's father sexually abused her and said because she was 'tainted' no one else would want her. How Bethany attracted someone like Andy into her world is all part of the tapestry of life, yet we do know at an unconscious level she was carrying on the relationship she had with her father because she believed no one 'better' (as in better I mean with higher self esteem) would be interested in her. Bethany's beliefs from childhood, which were mistaken, were ruling her life - and the ego was the voice in her head which would remind her daily she was unworthy and keep her trapped. It wasn't until Bethany went into therapy that she began to see the patterns evident in her psyche and how destructive they were to her well-being.

When we are children we are young, innocent and vulnerable, and most of our vulnerability is in what we learn to believe as we are growing up. We are completely dependent on our parents and give them our unconditional love, we see them as all knowing role models, and what they say to us verbally and non-verbally we generally take as truth. Our clean slate, as I mentioned earlier, is now being written upon. The problem is for us as children we don't know or can't assess whether what our parents are telling us is fair, right or appropriate. If we are told we are clumsy enough times we will believe it, if we are made to feel second best we will become it, and if we are told we are clever we will exhibit that too.

So as we grow we learn to believe that certain ways of thinking or behaving are absolutely correct (even if they're not) and so much of this can be detrimental to our development as children, but later on it can limit us as adults too. Some beliefs are handed down without our parents, carers or society even questioning the beliefs themselves like 'money is the root of all evil' or 'life is about luck' or 'get a proper job if you want security with money'. Some beliefs are created inadvertently when certain situations arise. For example, Paul's parents split up when he was a child. Paul suffered from epilepsy which was very severe when he was young, he later linked this to his parents separation which manifested into the belief ,"I am a bad person". No-one told Paul he was a bad person he created that for himself being too young to question it or decide if it was appropriate.

It's like believing in Father Christmas or monsters, for the child these figures are real, but after a while this concept begins to wear off as the child understands through time that they don't actually exist. Yet hundreds of other concepts are left, unquestioned in our unconscious mind.

Consider for a moment a child whose mother is going through a traumatic divorce, the child still needs to be cuddled, played with, looked after and loved. The mother on the other hand is too depressed and says "Sorry darling mummy's upset at the moment and needs a drink, please leave me alone." If this goes on for long enough the child will learn to believe that her needs are not important, or that she is not important. She will not have the adult reasoning to decide whether her beliefs are valid, and will assume they must be. She cannot understand her mother is going through a bad time and its her mothers inability to cope that is creating the child's neglect. The child is unable to distinguish that she is still a valuable human being and her needs are important despite this, so she takes it 'personally' and decides the opposite carrying these beliefs into adulthood. Then as an adult she may draw someone to her who will co-create with her a relationship where her needs will come 2nd, if not 3rd or 4th. The belief always successfully weaves its way through our lives, reflecting what we feel about ourselves unconsciously, showing up in relationships, work, home life etc.

So as a child your beliefs have accumulated from your experiences and relationships over the years, some of these beliefs may be beneficial, helpful and there for your general good. Others, as mentioned, will be inappropriate, negative and there for your demise or stagnation.

For you as an adult beliefs are very powerful, they determine the way you think, feel or behave. In fact they determine the very fabric of your life and literally create the very circumstances of it. If you look at your life and your relationships they will tell you much about your beliefs. Your beliefs pull to you all that you believe in.

Another point to note is that sometimes your beliefs may be in conflict, and this is where positive thinking can fail if our unconscious beliefs are not addressed. Positive thinking and affirmations work fantastically well but if at an unconscious level we believe something different to what we are telling our self, our unconscious will win. For example if you are going for a job interview and your friends say, "Think positively!" and you think, "Ok, I will" and repeat, "I am going to get this job, I am going to get this job" over and over, but what will happen if unconsciously you believe you are not good enough and change is scary? Well I can assure you it is highly likely you will not get the job because no amount of positive thinking contains enough power in it to over ride the beliefs of the unconscious mind. Once you have changed your beliefs within your unconscious in line with positive thoughts you have the power to move mountains! but until then you can only hope to create a breeze. This is why we often fail with will power alone, if you want to lose weight or stop smoking but unconsciously believe food and cigarettes are addictive, then will power will be over-ridden. Will power is no match for unconscious power.

'Nothing is beyond your ability to create
Nothing is beyond your ability to experience
You are limited by nothing but your thoughts'
Diana Johnson

Thoughts

Thoughts are the products of our beliefs, our beliefs are like small cyclones and our thoughts are the energy magnets which pull to us life circumstances and people which match our beliefs. Your thoughts have real substance (conscious and unconscious) and they are extremely potent because they are able to duplicate themselves in form (they also magnetize more powerfully if their is plenty of emotion attached to them). Everything you see in the world was a thought in someone's mind before it existed in reality. Cars, computers, homes, gardens, clothes, light bulbs, plates, ovens, playgrounds, schools, buildings, aero planes, knitting needles, marbles, they all existed as thoughts before they became real. The same is true for life circumstances, redundancy, money problems, divorce, arguments, stress, depression, as well as positive experiences such as marriage, childbirth, winning money, laughing with friends, holidays, good news, achievement, inner peace etc. All of these were thoughts before they became realities. Now I know what you're thinking, how can I have created my own redundancy, or stress, or depression or that car crash, I didn't anticipate that! I certainly wasn't thinking about that before it happened! No of course not, but then again your unconscious was. Your unconscious colludes with spirit, god/goddess, the all that is, to pull experiences to you for your growth. Yes it all happens for your own good. It may seem difficult to imagine that your painful times have come for your betterment, but they have. As I said before symptoms are messengers, symptoms from within and without, they have come to show you something, to tell you something, maybe change is needed or something requires healing. No matter what it is it all started within your mind, and it will always pull to you exactly what you need. Even the death of a loved one is giving us an opportunity to grow, nothing happens by accident.

So if thoughts attract to us our life situations then changing those which bring into being negative happenings or feelings at conscious and unconscious levels must be addressed if we are to gain control over our lives, and ourselves. It is like we are steering a carriage pulled by horses which for some of the time goes in the direction we want, and then for the rest of the time takes us through rough territory where we experience rocky roads, thick mud, frightening chasms and towering volcanoes -to places we would rather not go. This is why it is so imperative to change our beliefs (negative and limiting) re-programme them, and formulate thoughts (about us and life) that pull to us what we want and dream about.

What you can do now
Begin to pay attention to what you are thinking about during the day. Especially focus upon areas that are causing you unhap-

piness maybe money, your health or work. Focus too on what you say about yourself, constantly criticizing yourself or believing you don't deserve to be happy can have an astoundingly detrimental affect on your life. Negative thinking can also make us feel like victims, 'poor me' statements being fed into your unconscious which will dutifully bring to you experiences and people to validate this, a vicious circle is then created. So listen to yourself thinking, it is often surprising how many negative thoughts pass through our minds. If you become conscious of your thoughts now, and make some effort to change them (even if you just work on one area of your life or self) it will help accelerate your progress with this book. Here are some examples:

Negative
"I'm such a failure nobody likes me"

Positive
"I'm doing ok, I'm doing my best, I'm lovable and have many great qualities"

Negative
"I never have any money"

Positive
"Money flows into my life with ease"

Negative
"I'm always ill what's wrong with me"

Positive
"My mind is showing me the reason for my illness, I create good health and vitality"

So say for example you'd noticed yourself constantly saying,

"Everything always goes wrong, my life is a mess," each time you have that thought now say, "Everything now goes right, I am sorting things out and everything is going to get better." When you are thinking of positive thoughts its important to keep them phrased in a way that can be used by your unconscious for example don't think, "I won't have money troubles" as this focuses on the negative, instead say, "My money troubles are being solved." Or "I won't be tense" instead, "I am calm and relaxed." Tell your mind what you want to experience rather than what you don't. Also use the present tense instead of, "I will be confident" say, "I am confident." Even if the positive thought feels odd and untrue, don't worry! If they felt true you wouldn't have to do affirmations. You have to start somewhere, what you are doing is planting a seed which over time will germinate and grow as you repeat the thought. So it is important to keep repeating the thought at times during the day. It may be some time before you see the thought actualized, or sometimes you may see a difference in a matter of days. Whatever your unconscious is processing the information and will do all it can to produce that reality for you. I have a list of positive affirmations by my bed and each night and morning I read them to myself, they go like this:

I approve of myself
I support myself
I trust myself
I am my best friend
I love myself
Its easy to love myself
I have lots of friends who love me
I live in a loving world
I am so lovable
I attract loving, happy situations
My life is filled with joy
My life is full of abundance

I solve everything easily
I have the answers
I am worthy of success

You might want to take one of these or your own and practice saying it to yourself on a daily basis, use it as a mantra to confirm to yourself what you want to create, and as you say it really allow the feeling to arise that pulling this to you would bring. Don't repeat the thought in parrot fashion, imagine you already have it and let that feeling surge through you, really believe you will have this. The more you can imagine the feelings associated with the thought, even just for a few seconds, the more rapidly it will be manifest. Thinking positively must not become a chore either, if you choose to think positively about something only three or four times a week for five minutes that's better than doing it everyday for fifteen and secretly resenting it.

Be aware of negative influences around you, like negative people or stories heard on the news. These 'incidences' are occurring because you may have doubts in your positivity, so they mirror you. Try not to waver in your thinking even if the rest of the world seems to have a different view! Try to avoid the tabloids, nay sayers or negative friends if you can, they have a right to their own thinking but you have a right to yours too (if you have to spend time with cynical people, or those 'hooked' on drama make a conscious decision to not be influenced by them). Every positive experience is born of positive thoughts, and the same goes for negative experiences too. We create our own reality from our thinking, this is a valuable truth that so much of the world has yet to learn. Each time you hear or see negativity don't judge that situation instead send loving healing thoughts to it like, "I send love and healing to this situation, may this situation be resolved in the most positive loving way. I am strong and happy." If we send negativity or judgment to a person or situation we are then sending energy to help amplify their dilemma. Keep your thoughts as pure as possible for yourself, others and the planet.

Just to note, earlier I said postive thinking has no effect if it is in conflict with the unconscious. This of course is true but that does not mean you can't start thinking postively now, this sounds like a contradiction so let me explain. All positive thoughts are feed into and heard by the mind, which means they are getting through. If you think 'I create only happiness' and this is in conflict with your unconscious you may create the opposite, yet if you persist with the thought and *believe* you can create only happiness your mind will have to initiate a shift. This means if you say 'I create only happiness' and truly believe you can your unconscious will devise ways to bring this into reality. This then usually means any unconscious thoughts which are in conflict with the new belief (i.e I don't deserve happiness) will come up to be resolved. So positive thinking can bring results but only if you make up your mind that this is going to happen and are prepared to work with whatever your unconscious throws up to bring this about.

'The ego is not the bad guy; It is simply a collection of beliefs'
Burt Hotchkiss. Your Owners Manual.

The Ego

As you begin to help yourself either using the exercises in this book, changing your thinking and/or seeking out other resources or professionals to assist your ego is going to make its presence felt. The ego is the part of you that has been developed over the years by your perception. It is like the moving camera within us that shows us what is happening in our external world and this is then fed into our conscious awareness. Our ego uses the information which is promptly filed in the filing cabinet of our mind, whether good or bad, all these experiences become part of our data base and the conclusions you draw will be noted on your belief system file. So before entering into a similar experience you will refer to this data base and it will determine how you will feel, respond and perceive this event.

For example if as a child you were bitten by a dog and the experience frightened you, this would be noted by the ego and filed. As time goes by each time you see a dog your ego will warn you that dogs are frightening, even if this is generally untrue, and you will go out of your way to avoid them. This is one of the problems of the ego as it accumulates experiences and then refers to them throughout your life, whether they are relevant or not. Each time you refer to them and believe them, you nourish them and they continue to rule your existence. Most of these beliefs are from childhood and are no longer true, helpful, or relevant anymore.

The ego is the voice of our beliefs and thoughts and it is in fact a type of defence mechanism that has got out of hand. When you hear yourself saying, "I can't do that," "Its pointless trying I'll make a fool of myself" or "I'm not good enough," this is the voice of your ego. It doesn't want you to take chances, try to better yourself or be your true self because it wants to protect you from disappointment. This perception comes from the past and has been developed because of things that were said, or the way you felt about yourself when you were young.

For example, Jason was fed messages as a child that culminated in him believing that he wasn't good enough. His mother would say to him he had been a 'mistake' and if it wasn't for him her life would be so much happier, she would be free and not saddled with the responsibility of parenting. Jason believed he had no right to be on the earth and was unlovable. His ego filtered this information and filed it in his belief system database. As an adult whenever Jason thought about applying for a better job his ego would say 'No don't do that, you know you're not worthy you'll only feel stupid when you fail'. When he entered into a relationship he would set out to sabotage it before it even started, he'd be regularly late, extremely nervous and find numerous excuses as to why he couldn't spend much time with his new girlfriend. His ego was finding ways to shield him from getting to close, even though this is what he desired. Deep down Jason believed he would be rejected and his ego constantly filled his thoughts with doubts and fears to steer him away from encountering that outcome. It did this so Jason wouldn't get hurt but in affect it was holding him back, it wasn't allowing him to grow and change and to experience life to the full - it was over protecting him.

Like a parent who smothers their child, there is no room for experimenting and becoming autonomous, there is no opportunity for growth or freedom. Life is seen as threatening with no leeway for mistakes or failing, with no risk of getting hurt or feeling true joy. The ego overpowers your essence and causes you to believe this is who you truly are, but the ego is your false self. The ego is your mental energy field, it knows nothing of spirit and your true self. It can't contemplate love, success and abundance in an unlimited form, it would say that was selfish, impossible or not for you. It will pester you with thoughts of, "Why are you bothering this is crazy" or "Don't listen to her she's just found a clever way to make money out of a book!"

The ego will kid us that everything 'out there' is the reason for all our problems and discomfort, it doesn't want us to take responsibility for our lives because that would mean we would have to address our issues, see ourselves as the source and change. The ego doesn't like change, it wants to feel safe, to stay in the same relationship, to keep at the same job, to live in the same area. If we branch out 'this that and everything else might happen' says the ego. The enigma is if we don't grow, heal and move with life we will become stagnant. We will look to other sources to create that 'buzz', i.e. with drink, TV, shopping and other meaningless activities that the ego believes will make us happy.

In truth it is the ego which is the begetter of all our suffering, it is nothing we can point to 'out there'. We may believe that in changing others around us we will be happy, but in reality we need to change to create happiness in our lives, we will then 'attract' the right people, or the people around us will naturally change too. This doesn't mean that changing yourself to change others is down to you (there goes your ego!). Everyone is responsible for themselves although sometimes when we do begin the process of healing and finding our true self it can have a ripple effect on those around us. It's as if you have raised the vibration in your immediate environment, and as you do those open to it will respond (this does not always happen, in such cases we have to learn to be more tolerant of others or move on).

So we have to recognize the ego as a saboteur, it is limited and separate and not who we really are, it is all our negative thinking. It is the voice of our restrictive beliefs, it feeds off our inner child's fears and keeps us stuck, cut off and unhappy. It fills our heads with destructive thoughts and ignites self defeating emotions. We have to begin to recognize the ego and begin to take charge of our own direction in life. The ego was never meant to be in charge, it is inept as a manager, it just thinks it should be in charge for our own safety and well being - the ego is a cowboy (no offence to wild west cowboys!). It is us who should be holding the reins and steering the way, our true self.

Gill Edwards from her life changing book 'Living Magically' lists some tell tale signs that the ego has taken charge:

* We worry about trivialities
* Feel anxious and fearful
* Feel despairing, helpless and hopeless
* Feel resentful and guilty
* Want approval and admiration
* Take things personally
* Criticize and judge others
* Feel empty and dissatisfied

* Swing from one mood to another
* Feel hurried and 'driven'
* Strive to be 'perfect'
* Concerned with outward appearances and worldly success
* Focus exclusively on goals and results
* Cling to the past
* Are afraid of change
* Worry about failure, humiliation and rejection
* Compete rather than cooperate
* Are manipulative
* Harm and abuse others
* Are rigid and inflexible
* Are unable to live in the present moment
* Become addicted to drugs or alcohol
* Desperately seek love and security
* Want to be 'special' to someone
* Feel that life is futile and meaningless
* Take ourselves very seriously
* Wait for the world 'out there' to be OK in order to feel OK

I was recently reading a book by Paul McKenna entitled 'Change Your Life In Seven Days', in it he has an exercise which is great when wanting to deal with the ego and put it in perspective. Please try this out:

1. Stop for a moment and talk to yourself in your critical voice, saying all those nasty things in that unpleasant tone.

2. Notice now where you make that voice. Does it seem to be coming from inside your head or outside? Is it at the front, the sides or the back?

3. Extend your arm out and stick out your thumb.

4. Wherever the critical voice was, move it down your arm to the tip of your thumb, so its now speaking to you from there.

5. Next slow it down and change the tone of it. Make it sound sexy, or speed it up so it sounds like Mickey Mouse.

Now it should sound much less threatening!

> 'You will be free of suffering when you no longer see the
> benefit in it'
> Burt Hotchkiss

Victim Consciousness

When you become stuck in victim mentality it can mess up your life, it dis-empowers you and enables you to blame your parents, your spouse, your schooling, your job, your mother-in-law, your children and so on. Victim consciousness is a trick of the ego.

When my 2nd marriage broke up and I was left to care for our 7 month old daughter, for about 5 years following that I would slip in and out of victim consciousness. Deep down inside I felt like a failure and constantly reprimanded myself. Each time I saw my ex I would feel resentment and hurt wondering how he could have walked out on me at a time when I needed him the most. Because I had sunk into a period of depression I felt unable to see clients and look after a baby at the same time, so I stopped my practice and claimed state benefit to be a full time mum. Following this though my life circumstances led me to feel poor, lonely, incompetent and victimized. All this together eroded my self-esteem and I felt like the biggest loser ever! I was stuck in victim consciousness. Because I was stuck in this 'poor me' mental frame work I attracted trauma, money problems and further hurt, it seemed like a constant cycle which made me feel even more helpless and dependent on others to validate and support me. I felt angry with life and decided that I was put on the earth to suffer whilst others had a good time, I scolded god, the angels, my ex and anyone else I could blame 'out there' for my awful predicament. Then one day I recalled how our thinking creates our life and how we get what we focus upon, so I decided I'd better change my thoughts and attitude if I wanted things to improve. So this, coupled with me dealing with abandonment issues from my past, began to make the difference in my life. I decided to take responsibility. I saw the break up as 'meant to be' and learnt to grow from it, I understood the lessons and looking back can understand fully why we had to split, it was the beginning of the making of me. So as I changed my thinking from, "Life is a struggle" to "My life is filled with joy" or "I have to do everything myself" to "I have lots of support", my life finally began to change for the better. I stopped seeing myself as a victim and saw myself as a strong woman who was capable of anything! Life then reflected this back to me.

We all go through trauma, difficult times and get stuck in victim consciousness, unfortunately some people seem to be in it all the time. The problem with this ego illusion is that it can destroy our life and dis-empower us, it saps all our resources and condemns us to an existence of self pity. The ego constantly tells us we are bad, stupid, failing, hopeless, unlovable and whatever else it can think up, and because we attract what we think about we are then bombarded with problems and people who reflect our beliefs. We are having a bad day, a very bad day!

Sometimes though when I have tried to help clients, friends or family who seem 'trapped' in this reality they don't always want to shift. This is because there are payoffs to being a victim, one being it means we don't have to take responsibility. How often do you hear yourself or others blaming someone else or something else for things going wrong in their lives, yes all the time! It's so easy to do this, mainly because we've learnt to address issues in this way. Yet it also means we can avoid discerning what's wrong inside ourselves, we don't have to face ourselves, we don't have to acknowledge our shadow or what we see as our failings. Instead we can blame everyone else and feel fine. It can also give us permission to wallow in self-pity and punish others. I have seen many clients who seemed to sabotage happiness and success at every turn, everything always went wrong, relationships were difficult and they were never happy. As we explored this part that kept 'messing things up' we often found the client was punishing one or more parents. They believed that staging out this self pitiful life would eventually bring them the love they wanted from their parents or would make their parents feel guilty. Its a typical cut your nose off to spite your face scenario, but who loses really? Yes you do. This is such a dangerous game that the ego plays, and needs to be nipped in the bud.

Maybe you are angry with your parents but there are ways to deal with this so you won't suffer anymore, because it is only you who is suffering when you are stuck in victim hood. Now don't start to berate or blame yourself when you recognize those times you have been or are living as a victim, this is the voice of your ego again. Be gentle with yourself, recognize your reasons for 'playing the game' and resolve to do something about it.

Often when we have a lot of emotional pain to deal with from childhood victim consciousness can feel like an everyday occurrence, purely because we feel depressed, angry, hurt, worthless or in anguish most of the time. Please be reassured that healing does take time. If you recognize that the ego is running your life and you have a problem overcoming this, don't worry. As you use the exercises and begin to resolve problems you are going to find in time that the ego has less and less of a hold over you, so even if the mountain looks high now say to yourself, "Ego your days are numbered I'm sorting this!"

Another aspect of victim consciousness is martyr hood which can be more difficult to recognize as it doesn't appear to come from a victim perspective, but it is. Martyrs walk around with the world on their shoulders saying, "Don't worry I'm ok" they take on too much do too much and try to appear strong. Then deep down inside they feel resentful, misunderstood, unappreciated and burdened. They rarely ask for help or complain but secretly hope others will see how tough life is for them, and then see them as saints in some way. Ego is the self-righteous martyr within all of us and all it really seeks to do is punish. If you recognize this part within you then understand that this is a wounded part that wants to talk about its suffering, suffering that probably occurred in the past. The martyr is merely a reflection of our emotionally burdened inner child.

Remember times when you have experienced the victim or martyr hood persona, who were you angry with or trying to punish? Did you enjoy feeling sorry for yourself? Did it get you what you wanted rather than what you needed? Did it in some way make you feel powerful and more able to manipulate others? Do you feel unable to ask for help as you may appear weak, dependent or have to be grateful? Is there someone you find hard to forgive (even if that persons dead)? Do you believe one day something or someone is going to come to save you from all this ? Do you feel having problems is the only way you'll gain love or attention? Do you feel guilty about something and only feel ok about it if you're being 'punished', Do you cling to 'problems' because it enables you to fit in better with family or friends? Do you have a subconscious contract to never compete or do better than one or more parents? Do you feel powerful and enjoy seeing other's feel guilty or inadequate when you take on too much? Are you avoiding responsibility for your life?

Now assess your life and, if appropriate, see the price you pay for being a victim or martyr. How might you be different and your life be transformed if this part was given up?

The 'better than' illusion.

Have you ever met those people who walk about with an air of arrogance and superiority about then obviously believing they are better than everyone else? Now think of a time when you did this, yes we all do it! When we think or behave in this way it is just another mechanism of the ego to make us feel 'ok' in the world. Comparing ourselves to others who appear to be less fortunate, less able, less intelligent, less capable, less attractive, less wealthy, less liked, less accepted, less worldly, younger, a different color, or a different sex, is the greatest way the ego can ensure its not failing or looking stupid, no its doing ok because someone over there is doing worse than or is 'lower' than it!

The ego cannot bare to think that we are all equal as it then has nothing to compare itself with to make it feel better. Deep down the ego feels inadequate and a fraud. Its the part of you which longs to feel special - this need is developed from infancy. If we are seen as 'special' we are more likely to fit in, be loved and our survival continues. This is a childhood defence mechanism which unfortunately clouds our judgment as we believe money, talents, relationships, material belongings such as big cars and big houses, status, degree's and many other 'illusions' we acquire to make us feel special or better than others, or will ensure we will be loved or liked. This does not mean there's anything wrong with wanting a lovely home, qualifications or a partner who adores us, but when we use these to make ourselves feel better we are really coming from a sense of lack. This sense of lack is a lack from within - of low self- esteem. People with high self- esteem who feel good about themselves will not be racist, homophobic or chauvinistic. They will not need to 'flash their cash' or have the newest sports car to secure a date. They will not be condescending or superciliously kind. They will not have to wear lots of 'bling' to feel good or don the top high street fashions to get noticed. These are all accolades which serve the ego. Those with high self- esteem are already comfortable with themselves and do not require extra 'assets' to get by. They already know their greatest asset is themselves.

The People pleaser

People pleasers are those who need to please others at their own expense. They do this to feel loved, accepted and liked. Yet invariably people pleasers are used and abused. If you do a lot for others, want to help and are very giving this does not necessarily make you a people pleaser. Being loving, caring and compassionate is not the same thing. This is acting out of love, the people pleaser acts out of lack and fear. It is of course not the people pleasers fault, this is how they have learnt to respond. Often these individuals received little love or validation as children, and learnt to survive by putting others first. They may have needed to act in certain ways to keep their parents happy, or felt their parents saw fault with them and as adults over compensate so others don't see their 'flaws'. The people pleasers survival depends on pleasing. It is a disguise of the ego. This part finds it hard to say no and feels guilty if it does. Generally it gives to others to be liked or loved. Deep down these people have no self-respect or love for themselves. They think, "If I gain this persons approval I will feel OK, I will be safe." Over the years the people pleaser has buried their true feelings and have needed to turn their hurt, anger and frustration inward. They do all they can to disguise these feelings due to their fear of rejection or abandonment. They deny their true needs and listen as the ego tells them to care for others to acquire love instead of loving themselves. We must have all heard that phrase 'you cannot truly love others until you love yourself', the people pleaser has learnt that the opposite is true - but its a lie. When the people pleaser buries their true feelings this will manifest itself in other ways causing physical symptoms like backache, asthma, frequent colds etc. Or psychological complaints like depression, fears, shame and guilt, over eating or drinking. They will usually strike up relationships with controllers or abusers. Usually the type of person who personifies a parent. The people pleaser may also have strong urges (conscious or unconscious) to rescue others, they desire harmony at all times and dislike seeing others suffering as it reminds them of their own pain. They also need to be needed as it makes them feel worthwhile, they appear virtuous and kind but everything that they do is to make themselves feel better. People pleasers and victims are strong magnets for each other too.

So do you recognize the people pleaser in you, even if it isn't all the time? Do you feel guilty when you say "No"? Feel obliged to help, or put others before you regularly? Do you ignore your own needs to gain approval or fit in? Do you help others so much that they don't learn to help themselves? Do you believe that doing enough for a certain someone will mean they will love you in the end? Do you find that others take advantage of your 'niceness'? If so recognize your own feelings of inadequacy that cause you to do this. The next time it happens ask yourself what is motivating you, are you hoping to get something back? What are you afraid of? What can you tell about your own feelings of self worth? Did you have to please one or both parents to feel loved?

Everything has to be in balance and life is about giving and receiving. You have the right to derive love and care without feeling you must do something for it first, just as you have the right to say 'No' if something feels too burdensome or not right for you.

The Persecutor/Controller

In the other extreme there are some personalities who persecute or control others. Do you try to govern others by being critical, aggressive (physically and verbally), cruel, dominant, patronizing or rejecting? Do you isolate yourself, give messages of 'I don't need you' even though you know it hurts others? Do you often think and say "Pull yourself together"? Are your views of the world very black and white, or judgmental? Do you enjoy making others feel small, stupid, inadequate or afraid? Or are you in a position of power i.e. boss, therapist, policeman, teacher, supervisor, vicar etc and deep down know that without that label or position you would feel lost or worthless in the world? Do you need to be in control or looked up to feel OK? The persecuting or controlling personality appears to be the opposite of the people pleaser, yet deep within they too are coming from a place of fear, vulnerability, powerlessness and low self- esteem. They have just learnt to adopt a different approach. So instead of pleasing others to feel better they hurt or command others to feel powerful.

The ego comes in many guises, and we are all influenced by it to some extent, especially in this day and age. The above person- alities are just some of the most extreme examples of the ego, and you may recognize yourself in all of them at some level. If you do, remember this is the ego and not your true self. It is some kind of defence you have learnt to adopt because you have needed to. It does not mean you're a failure or deficient - no that's the ego talking. It indicates you have some inner child/adolescent healing to do. Look at Gill Edwards list again and tick those areas that you know you do or have done, the first step to tackling problems is to become aware of them so be honest with yourself and recognize the ego in you.

Why do we have an Ego?

The ego is not a separate entity within us, it is a part of us. It is our awareness. It has pulled together all our experiences and created a picture, this picture is how we view the world and ourselves. From when we were little to when we were big the ego, our camera of awareness, has been taking in all that was happening. After much sifting, analyzing and deciding, over many years, it brings us up-to-date to our current time. As you sit here reading this book your ego is also reading. In fact it may have raised its voice at times saying, "Tut that's silly" or "What! I wouldn't believe that." Whatever the day, year or month your ego has traveled that time with you. It has been with you since the womb. Some would say the ego is your inner child, some the voice of your parents and teachers. To me it's a mixture of all. The ego gets a lot of bad press, yet really it is merely the negative voice inside of us who expresses our fears, inadequacies and hurts. It would be easy to blame the ego when we feel unsure, cling to others or resist change, but ultimately it is us who brings about these limitations. We then use others, items, trophies, substances, work or denial to make our self feel whole. The ego is our limited part, and it is probably fair to say that the more troubled our childhood the more of a hold the ego can have upon us. This is because the ego is the voice of our inner infant (or adolescent), and if that infant was criticized, abandoned or hurt enough the more the self-deprecating part (the ego) has to chew on. This part will later tell the adult all that he believes about himself, from his past messages and conditioning.

So the reason we have an ego is that it keeps us informed as to how we really feel about ourselves or how we perceive situations, it is just telling us our truth. This though is never the truth. The reason why it is not truthful is because the ego is always negative and limiting as does not question anything. It lives by limitations. Our purpose for ourselves is to move beyond those obstructions. To let go of helplessness, guilt, dissatisfaction, appearances, worries, manipulation, self abuse, hurting others, addictions etc. We use these because we have not healed our past. When we heal our past we quieten our ego and move beyond our self made constraints. Eckhart Tolle, *A New Earth*, states "We are not here to experience limitation, but also to grow in consciousness by going beyond limitation. Some limitations may be overcome on an external level. There may be other limitations in your life that you have to learn to live with. They can only be overcome internally. Those limitations either keep you trapped in egotistic reactions, which means intense unhappiness, or you rise above them." When we heal the inner child, we master the ego. We then become the directors of our own life.

Our True Self

Our true self, which means the real us, is a limitless entity which all beings long to be whether their conscious of it or not. We all want to be happy, content, loved and secure. We all look for that higher knowing and inner sanctity. Our true self gnaws at us like a long lost love, we may ache, yearn and pine for it, and we may search high and low to get it. Think of those things you ardently long for, maybe it's a house by the sea, a child, inner harmony, a new love, freedom, money, happiness, intimacy, a holiday or new experiences. So long as what you aspire to is for your highest good and the good of all, it will be coming from your true self. It is only the ego who tells us we can't have these things (or can have it to inflate the ego or avoid issues) our true self says we can have it and more!

When we live as our authentic self we feel happy and fulfilled, open and heart centered. We know inner peace. We move toward our life purpose and take care of ourselves. We have boundaries and nurture positive thoughts. We are filled with joy and aliveness. We long to be all that we can be. We stay calm around others and see the bigger picture. We allow ourselves to receive love, abundance and all good things. We create a supportive environment and loving relationships. Joy flows through us, we are radiant beings. We are truly happy!

As you read the above your ego is going to be saying 'Its impossible to have all that, the author is in cloud cuckoo land' or 'Things like that just don't happen to me, never will I just can't believe it'. Yet this is how we are supposed to be living, this is where the evolution of mankind is headed. This is who we are, limitless, compassionate, forgiving, far reaching beings (no matter what your past or all the terrible things you've done - hi again ego!). We are all part of the divine energy of God/Goddess. Our natural self is spirit and spirit knows no boundaries. We have come to claim our power, to be true to who we are, to transcend the ego and to create a blissful reality on earth.

We will be exploring in more detail in the following chapters how to harness the amazing power of your mind, to change beliefs, question thinking, work through symptoms, understand illness, heal childhood memories, find your true self and enrich your life. Your mind truly is the treasure house that enables you to achieve this. It is your own inner gold mine from which you can extract all that you need to live a life which is advantageous and auspicious. Whatever you want you can have it, your mind is a miracle worker. You can make your dreams come true, discover amazing wisdom, develop your uniqueness and much more. You have the power to find solutions to every problem and the cause for every effect. I have witnessed miraculous healing within others due to the power of their mind, from debilitating illness to changing life circumstances. Everyone has this gift, this power.

'The mark of your ignorance is the depth of your belief in injustice and tragedy. What the caterpillar calls the end of the world, the master calls a butterfly'
Richard Bach

We Create It All – Judy's story

When we create our reality it all comes together with our current thinking, past experiences, thoughts we have about ourselves, and others. What follows is the story of Judy. Judy is a fictitious character, and this story is depicts Judy's week. There are many other characters in the story, but Judy is the main character. Just like you are the main character in your story. As events unfold for Judy I will be giving you the background information so you can see how Judy creates those events. I will also be giving you a brief resume of why the characters in the story are creating certain experiences. This will help you to begin to see how we all fit together perfectly, why outcomes occur and why certain people come to play a role in our story, whilst we play a role in theirs. It's quite magical, I have no idea how spirit or ourselves manages to pull it together in the present day, but when you begin to understand and appreciate that it does happen you can begin to re-write your own story.

Monday - Judy wakes in the early hours of Monday morning, she's had that dream again. She was at the point of being beheaded, there she was head locked in the guillotine and before the blade sliced her neck she woke up. (This dream signifies guilt from childhood and the fear of punishment. Judy has never resolved her guilt over her parent's marital break up). Judy sleeps again until she is woken by her 5 year old Toby, "Come on Mummy I'm hungry," he wails. When breakfast is over she puts Toby in the bath. "Why do I keep getting these panic feelings," she thinks. "What's wrong with me........ come on calm down......deep breath's that's what they said." (As a child Judy nearly drowned in the bath when she was left unattended, she has no conscious recollection of this). Later Judy sifts through the post and finds more bills, she feels dejected when she works out that the money coming in does not cover their outgoings. (Judy and her husband Iain both have scarcity beliefs, they believed as soon as you have children life becomes a struggle. They also have low self- esteem resulting in them feeling undeserving of money. Both beliefs come from the past).

At the shops Judy doesn't have enough money to pay for her groceries, she feels ashamed as she asks to return some items. "Everyone is looking at me" she thinks, "how embarrassing." (Judy suffered shame when she lost some money that was due to pay for her school dinners, her mother scolded her in front of her friends).

Tuesday - Judy has some friends over for lunch. Catrina and Zoe have been friends with Judy for two years, their children went to the same nursery. Catrina's car breaks down on the way, and she is stuck in a lay by. Catrina feels angry and frustrated in her predicament (these feelings emanate from when Catrina was unable to express her anger as a child. This has resulted in Catrina becoming a very frustrated and angry adult). Secretly Catrina enjoys the fact that Judy is coming to rescue her as it makes her feel special and important, missing ingredients from Catrina's chidhood. Judy enjoys rescuing Catrina it makes her feel worthwhile, missing ingredients from Judy's childhood. Sometimes though she gets resentful when Catrina demands so much, then feels guilty. (Like she did when her younger sister always had to have her own way, her mum would then make her feel guilty if Judy said it wasn't fair).

Everyone sits down to lunch. Judy feels inadequate next to her friends. She believes they are more attractive and interesting than her. When Zoe talks about her new boyfriend and her holiday to Barbados this compounds it. (Judy always believed her younger sister Jane was more interesting and special than her because she was the parent's favorite, now she feels inadequate to all females). Zoe is a constant sensation seeker and is always looking for new experiences to distract herself like new boyfriends and holidays (As a child Zoe was fostered, her mother was an alcoholic. Zoe now seeks outside stimuli to help her forget her inner pain and loneliness. Her feelings of low self worth come from her abandonment, she makes a great fuss of her personal appearance to help her feel better. She also dates men for short periods, ensuring she rejects them first to avoid getting hurt)

Wednesday - Judy has another dream, this time she is being chased by a man. She is desperate to get away and wakes up. (Judy's father had frequent affairs when she was young, sometimes he would move out for weeks and then return. Judy's trust in men was broken at this time. This dream indicates Judy's fear of sex, to Judy sex means to completely give of oneself. In Judy's waking life she withholds sex from Iain her husband, for fear of getting emotionally hurt). Iain wakes when Judy calls out, it's only 4 am. He comforts his wife and becomes sexually aroused. Judy pushes him away, Iain feels rejected and worthless. (Iain's mum withheld affection, now he has a wife who treats him the same). "Let me fix you a drink she says," trying to atone.

Thursday - Judy has a fear of enclosed spaces (linked to her near drowning experience). She is on the top floor of the multi-storey, she is forced to take the lift as the stairway is being painted and has been closed off. She enters the lift saying, "Please don't break down, please don't break down." As the doors shut her fear increases, "Oh God she thinks, hurry, I must get out." (Judy's thoughts have a lot of emotion attached, this makes the possibility of the lift breaking down much more likely). The lift stops. She presses buttons but nothing happens. "Its so hot, I'm trapped.....can't breath....please help me........please.......I can't breath" (feelings of her near drowning experience are occurring again although she doesn't consciously remember it). Judy feels utter panic actually believing she'll die if she doesn't get out of the lift. Then the doors open again. Judy runs out gasping for breath.

Friday - Iain is at work enjoying the attention he is receiving from a younger colleague. Isabel is funny and easy to talk to, not like Judy with all her hang ups, he thinks. Iain's inner child is also enjoying the recognition, (Isabel although younger is much more confident than Iain and his inner child is attracted to the potential mother figure she could be. Isabel's father was an alcoholic and never available for her, she has never learnt to be close to a man and unconsciously fears further rejection. As Iain is married he is seen as unavailable, this is the perfect set up for Isabel. Firstly because Isabel needs the excitement and emotional pain that desiring this man could bring - this is the only way she has learnt to relate- and secondly because she is terrified of true intimacy and commitment).

Saturday - Judy takes Toby swimming. When they approach the pool Toby protests that he doesn't want to go in. "Why ever not?" asks Judy "You're normally fine." Toby reluctantly gets in the pool but is initially afraid, Judy does not understand the change in him normally he loves swimming. (Judy does not know that Toby is picking up on her fear when near water, although she tries to hide it. Unconsciously Toby is learning to believe that water is not safe).

Sunday - Judy, Iain and Toby go to visit Judy's mum who now lives alone. Judy's mum Brenda was adopted as a baby, her adoptee mum was relatively loving but her dad was never home. He was a workaholic and had little time for Brenda, hence why Brenda married Judy's dad who constantly betrayed and rejected her. Rejection is the theme of Brenda's life and she makes Judy pay. She tells her how lonely she feels, how no one cares and why don't they come round more. Judy is racked with guilt, anger and resentment. She tries to comfort her mum like she did as a child when her father was running around town, and Judy was left to support her when she got upset. But she also feels angry that her mum depends on her so much, "I feel so guilty Iain" she whispers to her husband, "But I can't be here day and night I have my own life to lead." Despite this Judy feels responsible for her mum like she did as a young girl somehow believing her father's infidelity has something to do with her, as if she had done something wrong.

When they leave the house later Judy sees a bat flying passed, she points it out to Iain. That's odd she thinks I keep seeing bats this week, on TV, those ornaments in Debenhams, that book that Toby brought home, and now this. What Judy doesn't realize is that she is receiving a message from spirit. When we see something repeatedly this symbol usually holds a special message for us. For Judy seeing a bat means it is time for rebirth, it is time to let go of old stale habits and break the mould. Much in Judy's life needs to change, her fears especially. Life will keep sending Judy messages to sort things out and get help. She may switch to a TV programme about counselling, or hear about a friend who has done well in therapy. She may see frequent images of frogs which denote cleansing, or be asked to attend a birth representing her own need to be born again. She may be given an ornamental egg or break an egg in the kitchen signifying new beginnings, or she may trip over a bottle telling her to stop bottling things up. The messages are endless and everywhere. But if we don't heed them spirit just has to shout louder, and in order to do this sometimes our life has to become worse. Problems emerge more rapidly or something occurs to shake our world. When a crisis manifests itself there is always a reason. For Judy that crisis may come from Iain having an affair with Isabel, and although this is in no way Judy's fault it may be the wake up call they both have to suffer to get to the root of their problems.

4

'You are the most powerful magnet in the universe! You contain a magnetic power within you that is more powerful than anything in this world, and this unfathomable magnetic power is emitted through your thoughts'

Rhonda Byrne. *The Secret*.

How We Create Our Reality

In the last chapter I touched upon that we create our reality. Now let me explain this more fully. When you think about everything that has occurred over the past month it would be amazing to think that you created everything yourself. When upsetting things have happened to my friends they have usually remarked, "But why would I have created that!" Well quite. If you were happily dancing the Cha Cha with your partner in a glamorous ballroom and the ceiling caved in it would seem ludicrous to think you, and the others dancing, created it. Yet it is so.

When we think back to Judy in the previous chapter we only have to use the same dissection of internal thoughts, beliefs, past events, expectations etc to uncover why the ballroom ceiling had to land on your head! If after that event you came to my consulting room covered in bandages, wobbling on crutches it may not take us long to discover the truth. When a crowd of people create a catastrophe each individual person is responsible for that happening (and the outsiders affected by that tragedy). If you were there you were meant to be there because that unfortunate event had a message for you personally. Maybe a similar tragedy happened when you were young, or maybe you believe your life is full of tragedy or suffering and this is typical! Maybe your relationship is failing and you need a bang on the head to wake up to it. Maybe going to hospital leads you to find love and the synchronization of events made sure you got there on the right ward at the right time. Sometimes events can lead us to places or people and we get that, "Aha, now I know why that happened." Yet there is generally more to it than this. What we have to do is think about our thoughts and feelings before, during, or after the event to gather the clues. Almost always bad things happen because something needs to be healed. So when gliding across the dance floor you may happen to think about how angry you've been feeling lately, you may recall blowing up at the slightest thing, then suddenly the wooden ceiling falls down and you feel angry again. After all your dress/suit is ruined and it took ages to do your hair! Plus your night out is shattered. In this case it is your unresolved anger which has helped bring about that incident. Or maybe a large timber frame fell on your legs and you felt trapped and afraid. Perhaps your thoughts and feelings went a bit like this, "Help, what's happening? I'm trapped, panic, feel powerless, dizzy." In this case these feelings are directly linked to something occurring in the past which brought about the same thoughts and feelings. This is still an unresolved issue for you and the event was created to help you remember. Or after the event you went on to have nightmares about rooms caving in or feeling out of control, dreams of this kind can indicate feeling overwhelmed in your current life, being a victim to circumstance, or suffering guilt over something and constantly punishing yourself. If so this event was created because the inner is created in the outer and the caving in ceiling was reflecting your thoughts about your present life.

Everything thing that happens to us is created by us. If it's bad, unsettling, upsetting or horrible we can grow from this. When we learn it's lesson we stop it occurring again. Our own childhood is still running rampant in our mind, outside events and inner feelings will tell us everything we need to know to stop this. Our unconscious mind has moving through it thoughts and beliefs in every second. We are creating a reality to show us something is wrong or to reflect what we believe about ourselves or the world. Some of your realities have been decided weeks ahead. For example you may have been thinking today, unconsciously or consciously, "I'm no good, I don't deserve good things" only to find at the end of the month your salary has been cut due to some computer error and your going to be painfully short of cash for two weeks. This happened because of that thought, or other negative thoughts related.

It's important when thinking about these concepts not to get into the scenario of self blame. Maybe you live in an abusive situation, or have discovered one of your children are being sexually abused, or maybe you are poor, have a terminal illness or are in prison. Yes you have created that reality at an unconscious level, and you have something to gain from it. You can learn and grow from this. If your partner is abusive or your child is being abused this is reflecting something within you that comes from your past. Maybe the message is to remember your own past abuse. If you got into a fight with someone and then said, "Well you created it" your not taking responsibility. If an abusive person blames the victim they are not taking responsibility, likewise if you solely blame the abuser you are not taking responsibility either. The same is for poverty, illness or incarceration as well as the many other uncomfortable situations we find ourselves in.

Each situation is a lesson, each lesson is a blessing in disguise. We all create, we are all part of our own individual play. You are the star in your's, each person in your life plays a part. They all come at the perfect time and act in the perfect way. Your role in the play is to grow, heal, find happiness and achieve enlightenment. This is not always an easy role. Not everyone on earth at this time has this role, they may have different roles to fulfil. Maybe their next life will bring on this quest.

Now, at this stage you may be wondering why individuals in third world countries or war torn areas would be formulating a reality like that. Well of course the truth is they don't know they are creating that reality just like most westerners don't know they are generating their world. These people have been born into these situations or brought up where conflict or suffering either within the family or outside is the norm. They are just following the patterns of childhood teaching which may say 'I am always hungry' or 'I am always afraid'. This conception that we create our reality is secret knowledge which comes from the first world cultures of Taoism, Buddhism and Huna, the druids and Inca's - plus many more. It is not common knowledge - not yet anyway. As we approach a time where ideas on life itself are shifting we are becoming a more aware species. As we understand and harness the power within us we can begin to not just give physical aid to countries less fortunate than our own, but also educational aid. That is to teach each person globally that they create their own circumstance (either personally or collectively) through no fault of their own. It would take a long time and be many years before this idea could be realized, that is why we with the resources and education available have to get it. We have to get that we are the Gods in our own small universe, we are the manifestors. And if appropriate, and others are willing to listen, we can pass this message on. As Kuan Tzu said, 'If you are thinking a year ahead, sow a seed. If you are thinking 10 years ahead, plant a tree. If you are thinking 100 years ahead, educate the people'.

We co-create with spirit

We do not solely create events on our own. There is an even greater mystery to it. Somehow entwined within all these happenings is the power of spirit/God/Goddess/The All That Is/Angels however you would like to view it.

Judith Laura writer for *Beltane Papers* states, "We participate or collaborate in creating reality. We co-create our own reality. We do not need to stay in the role of victim because we do have some ability to change our circumstances. Regardless of how the situation was created, we are responsible for how we act or react to it. If something bad happens, if we find ourselves in dire circumstances, we almost always have choices. We can spend our time focusing on the bitterness of the lemon, or we can try to make lemonade."

Spirit, God, the Angels want us to make lemonade. They want us to be happy, abundant, fulfilled and joyful - everyday, every minute. The problem is God has had some bad press over the years. In the Old Testament God is seen as an all powerful being who creates havoc and tyranny when we 'misbehave'. He punishes us by famine, disasters, plagues and bad days. When the car breaks down, when we lose our job, when we have no money, when we get mugged, when our child becomes ill, when the wheat doesn't grow, we tend to think it has something to do with God and his/her displeasure with us. Or maybe he/she just doesn't like us?

In reality those who believe this to be true are not taking responsibility for their own creations in life. It is far easier to blame God than to accept we help to shape our experiences, problems, relationships etc. It means we don't have to do anything about it. If we begin to understand that God is not separate from us, not a bearded man sitting on the clouds deciding our fate, but a part of us we can begin to discover our true power, our true potential.

So what happens is this, from my understanding anyway, others may have an alternative view on it. As we go about our everyday business we have in our mind our thoughts and beliefs, we have our past, our conditioning, who we believe we are. When our childhood is still influencing us and we need to remember or heal aspects of the self-spirit will help us accomplish this. So lets imagine we are walking along a road, we want to get to a place in our life but the road is blocked. Living inside of us is God/spirit and our unconscious -these parts created the block. Living outside of us is also God/spirit who also helped create the block. Lets say the block is preventing us from finding love, Why?

Because we are afraid to love, Why? Because two years ago we were rejected by someone we loved, Why? Because as a child our dad left and we now expect rejection. Now the block may be that we just can't 'click' with anyone we date. Maybe we can't, but we are pulling incompatible people to us, we with spirit have the power to do this. We have so much power within us. We have the power to create blocks and create avenues for healing. We have the power to create happiness, abundance and success. We have the power to create trauma, failure and despair. God/spirit helps us to manifest these creations. We co-create. But why would God help us to manifest pain and sadness? Because he/she wants us to heal the past or change a current situation. All pain and sadness is really about the past and needing to change. Spirit will always lead us into situations to heal the past and change because when we heal this part we can find inner peace. When we find inner peace creating what we truly want becomes easier. This is what God wants. He/she created us in his image, this means he/she gave us power, his/her power. This power coupled with his/hers means we can move mountains, we can have joy, we can feel love, we can be happy. So if the car breaks down, if we lose our job, if our child becomes ill, if the wheat doesn't grow we are not to blame and nor is God. Yes we both created it, but it happened for a reason. We need that experience, there is a divine message attached, there is something to resolve. As Gill Edwards states, "Nothing happens unless we make it happen. Our thoughts decide which of an infinite number of possible and probable events will actually manifest in our reality. Thus metaphysics says nothing happens by chance. We create (or allow) each and every event of our lives."

'Seek not to change the world, but to choose to change your
mind about the world'
The little book of Miracles

Beliefs Create Experience

We transmit energy like invisible waves at all times, this energy is being transmitted into the world and pulls to us all our current circumstances. The energy you are broadcasting right at this very moment will bring people, situations, problems or happiness either in the next hour or days to come. Beliefs, as explained earlier, have an important role in what comes. Your beliefs create your reality. Because unconscious beliefs are just that, unconscious, they can be baffling to detect or work out, but all you have to do is look at your life, what you attract, what turns up regularly for you and recurring patterns. So for example you may consciously believe that women have equal rights in your place of work, yet find daily examples of their incompetence. Every day you see women messing up, getting it wrong and in your eyes being down right stupid. You really want to believe they have equal rights but you keep being shown that men are far superior, competent and smart. Now what you are seeing is a subconscious belief manifest, because what you actually believe unconsciously is that women are incompetent and have no right to equality at work. This belief came from your dad who would often express it. You took on the belief in the mistaken knowledge that he was right and it became embedded. The problem is that as you grew older you found modern thinking meant men had different perceptions of women. You really wanted to be one of those modern guys but it was difficult when you saw Mandy spill her coffee again or Jane mess up the faxing. What's really happening though is that women haven't suddenly become clumsy, inept or incapable, no, they are probably making as many foul ups as the men - but you're not witnessing it. Men and women are human we all mess up, spill things and get it wrong. But if you believe women are more likely too that is what you will see. Your unconscious will pull to you all that you believe, your beliefs will be played out right in front of you so you can say, 'there you go I told you!' This then means you will see the woman drop the paper on the floor but when a man does it you'll be out of the room or otherwise occupied!

You may be able to detect your beliefs more easily just by looking at your life. Your life is your greatest teacher, what you see around you, what you have created will tell you all about what's really going on in your mind. Here are some examples:

Your pay cheque arrives late and all your bills bounce - Belief: "Life is a struggle life is against me"

Your children are always fighting and you are always stressed -Belief: "Motherhood is difficult and stressful"

Your friends don't call you even though they know you're in a crisis -Belief: "No one cares about me, I am worthless"

You are attacked down a dark alley late at night - Belief: "I am vulnerable at night I will probably get attacked, I attract bad things anyway because I deserve to be punished"

You didn't get the promotion you were hoping for - Belief: "I'm a failure"

OR

Your pay cheque always arrives on time - Belief: "Life is for me I always have what I need"

Your children get on most of the time and your house is a happy place to be-Belief: "I love being a mum motherhood is a great experience"

When in a crisis you always have a lot of support-'Belief: "I am loved and cared about"

You got home safely even though you were walking late at night -Belief: "The world is a safe place, I deserve only good things"

You got promoted-Belief: "I am a success!"

Some would say experience creates belief, but the reverse is true.

So the next time you hear someone say, "See I told you things would go wrong today with it being Friday 13th and all" or "I never have any luck with the opposite sex I'm not attractive enough" or "See I told you it always happens to me" or "That's typical sods law," just remember that belief creates experience not the other way round.

A Scientific View

Science and spirit are moving closer together. Scientists are beginning to realize that consciousness has an effect on matter. Seth (a channelled source) says, "Your scientists are finally learning that mind can influence matter. They still have to discover the fact that mind creates and forms matter." The old world view tells us that consciousness is created from matter, when we change this view and realize it is us who is creating our world globally and personally we can begin to transform everything.

In brief this is how it works; Don't worry if you don't get this mind boggling concept, its not essential!

"Particles of atoms are trapped light, and everything on earth contains these particles of light, and the only difference between a stone and a dog is the frequency at which these particles vibrate. Everything is trapped light vibrating at various frequencies. The light as we know it is energy, and this source of energy is consciousness. So thought creates energy, energy creates light, light creates trapped light, which then creates atoms and molecules, which then creates matter, consciousness creates matter! So as consciousness creates matter, nothing happens unless we make it or allow it to happen"
Gill Edwards.

We don't have to be a metaphysician or scientist to grasp the theory that we create our life, we just need to become self-aware. That is to have awareness of what is happening inside and outside of ourselves. As we begin to trust that we do create it all and then take steps to note what is happening to us each and everyday environmentally, physically, emotionally, mentally and spiritually, we have there the very power to create the life we actually want and not the one that is being created by our deeper childlike self.

'Rather light a candle than complain about the darkness'
Chinese proverb

Your Psychology
Before we move onto Chapter 5 let's touch upon some of the more common symptoms/issues people suffer from. Sometimes a problem is not always what it seems, we may know what ails us but find we are groping in the dark as to what it really means, that is, what our unconscious is trying to tell us. It is often helpful to know what is fuelling a symptom before we trace it back to it roots.

Depression
Depression occurs when we have to deny or push down emotional reactions which we learnt to do as a child, emotions like discontent, pain, anger, rage or hunger. It is also related to unresolved grief due to rejection, abandonment, betrayal, humiliation or upheaval. Depressives often experience childhood pain in isolation and had no parental support. The suppression of such emotional wounding may still be festering inside, this coupled with feelings of poor self worth and believing you are unlovable adds to the problem (not to be confused with burnout as below)

Shop-a-holism
Emotional deprivation as a child, or neglect can cause individuals to compulsively self nurture. Their inner child longs for love and

affection and as an inner substitute seeks it through shopping. Shopping is also used as a distraction from other painful issues or uncomfortable feelings, it can be used to avoid anxiety, loneliness, discontentment, emptiness, sadness, anger, fear or painful memories from childhood. The spending of money or getting into debt on the other hand may be related to guilt with having pleasure or the things we want. Self-punishment can be very unconscious and shopping may be leading us into poverty or crime to pay for actions we harbor guilt about. All these issues are rooted in the past.

Jealousy
Jealousy is usually the result of trust being broken as a child. The parent we loved and trusted may have rejected, constantly hurt or abandoned us. Or we received so little validation and love as a child we believe we are not good enough, we feel everyone else is better and our partner will soon realize that for themselves. Jealousy is the fear of loss due to low self worth.

Alcohol and Drug addictions
Addictions are used primarily to camouflage internal pain. When the addiction is let go of i.e. as a result of being in detox, the feelings you have been trying to numb will begin to emerge. Everyone's pain is different and there for different reasons, the underlying distress you have been trying to mask could be for a number of reasons. This pain comes from childhood and may have to be resolved for the addictive substance can be released for good.

Food dependency
Food dependency is on the increase and most dependents don't even know they have a problem as food addiction is a relatively new concept, although the issues have been around for years. When we look at overweight or obese people we can wrongly

assume they are greedy or weak willed and if they really tried they could lose the pounds. This though is not the case as food dependency, which these people suffer, is a progressive all consuming problem. Food dependents are obsessed with food, preoccupied with their weight and how they look. They are often yo yo dieters always looking for the next diet which will do it this time. This dependency can have fatal consequences (diabetes, heart disease) as the addict has to increase their food intake to get the same feeling of well being. Food in fine carbohydrates is the most commonly sought, these carbohydrates stimulate dopamine and serotonin which create euphoria and the craving for more. These foods include wheat and flour products; cakes, bread, pasta, biscuits, pizza, crackers etc, and sugary foods; soft and canned drinks, cereal, sweets, chocolate, sauces, ice cream, pastries, puddings etc. Because some dependents go through periods of fasting, binging, often purging to get rid of the food or drink through vomiting (bulimics are food dependents) taking laxatives or diuretics the problem has long term physical and emotional consequences, as well as disrupting family life, work and relationships. In the short/long term depression, poor sleep, irritability and lethargy is experienced. Just like addictions its primary use is to create feelings of happiness and calm, masking pain, loneliness, fear and hurt felt as a child. In fact this problem is usually initiated in childhood.

My own food dependency began in infancy when my father used to shower me with attention and then ignore me for days, so as a five year old I learnt that sugar made things feel a whole lot better. I used to scoop a couple of teaspoons in my mouth at regular intervals to curb my anxiety and distress. As I got older food would preoccupy me as I snacked on cakes, biscuits, bread and cheese. Meals were eaten at a rapid rate to keep hurt feelings down. In my late teens I swapped the food for alcohol, another fine carbohydrate, and began to lose weight (also when alcoholics abstain they often turn to sugary food). Being in a relationship helped too as I was obsessed with keeping slim to keep my partner interested. At this time I was purging on laxatives and eating zilch. Five years later I began to worry about the laxative abuse as I was now taking 15 at night and lunchtime. Then I saw a newspaper clip which described how the TV presenter Ann Diamond's nanny had died of a laxative overdose, this terrified me and I got help. My fasting, drinking and obsessive exercise though continued until I had my daughter at thirty four. When my baby was seven months I was single. Getting out to exercise was difficult, I was growing more and more intolerant of drink, and there was no man to get me worried about my body. At this time sugar became my companion again along with bread, pizza, cakes etc. I didn't even know I had a food addiction until six years later when I found some info on the internet, but by this time I had gained 20lbs.

To better understand if you have a food dependency answer these questions; Do you eat large amounts of high calorie food in a short time? Do you eat in a response to stress, anxiety or sadness? Do you worry about your weight and weigh yourself regularly? Do you eat more than you feel you should? Are you a yo yo dieter with little success? Do you binge then get rid of food through vomiting, exercise, laxatives etc? Do you have a weight problem? Do you eat when you're not hungry? Do you eat in secret? Do you have periods of fasting or severely restricting food? Do you feel ashamed and guilty about your eating? Do you hide food so you always have enough? Do you overeat more than twice a week? Do you gain more weight than you lose after a diet? If you have answered yes to any of these questions you may have an issue with food.

Food provides nice warm feelings, eating feels good, it is a great comfort when we are in pain. Likewise alcohol and drugs service to provide a better state than the one we find ourselves in. We do become tolerant of them though and need to increase the intake or try stronger remedies. Addicts/dependents are not bad, have behavioral problems or are weak. They began to take a substance to relieve emotional pain (sometimes physical too) and lost control as the body demanded more and more of the substance to get the same effect. When a person begins to abstain from the addiction, or detox, getting help to then deal with the underlying issues is essential to remain free.

Illness

Our body becomes ill when it wants to tell us something. This is where the word disease comes from, we are at dis-ease with ourselves. Our body is saying that our way of thinking (mainly unconscious) is out of harmony with what is best for us. When we are ill we need to address our thought patterns and how we feel about ourselves. Every illness has a different message from warts to bronchitis. (Please see appendices for a directory of ailments).

Stress/Burnout

Symptoms are similar to depression including fatigue, listlessness, lack of energy, poor sleep etc but the cause is different. Stress and burnout usually occur when the demands of everyday life have become overwhelming. People who suffer with this usually have an underlying need to prove something to a parent (very often the same sex parent). They believe if they do more they will gain the love and recognition they yearned for as a child. Deep down they lack the capacity to love themselves as their feelings were not validated in infancy. Co-dependents and people pleasers are vulnerable to burn out.

Anxiety/Worry

When we feel insecure or out of control due to events in childhood we carry this knowledge (unconsciously) into our present and worry about the future. Our ego is on the rampage as we listen to it telling us what terrible things will happen to us if we do this or that. Most of this is in our imagination but can be created in reality if we don't look to the root and resolve it. Its roots lie in the past. Extreme forms of anxiety can result in Obsessive Compulsive Disorder (OCD) which is a form of worry that renders your thoughts as scary or upsetting. Some actions have to be carried out to prevent 'bad' things happening in the persons mind. For example, cleaning self or environment, things being even or straight, doing things in a ritualized manner. If these repetitive actions are not carried out the person believes they or someone else will get ill or die, or some other trauma will befall them. The adult then uses obsessional thoughts and actions to 'feel' in control. They create this make believe reality to feel safe. Or the adult is trying to correct something from the past, i.e. if he washes his hands constantly mummy won't be angry, or if he keeps the house nice just as daddy likes it daddy won't leave. Bad occurrences will be averted.

Panic attacks

Panic attacks seem to emerge for no apparent reason bringing intense feelings of overwhelming terror and fear. The usual symptoms suffered are chest pain, palpitations, sweating, hot or cold flushes, trembling, dizziness, choking or smothering sensations and/or shortness of breath. When we look at these symptoms we are seeing a recreation of a reaction experienced as a child. The clue to what this experience was, as it will probably be unconscious, is to do with what happened just before the panic attack. So if you have panic attacks think about the last attack you had, try to remember what you were doing, thinking or feeling just before it came on. Was there a particular smell? Something you saw? Something that was said? Did you hear a noise? etc. Do some detective work on yourself. If you have another one think about what occurred before the attack because the clue is in this time frame. Or recall past episodes and try and find a common theme, like Lindsey who had a panic attack every time she went on a train. Her unconscious was warning her to get off as she had been involved in a train crash as a child.

Loneliness/Intimacy problems

Relating to and being close to others begins in the family unit. Relating means sharing feelings and thoughts and being accepted by and of others. The person who finds themselves lonely for years or unable to connect well with others is re-enacting their childhood. They may have been lonely as a child even if they came from a big family, they may have had playmates but the parents did not interact with them adequately or were too busy. Often they feel unworthy and unlikable. These problems will also emerge if the child was abused or rejected, they learn to fear close relationships to avoid further suffering and therefore find safety in solitude.

Homosexuality/Lesbianism

Some of you may be surprised to see I've included this, because generally it is not regarded as a symptom but rather just the way some people are. But is this really the case? Are we really born to have desires for the same sex partner later in life, or are we reacting to the influences of our past? I could probably start a debate here but I believe it is possible to be born straight and become gay. Now I have no prejudice against gay people in fact some of my friends are gay. Those same friends though do have the kinds of background which would back up my theory, and that is; same sex relations are a result of nurture not nature. One of the ethics I have to abide by when seeing clients is to tell them, if they are gay, that the inner child work we will be doing could change their sexual drives for life. That is if they desire men, and are male, and we get to the root as to why that is they could very well begin to desire women instead. So if you are gay and are considering therapy please be aware of this likely transformation, and if it doesn't happen you may need to ask why? What else needs to be resolved?

The reasons for wanting a same sex relationship are numerous, and individual. Some of the causes I shall touch upon may not relate to your own psychological make-up, these are just a guideline.

If you are homosexual you may have difficulty accepting your maleness. Probably since adolescence you have felt negative toward your father. You have probably disliked his behavior, attitudes and/or lifestyle, so much so you would prefer not to be a man. If you are a gay female the same applies, that is you have problems accepting your femaleness. You dislike your mother's role or your mother and do not envy being a women. You feel being a man is a better deal. This is why in the gay scene gay men often act or look like women, and gay women often act or look like men.

Other scenarios include children being abused by the same sex parent or carer and acting out that relationship as adults. Or children being rejected by parents because the child was the 'wrong' sex. The child then unconsciously strives to act like a man or a woman to win approval and be accepted in the world, believing their natural sex is less than or not good enough.

People have said to me but what about people with opposite sex physical characteristics? Like woman who have predominant facial hair, or men who appear physically 'feminine'. Are their sexual preferences related to childhood? (supposing they have same sex preferences or are confused about their sexuality). And are their physical characteristics the result of childhood influence too? I say, in relation to physical attributes, it is always related to childhood. If these individuals were born one sex but became biologically like the opposite sex they are being influenced by their childhood or womb experience. They are reacting to the environment they are in, or about to be born into. So a girl child in utero, or in infancy, may sense her parents desire for a boy and as she grows begins to physically become like a boy. Foetuses, babies and children all have an inbuilt need to survive, if this looks to be compromised then 'changing' to increase the likehood of survival becomes imperitive. This may then lead to sexual preferences being different, because when a girl feels physically like a boy, or visa versa, their sexual preferences will naturally fall in line with this. That is, when a girl grows to be like a boy she may naturally be attracted to girls just like a boy would be.

Low Confidence/Self-esteem

Our relationship to ourselves and the world depends on our self image. Our sense of self develops when we become aware of our parents views about us. If they made us feel loved and respected we learn to love ourselves and our self-esteem remains intact. If they criticize, reject, hurt or abuse us we learn to regard ourselves as worthless or tainted, damaging our self esteem. How we value ourselves is very important in the way we deal with others, work, family and life because it affects our self-confidence and fulfillment.

Sexual problems

Impotence - Some causes of impotence can be; feeling powerless over some issue in your life, past unresolved negative sexual experiences linked to guilt, shame or fear; wanting to deprive or punish your partner or you seeing your partner as a mother/father figure; fear of intimacy or closeness due to childhood hurts, fear of failing, guilt due to betraying a partner. Premature ejaculation- Some men, and women, have high expectations during sex yet according to sexologist Robin Saxon, the normal range for ejaculation is ten seconds to three minutes, he believes premature ejaculation does not exist. If you're a man and feel you do have a problem or ejaculate before penetration then the underlying reasons are the same as impotence.

Frigidity - Sex may be seen as wrong, sinful or dirty or penetration may be feared due to pain emotionally or physically. These may be linked to sexual abuse, or parental attitudes, but not always, for example women can be predisposed to frigidity due to fatherly rejection. They are literally afraid to let another man in, or to get close. It is also linked to fear of losing control.

Sexual disorders or problems can be numerous. If you have a fetish or are turned on by something unusual then it must be assumed that some time in your past sexual arousal and the unusual things were linked. For example if a child was spanked and then sexually interfered with they will later associate the two and perhaps seek a sadistic partner.

Self-harm

When individuals self-harm they inflict deliberate injury to their body, the most common being lacerations to the arms or wrists. This is done to relieve intense emotions or feelings of numbness usually related to past trauma or abuse. The person may not be aware of these past problems but the body is generating the emotions linked to those times. When the person sees their own blood they begin to feel calm or alive again as it gives relief. This behavior is akin to crying as the individual who usually keeps emotions suppressed finds an outlet for release through opening up the body and bleeding. Often the behavior is used to gain attention or nurturing so the inner child feels loved or fussed over, an important element missing from their childhood. Sometimes self-harm is a way to self punish if the person has past guilt or shame issues. Burning yourself is also related to guilt and self-loathing.

Scarcity of love, money, friendships etc

If you feel you are lacking in any area of your life this is related to your beliefs and how you feel about yourself. So if money is always tight you may have the belief, 'Its wrong to have money when others are suffering' or 'Life is always a struggle'. Maybe the scarcity in your life relates to feeling undeserving or bad. If you lack friends or a close companion you may have an unconscious fear of being rejected. Our childhood experiences help shape our beliefs, fears and self image so we have to go back there to undo the damage. Remember our beliefs and thoughts create our reality, so if we created it we can change it.

Anger

Some people are overtly angry, constantly fighting in their relationships, beating their wife for small indiscretions, getting into fights after the football match, hitting their children to gain relief, the list goes on. These people are aware of their anger, and although they express it frequently they never quite discover what they're really angry about. For example, you may drive your car daily and always find you're getting angry with other drivers, if this is the case you may tell others, 'Those early morning drivers are so incompetent, what's wrong with everyone always cutting me up or getting in my way'. We all get annoyed on the road from time to time but if we are always getting angry when in the car then we have unresolved anger. Anyone experiencing frequent bouts of anger or aggression have anger from their childhood to deal with. This is a fact, it's not to do with Liverpool losing to Manchester United or your wife going out on the town, it's not your kids, or your mother-in-law, or that restaurant, or those drivers, it's you! If you keep generating that emotion then your unconscious is trying to tell you something. Something like "Well you know that time mummy walked out and never came back, well you're still angry about it."

More commonly though anger becomes very repressed, especially if as children we were made to feel bad when angry. This means we don't express it overtly but covertly often taking our hostility out on ourselves or others without even realizing it. What follows is a list of examples of symptoms, emotions or behaviors that indicate underlying rage and anger.

Frequent illness

Terminal illness

Obesity

Depression

Smoking

Extreme exercise or sports

Manipulating others

People pleasing or being controlled by others

Abusing another (including animals and plants)

Self sabotage

Poverty

Loneliness

Drinking and other addictions

Bulimia and anorexia

Binge eating

Gossiping

Bruxism (grinding teeth when awake or asleep)

Insomnia, or dreams about aggression or fighting

Homicide

Jealousy

Being difficult, controlling, obnoxious, rude or critical

High sex drive

Rejecting others or playing mind games

Frustration or tension

Frequent stomach or head aches/migraines

Frequent injustice happening to you

Guilt

Lethargy

Anxiety

Frequently desiring chocolate or ice cream which is crunchy or has nuts.

Frequently chewing gum

Going to war

Lack of sexual interest

Ignoring bills, poor credit rating, irresponsibility

Committing a crime

Being the victim of crime

Blaming others

Keeping 'busy busy' or being obsessional/perfectionism

Watching violent and horror movies

Always wanting revenge

Skin disorders

Aches and pains

High blood pressure

Low self esteem

Promiscuity

Arguing or bickering in relationships

Ridiculing others (including humorous)

Psychosis

Frequently hurting yourself accidentally (i.e. stubbing your toe)

Clumsiness

Hyperactivity

Poor concentration

Habitual constipation

Painful menstruation and PMT

Peptic and gastric ulcers, hiatus hernia

Asthma

Heart disease

Owning aggressive dogs

Participating in protests

Bullying self or others

Enjoying loud or chaotic environments.

Working as a policeman, prison officer, psychiatric nurse or any other work which involves control and restraint

Terrorism

Need to watch competitive or aggressive sports

Feminism and chauvinism

Co-dependency

Co-Dependency is a form of people pleasing/victim consciousness where the individual attracts relationships which are one-sided, emotionally destructive and often abusive. Co-dependents take the role of the caretaker because they need to be needed, which means they are involved with others who depend on them or are irresponsible. They are attracted to addictive, detached, alcoholic, or abusive out of control partners. Co-dependents have very low self esteem and their repeated rescue attempts allow them to feel worthwhile and wanted, their inner sense of loneliness though often leads them to have their own addictive problems with drugs, alcohol, nicotine, work-a-holism, gambling etc. In fact the highs and lows of a co-dependent relationship are addictive in themselves. Co-dependents always come from families which are highly dysfunctional, this means the members suffered fear, pain, shame or anger which was ignored or denied. The National Mental Health Association states that the underlying problems in a dysfunctional family usually include the following;

* An addiction by a family member to drugs, alcohol, relation-ships, work, food, sex or gambling.

* The existence of physical, emotional or sexual abuse.

* The presence of a family member suffering from a chronic mental or physical illness.

They go on to say, "Dysfunctional families do not acknowledge that problems exist. They don't talk about or confront them. As a result, family members learn to repress emotions and disregard their own needs. They become 'survivors'. They develop behaviors that help them deny, ignore, or avoid difficult emotions. They detach themselves. Attention and energy focuses on the family member who is ill, inadequate, unavailable or addicted, in this situation the co-dependent (which involves the children) sacrifices his or her needs to take care of the person who is in need. When the co-dependent places others peoples health, welfare and safety before their own, they lose contact with their own needs, desires and sense of self." Co-dependency is born when there is any sacrifice of self as a child, which means someone else's needs constantly came before their own. When we look at abuse the abuser is using the child to meet their needs. The child quickly learns that she/he are not important, have no say and are there to be mistreated.

As adults the co-dependant will always look for a partner who needs them, they believe they can help them, change them and make things better. As children they longed to make everything right, maybe if they had been smarter, prettier or better in other ways daddy wouldn't have left, or mummy wouldn't have got sick. Their adult relationships provide them with a chance to start over. This time they will be good enough, try harder and make it work. All they end up doing though is to exhaust themselves and keep the other person dependent. What motivation has the dependent person got to change when they have now replaced their abusive/cold/rejecting parent with a pseudo-parent who loves and takes care of them constantly. In this situation both partners have to heal their own inner child instead of trying to find a way to fix or avoid their past in their current relationship.

Co-dependency in dating

If you're single and find you are continually attracted to the type of person who leaves you waiting by the phone, proves unreliable, makes you feel good/bad about yourself, showers you with attention and then ignores you for days - you could be a co-dependent dater. Do you find nice guys/girls boring? Are you in some way hooked on the highs and lows of a painful relationship? Do you find it exciting or stimulating when that person is nasty or cruel to you? Do you feel there is a deep connection between you both which feels like a spell that can't be broken?

When you first met this person it is highly likely there was a strong pull on your part toward them, you didn't know why and now you're still flabbergasted as to why you're always attracted to this type. Well it will be no surprise to discover that this magnetic creation of the wrong guy/girl comes from your past. Usually to do with the opposite sex parent and their treatment of you, which will in some way resemble your dating anguish.

In this situation where you do all the giving, loving and running - you are the co-dependent. The person receiving all this attention but gives very little back is the taker. Sometimes you may find yourself in the role of the taker, or the taker in the role of the co-dependent. The taker has usually experienced a fatherless upbringing, rejection from a parent, or abuse. This type of personality enjoys the attention that is usually lavished on them, it can allow them to feel taken care of, loved and important. The co-dependent becomes the parent they never had. Yet it is a dangerous dance because it keeps the taker needy and the co-dependent in sacrifice. Should either of these two become 'healthy' the dance would stop. The taker would run at the possibility of having a close intimate relationship due to fear, and the co-dependent would become bored with Mr nice-guy/Miss nice-girl who doesn't provide the addictive heart pounding stomach knotting feeling they believe to be love anymore.

Kiki Anniston writes in her article *The 'secret reason' why women are attracted to Jerks, players and just dangerously wrong guys.* "Every time this happened I thought I was feeling passion....or love at first sight. Little did I know I was deeply attracted to a socio-pathic personality type because of my own dysfunctional psychology. I now know that my concept of passion was really my addiction to the wrong type of guy....It turns out I was addicted to the emotional highs and lows that socio-paths bombarded me with that kept me hooked. In normal relationships everything is more steady so you feel something is missing. I was amazed to learn that our brains actually become physically addicted to emotional intensity and the more we subject ourselves to roller coaster relationships of hot and cold intensity, the more addicted we get (just like a drug), this happens for those with a lot of dysfunction in the home. Well it didn't take my therapist long to reach a very common conclusion - I had a co-dependent personality. Because co-dependents live through or for others, have a strong need to 'fix' people, seek out relationships where they play the victim role, and because socio-paths thrive on control and manipulation when the two get together it's like Nitro and Glycerin - Boom!"

Although Kiki's article is written for women the same applies to co-dependent men, and if we come from a childhood where emotional pain and intensity are the norm we can get hooked on that experience and become bored if we don't have it. This doesn't mean we want trauma or bad things to happen, but when things are going smoothly it can often seem alien or humdrum, so our unconscious will pull some upset to us so things feel 'normal' or interesting again (this is also a strategy to avoid intimacy).

And remember when dating, that 'deep connection' you feel to this 'wrong type' is really your unconscious (and spirit) pulling to you what you need. You are setting the scene to play out your childhood. Once you heal these past wounds that person you can't live without will become as unattractive to you as flu on your birthday!

5

'A clay pot sitting in the sun will always be a clay pot.
It has to go through the white heat of the furnace to
become porcelain'
Mildred Witte Stouven

Inner Child Healing

Beneath every painful emotion, every tear, every problem, every illness, every disappointment, every rejection, every failure, every discomfort, every embarrassment, every frustration, every angry outburst, every fear, is the voice of your inner child. Almost every situation, emotion or issue you desire to change is in some way supervised by your inner child. Some would like to believe that our childhood is of no consequence but how can this be? We are still the same person we've just got bigger! In being the same person all the negativity, mistaken beliefs, suppressed emotions and learnt behavior from youth have come too. How can a child who lost a parent and was never able to grieve really be ok? Did all that pain, fear and confusion just disappear? How can someone who was told they were useless grow up to feel of any use? Did they reason it out as a child and think their parents were mistaken? A psychologist would argue it highly unlikely. Do obese people come from happy childhoods when we now know obesity is linked to emotional clampdown and often abuse? If you have a panic attack when boarding the bus is it reasonable to assume that your adult self has just developed a fear of travel? It only really makes sense that our current problems and feelings must have deeper roots. Those who scoff at the possibility their childhood holds the key are too afraid to venture there, those who don't are on their way to freedom.

Your inner child holds all your childhood memories - nothing is omitted, not one cold, not one scraped knee, not one Christmas. You on the other hand would have forgotten the small details and day-to day happenings, and then signed to oblivion uncomfortable or painful memories you'd rather not know about. The little you though, remembers it all and due to this it carries all your fears, hurts, shame, inadequacies, guilt and powerlessness, as well as excitement, the need to play, your sense of joy and wonder. Your inner child clings onto what it has learnt, and it clutches at past patterns, even if they're negative, to feel safe. If you learnt to believe 'life is full of problems' or 'money is hard to come by' your inner child will still believe it. If you learnt to believe you are unlovable your inner child will avoid intimacy and attract rejection to stop getting really hurt. Your inner child is such a powerful player in your psyche that if not kept in check could potentially ruin your life. It doesn't do it on purpose but out of a sense of security will repeat the past, and work on fulfilling its beliefs. So if you were neglected as a child you will attract neglectful partners or if you were poor then hardship may be a common theme for you. Your inner child runs the show! This is why it is so important to connect with your inner child, let it show you its memories, hurt, pain, frustrations and sadness, and allow it to take a back seat so you the adult self can begin to take control. Your inner child wants you to take command, it wants someone to come along and free it from its burdens. It wants to share with you all its upsets and traumas. It wants you to come along pick it up and make it feel safe. It needs a responsible adult in its life to show it the way. Your inner child is willing to learn and be lead just as you were when young. It just hasn't quite worked out that negative beliefs or behaviors are unhelpful. It doesn't know that it can stop crying about what daddy did, or stop raging about what it lost. The inner child is stuck in a time warp still living out the childhood you left behind many years ago. This is why some feelings and thoughts can be so perplexing, like when we over react and think 'why?' Or when we think bad things and feel ashamed. Likewise if your inner child experienced so much hurt that it shut down it may feel indifferent to others pain or suffering and you may feel guilty at sometimes having little compassion.

Do you want to remain forever in this time capsule? Or do you want to heal the past and let it go? Your inner child is waiting for you. When you transform the inner child it lives in peace inside of you and your life becomes peaceful. You no longer attract trauma, pain, difficulties or hardship based on your childhood. You no longer repeat the past or invite others into your life who represent your parents or past abusers. You no longer pull to you scenarios that confirm your low self worth. You no longer live on a roller coaster of arguments, frustration or stress. You become free. You become who you were meant to be before all this other stuff got in the way. Your true self.

Before we look at an issue in your life and begin to take it back into the past with your inner child it would be a good idea at this stage to introduce you to your higher self. Your higher self is your future self, the self that is wise and enlightened. Many do not attain to their higher self in this life-time, but they will attain to it eventually. Our many lives are leading us to a state of enlightenment with a myriad of lessons and journeys along the way. To become enlightened we need to learn much and your higher self is already at that place. This is a true aspect of you and you can call on your higher self any time you need support or guidance when working with your inner child or past memories. Your higher self will be only too happy to assist because it comes to you as a parent figure, it loves you unconditionally. It wants to guide and help you and it sees passed all the fear and negativity, the blame and doubts. It sees your life from a higher perspective and knows where you are going even if you feel confused. It also sees you for the beautiful unblemished being you really are. You can ask your higher self for help at any time anywhere, it will always serve.

To meet your higher self begin to relax.........relax your head all the way down to your shoulders, breath away tension...............let your shoulders go limp...........let the weight in your arms and hands drop...........relax your body..........all the way down your legs.............let it all go..................breath away stress and tension................................now imagine yourself sitting by a beautiful water fall. The water cascades down into the pool below which gently rushes into a long meandering river. As it does it tumbles over rocks and stones splashing and swirling on its long descent. The sound of the waterfall is so relaxing and you begin to walk down the hill to a quieter part of the river. As you walk down you relax more and more. Feel the warm sun on your head and shoulders and notice the pretty spring flowers at the waters edge. The sound of the waterfall becomes quieter as you walk down the hill. You come to an open green pasture by the river where the rapids begin to slow down. You sit down on the soft green grass and bask in the sun..................suddenly you see a light approaching from high above. As it gets closer it becomes larger and larger the light brighter and brighter......................when the light is close it begins to dim and within it you see your higher self..............this is your wise enlightened self. Feel the love emanating from this aspect of you as you greet each other. Feel the warmth of this high being, he/she loves you without question. Notice how your higher self looks, they may be bathed in light, or look different to yourself. They may have the appearance of an angel or wise man. You higher self sits by your side and you tell it what you need help with. You tell it what you want to achieve personally and in your life. You may talk about your hopes and dreams or issues you feel stuck on. You may ask it to help heal you or give you guidance..notice how comfortable you feel with your higher self as if they had been with you always...................................now listen to what your higher self says, hear its gentle wise voice...............................thank your higher self for coming and know you can call on them at any time...............your higher self is available for you throughout all your inner child journeys, to give guidance support and love.............................now come back to the room you're in.

Working With Your Inner Child

To begin working with your inner child think about an emotional pattern, problem, issue, or fear you would like to know more about. Or a behavioral or psychological concern like a repetitive negative thought or action. Or you may have an inner blockage you wish to overcome like a fear of success or intimacy. Or perhaps you'd like to heal and let go of something from your childhood. Or maybe you have a situation in your life which is bringing up a great deal of emotion, even if someone else is involved and you think if only they'd change I'd be ok. Whatever the emotion is it is time to take that back into the past and to begin to understand how you are creating it and what it means. The other person or situation is merely a catalyst for what requires healing in you. Once you change this aspect of yourself you will either no longer attract it or the situation or person will not affect you in the same way.

When you have something in mind make yourself comfortable and begin to relax...............relax your feet and toes...................that kind of feeling you have when you take off a pair of tight shoes you've had on a for a long time............feel the muscles of your feet letting go all that tension draining away.........and feel the relax-ation working its way up your calf's and thighs......................your legs becoming heavy lose and limp.................relax your hips and lower back............sense any tension in your back and allow it to melt away......................feel that soothing relaxation move through your tummy.........all your emotions feeling calm as you let go of stress and tension from your tummy.................that's right letting go becoming more and more relaxed....................the relaxation is moving through your back and chest...............your breathing is becoming easy.....so much easier...............breathing away tension.................letting it all go....................so calm...................so relaxed...................feel your shoulder blades and shoulders releasing tension.................let your shoulders become lose and limp.......sagging down................relax your neck all the way up the back of your head.....................release tension from your head and scalp...............let your scalp and forehead become smooth as the comfort flows down into your face................feel any tension and tightness wash away..........flowing down and away.............feel yourself relaxing more and more............going deeper and deeper down...............letting go now....................let your arms become heavy...............feel the tingling in your finger tips as your hands let go...........................and relax...........................let yourself go deep.................deeper now...............that's right......................sense yourself somewhere with the sun on your skin...............it maybe a sunlit forest, a beach, a meadow or maybe a country house with you sitting by the window.................let yourself be wherever you choose....................make it as vivid as you can................notice the colors around you................what do you see................what time of day is it..................what do you hear.............what are you sitting or laying on, or maybe your walking about........................let yourself be there.................touch something in this serene place............no one can bother you here....................and relax some more...........................Now think of that issue or feeling you'd like to transform. If it is an issue think of the feeling/s you get about that maybe hurt, anger, resentment, guilt, fear, shame or something else..............................feel it in your body....notice where you hold it...................now think of the most recent time you experienced that feeling.........let that memory come...............notice who else is there and what you are doing..................now in your thoughts ask your inner child to join you.........................and see them approaching ....getting closer and closer......................notice how old the child is.......................how they are dressed......................how they look............................if ok give your inner child a hug.........show it your unconditional love..................let your higher self join you now, even if they remain in the background........................the child knows the issue or feeling you are working on and is now going to take you back to where this issue of feeling was formed...........let the child take you back as you move through time and begin to get an image from the past...............allow yourself to be somewhere even if it doesn't make sense at first or it feels as though you are making it up....... just allow a memory to come...............and be there now..................that's right somewhere way back in your childhood..........notice what you see, how old you are and what's going on....................................are you alone or is someone else there?..................let the memory run..............let your imagination show you............just go with what your unconscious and inner child are showing you...........and be the child you......... see out of your eyes.........hear with your ears..........feel with your emotions.......................take your time..............let that feeling come...........understand why you are being shown this memory............. see the links to your adult life..........let your higher self be by your side if you wish............now ask yourself what negative beliefs, thoughts or fears have come from this experience?.............What decisions are you making about reality?..........What decisions are you making about yourself or other people?.............What effect did this have upon you?............ let the answers come now...........Now imagine you your adult self is entering the scene, the self you are in your current life, imagine you are your most confident and assured self..................see the situation there and take your inner child away from it.............bring them back with you to the beach, meadow, forest or country house, the place where you first met you inner child..........now sit with the child and hug them............tell the child you have come to help them now, you have come to listen. Tell them when they need to show you a memory or painful feeling you will work with them to heal it. Tell them you will never leave them and that you love them..........let your higher self be with you to.............now ask the child if they have any questions or concerns, and ask your higher self to help if you need any assistance in answering or explaining anything............now hold the child close as they merge into you, they may get smaller to do this............imagine them merging into their safe place inside of you............and come back to the room.

The above inner journey introduces you to childhood regression. In Chapter 6 we can look at the same issue (unless it has been resolved with this exercise), or another problem in a more detailed and thorough way. You can do the above journey as many times as you like to gain insights, change beliefs, create healing or strengthen the bond between yourself and your inner child.

Problems In Relating To Your Inner Child

Rowenna is a 15 year old client of mine. When Rowenna was only two years old her mother was murdered. The man who killed her had broken into the house when Rowenna and her father were out. On returning to the house Rowenna needed to use the toilet, but her father was unable to get in. He decided to take her to his sister's house who lived close by. As Rowenna got older she felt the incident of needing the toilet cost her mother's life. "If only I hadn't needed to go we could have saved her," she said to me recently. As noted earlier when a parent dies or leaves it is very common for children to blame themselves even though naturally these traumas are never the child's fault. For Rowenna this was amplified when she was told what had happened. As Rowenna was progressing through therapy she began to realize the animosity she felt toward her inner child, "I don't like her" she'd retort when recalling a memory, "she's nasty, there's something bad about her." In the following session Rowenna gave me a list on her feelings surrounding this area it read, 'Guilty, Betrayal, Shameful, My fault'. Whilst relaxed we took the feelings back and Rowenna remembered being on the sofa shortly after her mother's death, "My arms and legs are crossed, I'm wondering where everyone has gone, I think they've gone because I've been naughty. I'm so confused and sad. My mum has gone I don't have a reason for being what's the point of my life (begins to cry). I'm ashamed, I've done something wrong but I'm not sure what it is, feel I've betrayed someone, I've betrayed my mum, now I'm all alone." As a child Rowenna had begun to blame herself. Children need to make sense of situations, they need to fill in the missing pieces. The problem is they don't have the skills or information to interpret these happenings accurately, and the adults around usually dismiss the need to explain. So with no way of working it out they resort to self-condemnation. This disapproval is what often lies at the heart of all inner child renunciation.

Victims of sexual abuse often have problems relating to and comforting the inner child. They often feel dirty, tainted and damaged and see their inner child as party to the abuse. Sometimes this is due to the reminders of the abuse which the adult would rather not face, but generally it is from the child's internal guilt and shame. Abusers regularly use emotional blackmail on their victims to keep them quiet saying things like, "You made me do it" or "If you tell the police will be called and everyone will know what a bad girl/boy you are." The child then feels they are in some way to blame and are culpable in the act. To exacerbate this children often feel pleasurable feelings when being touched in highly sensitive areas, the child may be thinking, "I wished he'd stop," but the body is responding sexually. This rapidly increases the child's guilt as they feel bad for having these feelings. Penny Parks author of *Parks Inner Child Therapy* states., "Our genitals were designed to be responsive to touch, it is not 'bad' to feel good when our genitals are touched. So, the act itself is not 'bad': what is 'bad' is the fact that an adult is doing the act to a child. So, having pleasant feelings does not mean that the child is 'bad' or wants the abuse to happen, it only means their genitals are working properly." The child is being introduced to sexual behavior at an inappropriate age, and pleasurable physical feelings are normal. The child cannot work this out for themselves and the abuser often takes advantage by saying 'see you like it', even though the child was probably screaming inside. Remember abusers are very manipulative and will do anything to make the child feel ashamed ensuring the secrecy of the situation continues.

Some clients say to me, "But I kept going back to him, I must have wanted it to happen!" If we were starving eventually we would go to the dustbin for food, the same is for attention and 'love'. For most abused children the abuser is the only person giving them attention, and who seems to care. Abusers can be very 'nice' to the child giving time, recognition, affection and often gifts. To the child the abuse may be worth the price, as they need attention and concern like they need air and water. Of course the abuser has no concern whatsoever for the child, they just know they can overpower the child with false kindness. Some children are coerced back due to threat and fear, and may have been told they will go to prison if they don't. All in all, the whole scenario, whatever form it takes, is set up by the abuser and they are ultimately responsible. The adult always has a choice, even if the child is a teenager and they say, "She flirted with me." The abuser has unnatural sexual feelings and is exploiting the child, the adult knows these are unnatural and harmful and should seek professional help. The responsibility is always the abuser never the child, in any circumstance. For more on the subject of sexual abuse please see Appendixes II at the back of this book.

In other situations how often when things go wrong does the child get blamed? How often do you hear parents say, "If you hadn't done that it wouldn't have happened" or "You make me so angry/sad/frustrated." The child takes this all on board and believing their parents to be right they generally blame themselves.

So if you have any problems hugging, loving, feeling affection or talking kindly to your inner child find out why. What are you blaming yourself for? It is now time to find out and put things right. Your inner child has done nothing wrong, your inner child is innocent. You the adult are the only one who can help the inner child, it is time to put things into perspective and free yourself from incrimination and self-dislike.

In retrospect it may feel odd to show affection to your child because it was never shown to you, if so hold your child's hand or sit them on your knee. In time, as old wounds are healed, you are going to find you have a great capacity to love, and displays of affection will feel more natural. In a sense your reluctance to show tenderness may reflect a fear of rejection, and your child may also hold this fear. If you or your child are afraid this is natural, the relationship can feel very new even though you've 'lived' with each other for years. You need room to build a friendship, and the younger you may need reassurance that it is not going to be abandoned, betrayed or hurt if it has been in the past. It just takes time, patience and treading lightly with each other.

When we explained to Rowenna's inner child that her mother's death was not her fault and was the responsibility of the man who killed her Rowenna was able to hold her child self and show her love (albeit for a short time, as we are still working on Rowenna's relationship with her inner child), and this kind of self love is crucial for recovery and for the creation of a happy life.

'Never measure the height of a mountain, until you have reached the top. Then you will see how low it was'
Dag Hammarskjold

Overcoming Blocks On Your Road To Recovery
One of the biggest blocks to therapy is fear. Fear can be broken down into two areas.

1. The fear of facing the past and dealing with the emotions/thoughts therein.

2. The fear of recovering from the past and becoming a healthier and happier person.

The fear of facing the past and dealing with the emotions/thoughts therein

Going back to your childhood, even if it was basically good, takes courage. I always say to my clients how much I admire them for facing their 'ghosts' and for recognizing that this route is requisite. Only a small percent of the population are willing to see that their childhood counts, the rest of citizenry avoid the concept either through ignorance or fear. Fear is a powerful obstacle because we fear fear itself. This means we assume some memories are going to be so painful, hurtful or scary we fear them. We are afraid to feel what we need to feel and afraid to face what we need to face. When we look at this feeling closer though we see it comes from the inner child. The child is in conflict, it wants help but it doesn't want help. Like the lyric from Pink 'Go away come back, go away come back', you will probably feel this push pull energy throughout. But you know as the old saying goes the way to resolve your fears is to face them. Decide to take the challenge no matter what and slay that dragon called fear.

When clients sit in my office during a consultation they usually say, "This is the last resort, there is nowhere else to turn, I've tried everything else I really hope this helps." Then they find the last resort was the first place they should have come! Don't let inner child healing be at the bottom of your list, don't let fear stand in your way. If you do you put your life on hold, all those things you dream about having -not just material but good feelings such as peace and joy - will remain out of reach. Inner child therapy is a revolutionary therapy, hundreds of people are being freed from illness, phobias, suffering, impediments and much more on a daily basis. It works! I know that facing abuse is horrible, I know that divorce or bereavement is painful, I know that the slightest criticism can be devastating or that embarrassing incidents are humiliating, especially for a child. But these experiences are in the past, which means they can't really hurt you anymore. Going back to them may bring up distress, sadness, fear, grief etc but these feelings, if they linger, will pass. The obstacle of fear that you feel is your inner child's fear, you as the adult have enough resources and far sightedness to help the child. After all the child needs your help, and unless you go to your child and free it from the past you will go on creating the same patterns, relationships, problems and issues. Of course it is your choice freedom or entrapment? When you face the fear you will find recalling memories not as awful as you first thought, because once faced and resolved you will be liberated. This is the prize, the incentive. We are all looking for freedom in one sense or another. Here are the Keys - will you open the door? My publisher John Hunt wasn't sure about the title of this book he thought it sounded like a prison break out and I thought 'mmmm.....he's right, that's exactly what it is!'

As you progress with your healing you may be fortunate enough to have the help of a therapist. Therapists are invaluable for obvious reasons but they will also understand to some extent what you're going through (so long as you're seeing someone who has been through analysis). This journey is by no means the easy route, but it brings the greatest return. During your travels you may get depressed, angry, exasperated, confused, pitiful, frustrated, stressed to name but a few. You may feel worse before you get better, or you may be up and down over time having good days then bad days followed by good. Be assured though that you are making progress even if it feels you are not. This is why it is a good idea to get as much support as possible whilst also learning to rely on yourself. Make sure it's the right support though, going to people who may have been involved in your past is something you have to judge. Most of my clients and friends who been though analysis find their parents unsupportive, many may deny claims you make or tell you to stop overreacting. This is not true in all cases though and one or both parents may want to help. Siblings may be supportive or not, it depends on your circumstances. If you start to talk about traumatic memories and a sibling is still in denial you may find they don't want to carry on with the conversation. Seek out assistance from those who don't put your inner work down or tell you must be imagining it, or to pull yourself together. You will know who you can talk to as time goes on. You may even find as you grow some people moving away from you as your transformation poses a threat or feels uncomfortable, that's ok it's all part of the process. For many there is no support and self reliance is the key, it is often at these times that we find solace in spirit and increase our connectedness to our guides and The All That Is. Spirit is probably the highest and most natural form of assistance you could ask for, and can also bring situations or people to you that can aid your healing, you just have to ask.

All in all you may find on this pathway to health and healing fears rearing their heads at every juncture. The fear of facing the past and the fear of the feelings it uncovers. See your destination, or the many goals you want to overcome to reach it, and be a brave warrior. Living the life you dream of doesn't always have to be a dream, have courage and walk the path.

The fear of recovering from the past and becoming a healthier and happier person.

Most fears in this area come from negative beliefs and the fear of success. Some of you may be afraid to change. These fears may come from beliefs you acquired as a child and are based on what might happen. If I say to clients this process is transformational and you are going to become the person you are truly meant to be they sometimes say things like, "Look I know he treats me badly but I really don't want to leave him," "I know my jobs not much but I can't imagine doing anything else," "It would be odd to lose weight I'm not sure I'd be comfortable with it now," "I don't really deserve good things," "Yes I'll probably feel good for a while but it's hard to believe it will last, you know what life is like" and so on. It can be disquieting to imagine yourself as so different so you continue to choose the place of comfort.

Some of these beliefs change as you change, sometimes you have to gradually shed the old skin before you feel the benefit of the new. For some though the thought of changing can put them off personal growth completely. This is a shame because growth in this way is very positive. Working on your inner self can have many amazing and beneficial effects such as feeling more balanced and stable, calmer and in control, feeling happier and more creative, overcoming physical dis-ease and poor health, unlocking your true potential and gaining a clearer perspective on life. As well as attracting more joyful and harmonious relationships and events. Yet even if I explain this peoples egos have an opinion on the matter. The ego promptly reminds them, "If you're that well no one is going to take an interest in you," "What would happen to all your motivation if you were peaceful all the time," "Who could you trust if you had lots of money, they'd only want you for that," "What would you have to complain about if you got better, you know you love the attention," "Working for yourself is beyond your capabilities" etc. Underneath all these excuses is fear - the fear of not being good enough, able enough or deserving enough, the fear of abandonment, or negative fears about life like; 'happiness never lasts', 'Life is a struggle' or 'I could have it all then lose it again'. All these beliefs and thoughts are mistaken. Some are there to falsely protect you, others are what you've learnt to believe over the years. They are all detrimental, inappropriate and holding you back. In truth you are here to reach your highest potential, discover your greater purpose and unlock your greatness. We were all born great and are supposed to be great, not just existing and getting by. If you want to live in this stifling reality you will miss out on the immense pleasure and reward that inner healing can give you.

Other Blocks
Victim consciousness

In Chapter 3 we talked about victim consciousness, and this kind of consciousness blocks recovery. We have all been there and our ego tells us the benefits outweigh the sacrifices, but the opposite is true. When you walk around in 'poor me' mode you are handing over control to others. You are not taking responsibility and take pleasure from the care and attention you receive from being poor, ill, lonely, depressed or whatever else it is. Or some create painful or stressful situations to punish others, usually one or both parents. When Lucy was poor, lonely, burdened and depressed she knew it worried her mum. Because of Lucy's past and her mum's lack of protection she wanted to punish her. So Lucy told her mum all the abuse that had happened when she was little, and then unconsciously kept herself in a state of victim hood. Part of Lucy hoped her mum would see the effects of her childhood and feel guilty, another part of Lucy hoped her mum would come and rescue her. The same false hopes she'd had as a child. Either way Lucy wanted to affect her mum, but the only person being affected was Lucy. It wasn't until she 'woke up' to how unhappy this was all making her that she decided to change. It was a huge block in Lucy's recovery but it transformed everything when it was liberated.

Sometimes victims enjoy the thrill of trauma and drama, just being in the status quo can seem boring so they unconsciously create a catastrophe to get the roller coaster going again. As mentioned before, the adrenalin rush of stress can be a well laid out route in our mind conditioned and reinforced by a dramatic childhood. Sometimes we can't let go of the fix.

If you recognize yourself as playing the victim role at times and it is troubling your life don't feel bad, this is how you have learnt to cope and adapt. Often well meaning friends enjoy us being victims so they can rescue us, or society enjoys drama because its 'exciting', or being a victim is just part of the culture we're in. Most victim consciousness is learnt from childhood though as a way to attain love, or get at and blame others. The first step is to recognize the problem, the next step is to see the pitfalls and have a desire to change. You have to realize that this way of operating is only hurting you and is preventing you from having a happy life. When you see that blaming others disempowers you, when you see that punishing others is futile, when you see that you will gain so much more love as a well person, you are on the way to removing the block that trespasses on your path to greatness. It's your choice would you rather have problems, pain, sadness and stress, or joy, power, health and peace?

Sometimes we may become aware of a block but don't know why its there or what its about. For example you may wish to attract more money, a soul mate or a better job but it always seems to elude you. Or you may wish to acquire something, be somewhere, see someone, make a dream happen etc but something always goes wrong. What we must remember is we create our own reality so we are blocking the very thing we desire. Once we understand why we are blocking it the block is released (unless what we desire is not for our higher good). What follows is an exercise to help with any block in your life, no matter what it is.

Exercise to overcome an inner block

Now make yourself comfortable and begin to relax. Breathe deeply and let go of stress and tension. Relax your body from the top of your head to the tips of your toes. Let your shoulders become limp and your jaw relax. Let your forehead smooth out. Breath in and expand your tummy, feel yourself relaxing as your breath out...........do that a few more times..........relax.............any sounds you hear relaxing you............letting go............just letting go now................deeper down...........becoming still.........becoming peaceful........becoming centered.............your mind quiet.........now think about a problem, fear, or block you want to overcome, or think about something you want to create...........now imagine you are walking along a tunnel or corridor..........imagine this tunnel or corridor is a passageway in the deepest part of your unconscious mind.........as you walk along you become more and more deeply relaxed............you feel safe and calm..........now notice ahead something is blocking the tunnel or corridor........it might be a wall, or a gate, a person or a child, it might be a thorny bush or a giant rock just go with the first image that comes to you, the first image is the right one..........now ask this block why it is preventing you from getting through, why is it blocking the way? Why does it believe it is better for you to not have what you want? The answer might come as a memory, a thought, an image or some other form..........just take your time now as you allow this block to talk to you..........now this block has been trying to help you in someway, maybe it has wanted to protect you, but the block has served its purpose and can no longer block your progress like this.......... thank the block for helping you in the best way it knows how............now show the block why it is a good idea to let you through, show it images of what you want to create and your future. Show it how you want to change and why this is so good for you................now see the block becoming light filled, perhaps changing its form or turning into light...........this light illuminates the passageway and you are able to move through..........continue to walk through the tunnel or corridor and see the light at the end, a beautiful bright light that beckons you...............move through the light and see yourself in a future situation now that the block has gone, so if you were being blocked from addressing your childhood see yourself resolving your past and creating a happy life, if you held a belief that life is full of struggle see yourself creating an easy abundant life, if you've had poor health see yourself completely healed and doing those things you've always wanted, if you believed love brings trauma see yourself problem free amongst loving friends even if you haven't met those friends yet..........let yourself see yourself now that this block had been removed. See what you can achieve, see what you can have, see that removing the block was for the best...........................really be in that situation now...............feel the feelings of joy, strength, contentment, bliss or whatever it is......................and enjoy that for a bit longer before you return back to the room.

'Words that enlighten the soul are more precious than jewels'
Hazrat Inayat Khan

Letter Writing

Letter writing is a very direct way to communicate to the inner child, and for the inner child to communicate with you. To begin with it is best to write to the child without a particular problem or worry in mind. Once this link has been established you can then ask the inner child specific questions about feelings or concerns you are experiencing in your adult life to gain some idea of what the cause may be. When you talk to the child through letter writing the results can be remarkably profound, and often moving, as well as creating a close bond between you. The technique can be done at any time and anywhere you feel moved to do it.

To begin with take a piece of paper, relax and see as clearly as you can an image of your inner child. If you have a photo of yourself as a child this would be a helpful way to get things started. Then write Dear........adding your name, or what the younger you was called as a child. As you become familiar with this you may want to give your inner child a special or pet name. Some people like to add little or darling before the name so it reads Dear little Jonny...... or Dear Darling Alice........or you could just say, Hello sweetheart .... Be as affectionate and loving as possible and remember this exercise is to create an atmosphere of love, trust and safety. If part of you feels angry or affected by the child you need to work on this before letter writing can

161

commence. Next introduce yourself if you feel its necessary and ask how the child is, tell the child you are here to listen and care. Ask if there is anything the child needs to talk about with you, any concerns they have or worries (or they may have something good to tell you). Here is an example.

Dear Tilly,

Hello sweetheart it's me your grown-up self, how are you today? I thought maybe we could write to each other from time to time so you could tell me if you have anything you want to talk about. I am here for you now baby and I'm not going anywhere, I want to know that you're safe and well. I want to take care of you. You can tell me anything, I won't be sad or cross like maybe mummy and daddy used to be. I love you so much, you're my special little girl.

Lots of love and hugs

Grown-up Tilly xxxxxxxxxxx

It is important to remember your talking to the child so keep it simple and child friendly at all times, adding lots of love and affection! Now with the hand you don't normally write with imagine you are replying to yourself as the child. This may seem odd at first and you may need to relax some more and focus on that image of you as your younger self. Put pen to paper and then let it flow, when you begin writing it may seem as though the pen has a mind of its own, that's ok! Just keep writing whatever comes to mind, you may find your scribbling if the child has lots to say or is upset so just go with it. Don't be surprised if you start crying or are shocked by how much information your child gives you. Be aware that this is the infant you communicating with you so touching and arousing emotions are normal (some people actually have a clear image of their child and can imagine hugging and stroking the child's hair to give comfort, or make friends).

When this is done you need to reply to the child and your response should be loving, non-judgmental and supportive. Your inner child needs your reassurance and approval, and you are the only one who can give it. When you re-establish this link and allow the child to feel secure and cared about you are giving to yourself, Love. This self- love is essential for your growth and recovery. If you show the child you feel negatively toward them this will ultimately affect you because you are berating and rejecting yourself. This then leads to a downward spiral of self-sabotage and stuckness. Remember if you need more information so you can connect with and help the inner child read up on the problems your dealing with. Look up information on how children are affected by divorce, abuse, bullying, favouritism or whatever it was you went through. Any counsel which addresses the plight of the child and long term affects will be invaluable to you and your younger self.

Just to note never call yourself mummy or daddy when addressing the child. It is important to maintain a separate identity from your parents and not to confuse the child, or try to replace your parents with yourself. You are a parent figure in your child's eyes, you are their present and future parent figure. The one who loves the child unconditionally, is always available, and is filled with love for the child. Not a past parent whom the child may have some antagonistic or negative feelings about to a larger or lesser degree.

As you progress with letter writing and establish a bond with your inner child you may find it helpful to address specific problems. This then allows you to gain more understanding of what is going on in your unconscious mind, the place your inner child resides and influences. Here is an example from Joshua, a recent client;

Dear little Josh,

Hello there little man, how are you feeling today? I hope you will come and talk to me I've missed you since we last spoke. I wanted to ask you about these panic feelings I keep getting. You know the frightened feelings we get sometimes, that scary feeling in our tummy and chest, which makes us want to run. I know it may be hard to talk about but I am here for you now, I will help you with any bad feelings. It is ok to tell me if someone upset you or hurt you or made you scared, they cannot hurt or scare you anymore because I am going to take care of you. I am going to protect you and love you no matter what.

Love and cuddles, Big Josh

Little Josh's reply: Hello, I don't like those feelings they make me feel bad, they make me want to cry. I wish I could tell you why they come, they make me feel bad. I want my teddy, where's mummy. Mummy, mummy it's dark here mummy. I can't stop crying don't tell me to stop, please hug me mummy.

Big Josh: Tell me where you are little Josh, tell me what's happening.

Little Josh: I think we are on holiday, I don't want to stay in this room on my own it's dark, it's strange, it's scary. Help me. I can't see it's so quiet. Mummy don't go downstairs, please don't. I'm scared, my tummy hurts it hurts real bad. I feel frightened I want to run, run to mummy but I'm too scared. Scared, scared, scared I can't stop crying. It feels horrible, the hotel is so big. She's been gone ages.

At this stage Big Josh imagines hugging the child in the hotel room.

Big Josh: It's ok Josh I'm here now, I'll look after you, there's nothing to worry about. I won't leave you your safe, you can go to sleep now.

In Joshua's case his inner child took him to the cause of his nightly panic attacks, but often it may take a few letters and regression journeys to get to some causes. Letter writing is a good way to instigate the recall of memories, so you could start with;

Dear ....

Can you tell me about your experiences of school, or can you tell me about your trips out with Uncle Bob, or what was it like at home with Mummy when you were little?

This also allows you to develop the relationship gradually. Remember to treat your inner child like you would a child, they have to learn to trust you before they will tell you their inner most thoughts, memories and feelings. For issues of abuse Penny Parks book 'Rescuing The Inner Child' has many good examples and ideas on how to write to the inner child.

Letter writing to a parent/carer/teacher etc

Letter writing is also a good way to release pent up emotions. These letters are not written to the child but are written by you to whomever you feel aggrieved with. This could be anyone from your past who you feel the need to say something to. These letters should not be posted, they are purely to get emotions up and to get your thoughts out of your head and onto paper. If you wish to write a letter for a parent, carer etc to receive we will be talking more about this in Chapter 7.

Letters that release emotion and thoughts are for therapeutic purposes and most people tear them up or burn them to help put issues to rest, unless you are seeing a therapist who may find it helpful to read them. Sometimes when you are writing to someone who has hurt, troubled or affected you the letter can get quite heated. In this case you must not censor the letter or hold back, swear, throw insults, say whatever you like, whatever you like! This is very important. Being polite, holding back and not saying what's really in your mind and heart is how you had to behave as a child, this is no longer necessary and is certainly not helpful. Let it out, let it go, if need be say things like, "I'd like to punch your face in" or "I f**king hate you for what you did" and worse if you need to!! Of course not all letters are like this, you may just need to voice some thoughts or ask a question. Yet emotive letters can be very powerful and many times I've started with a letter and ended up bashing the pillow! It's great and I always feel much better afterwards. Here is an example from Kevin;

Mum,

Why did you sit by and watch Dad hit us all the time. Why did you start crying what bloody help was that to us? Weren't our cries louder? Didn't it bother you that he was hitting us with a belt, punching our little faces and screaming at us. How could you have sat by and watched him you stupid stupid cow, you stupid weak pathetic cow. You were supposed to protect us, what's bloody wrong with you?? I hate you, I hate you as much as him. Didn't you love us? Didn't you care? I don't get it mum I never will. You didn't even hold us afterwards, are you so cold? So cold to watch three of your children crying and not wanting to comfort them? Oh yes you tell me you were scared, well you should have got out of there taken us away, away from that monster. You're so weak, so useless, so pointless. What was the point of you being there? The shadow in the corner, the one person who could have saved us but instead you betrayed us. There's so much hatred for you, I want to hurt you, kill you, injure you. I want you to feel what I felt, what we felt your little children. God I hate you, I'm sorry but I do.

Kevin

Kevin wrote many letters to his mum and dad. When I used to write letters I must have written hundreds, there was so much I needed to say that I couldn't say as a child. There were so many people I needed to say stuff to, no one was left out. Also writing letters that contain scenes of killing, hurting or even torturing a carer will not turn you into psychopathic maniac. Its better out that in, if your having thoughts like this get it down on paper, express it in all it grotesque forms. Its important to make you feel better. Therapeutically working through your feelings and thoughts will help you become a much calmer person, and your perspective on others will change. You can only really forgive and let go when you have processed the pain and 'mad' thinking, whatever form that takes. If you find letter writing brings up a lot of anger do the pillow bashing exercise as described in the next chapter.

Please don't worry about spelling or grammar when writing letters, just let the words flow. You may find the writing speeds up as you go and can get more like a scribble. Many of my clients' letters are illegible when they give them to me and this is a good sign! You can also write letters from your inner child to the parent/carer etc. To do this you just need to relax and imagine yourself as the child with the person you wish to write. Here is another example from Kevin written by his inner child.

Daddy,

Why did you hurt us like that you were so scary. Didn't you like us? Did we do something wrong? Big Kevin says we didn't so why did you do it? It scared me a lot and I sometimes wet myself when I heard you come in, why did you hit me for that? Why was I hit for being scared? If I was big and strong I would have hit you back but I couldn't I was too little. I only wanted your love, I only wanted you to play but you didn't. You made my life really bad and when I got big it made me really sick. Why couldn't I have had a normal nice daddy. You made me so sad.

Kevin

If it feels right you can always imagine the parent answering the letter. Sometimes this can comfort the child to get an explanation, but can never excuse what happened. These letters are usually written when the issue is completely resolved and your ready to move on. It is when your ready to see the bigger picture. Here is Kevin's example;

Dear Kevin,

I know what I did and I'm so sorry. I was so full of anger and I took it out on you which was bad. I think because my own dad was violent I learnt to be this way, but this doesn't mean it's ok, of course not. I was very wrong and it was very bad, I should have got help but I didn't. I didn't get help because I was a coward, I was too scared to face my past and to face the fear I felt as a child. Instead I took it all out on you, you the innocent child who couldn't defend himself. Isn't that typical of a coward, I'm so ashamed. I don't blame you for hating me I deserve all the hatred you have. I am weak, inadequate and a pathetic example of a father. So sorry.

Your dad

Of course you and I know that Kevin's dad didn't really write the letter and the chances of him writing such a letter are pretty slim, to say the least (most parents won't even acknowledge they were wrong). The letter has truth in it though and comes from a higher perspective. This means you are able to see that people behave in certain ways for a reason, and not because the child is deficient, inadequate or a failure. This can be very enlightening for the child and the adult alike. To finally realize that your parents acted inappropriately because of their childhood and their problems is a good way to release self-blame and feelings of worthlessness. What we need to remember is that if Kevin's dad finally 'woke up', went into therapy, healed his pain, and once again became the person he truly is (before his own father turned him into a cold child beater) this is the kind of letter he would write to his child, and it would be sincere. This is because underneath all of us is a kind, compassionate and warm being. This is who we truly are no matter what we've done. The problem is most people have been well and truly messed up by the impact of their childhood, and gaining access to the good inside them is sometimes impossible. Always seek the guidance of your higher self when answering back to the child or adult self. Also note this type of letter must only be written when you have dealt with your anger and pain. Saying to the child, "Dad only hurt you cos he was hurt" will not allow him to express his feelings fully. Sometimes you have to become blind to why your parents failed until you are more sorted. Also your inner child never has to or shouldn't be expected to excuse an adult who intentionally hurt them. They may gain some understanding but exoneration is not required at any stage for growth and healing. (More on forgiveness in Chapter 7).

Some letters to the carer/parent/teacher can also be about a small issue which was very important to the child, like in Karen's case;

Dear Uncle Jim,

I am so angry that you laughed at me with your friends on my birthday. Just because I fell in the pig pen gave you no reason to laugh. Didn't you see I was embarrassed and humiliated? Why did you keep laughing even when I'd started crying? Are you so uncaring? It may have not been a big deal to you and I remember you telling me to stop being silly, stop being silly! I'd just fallen in all that muck in my beautiful party dress and you said stop being silly! How could you, you made me so mad, you embarrassed me so much. So stop talking about it, stop telling the story I'm sick of hearing it. I'm sick of it. Just shut up and get a life.

From Karen.

Even if it may seem like a small issue to others and you scold yourself for being silly, remember children feel things more intensely and are usually affected much more so than adults. If your inner child says it was bad then it was bad full stop. Therefore don't overlook it if it needs expression.

Some clients have felt the need to write letters to other children, for example school bullies or a sibling that was cruel or abusive. It is essential to release painful feelings toward everybody in your childhood who hurt you. Yet when it comes to children I always ask my clients to do an answer back letter like above. This is a letter from the bully, sibling etc explaining why they behaved like they did. I think its important to see the bigger picture where other children are concerned because they are always acting in response to something that is happening to them. Bullies feel out of control at home or victimized, cruel siblings may be jealous if you were treated differently or abuse you if they are being abused. Children don't always have the adult reasoning to assume that what they are doing is harmful. Adults always have this reasoning, even if they don't acknowledge it. This is why I find forgiving children who may have hurt us becomes easier than forgiving adults because we know they cannot be held fully accountable. They are just kids after all. It is down to the adults to take accountability for a child's behavior. In this sense you may wish to write letters (not to be sent) to the child's parent or carer (who may be your parent or carer too) expressing your anger at their negligent parenting, and explaining that their behavior has affected the child and in turn affected you.

6

'The more you connect to the Power within you, the more you
can be free in all areas of your life'
Louise Hay

The Gold Counselling (TM) Technique

Gold counselling is a structured technique created by hypnother-
apist/psychotherapist Georges Philips, which allows you to pin
point very accurately the core of any problem. This then makes its
much easier to seek the cause, and alleviate the difficulty. The
technique is very simple yet very effective once you get the hang
of it.

To begin using Gold and exploring the cause of your current
problems you need to think about something to work on, you
need a heading. You may want to use the list that you put together
in Chapter 3, or you may want to work on something else. Here
are some ideas;

A recurring pattern - Rejection, overeating, angry outbursts in
certain situations etc

A feeling you've experienced this week, or keeps cropping up -
Embarrassment, fear, tension, headaches etc

An area in your life which is bothering you - A relationship, work,
money, home etc

A past condition you'd like to explore further - An illness, a past
relationship, a habit etc

An area which makes you feel out of control - A fear or phobia,
intense feelings in a situation, jealousy etc

An addiction/dependency issue - These areas are best dealt with when you are no longer taking the substance depended on, as emotions and issues will then arise for you to look at. Until then the addiction will continue to mask the real problem which will render it less accessible. Also substances like drugs or alcohol affect the mind's capacity to think clearly and if they are in your system will hinder the overall outcome of any work you do. As stated before you may need to seek additional support when letting go of addictions or dependencies. Maybe though you feel you can deal with, or have let go of your particular habit - if so work with whatever feelings, thoughts, problems or behaviors that have come up for you or do come up for you. Remember to keep off the substance depended on you need to address the deeper issues and understand why you required the sugar, drugs, alcohol or whatever it is. This is necessary for long-term success. If your dependency is not related to a substance but is do with say shopping, sex, or exercise then the same applies. Prepare to abstain from the desired activity for a week to ten days, and work on the issues which arise. It is often surprising to find how much you've been avoiding for so long.

Or you may be in a crisis - If so explore your feelings around this, i.e. out of control, powerless, panic, confused. Recollect your thoughts before the crisis, did you believe 'happiness never lasts' or 'I don't deserve for things to be this good'. If so put these as headings. Have you created crisis or trauma to punish yourself or to punish others? If so put 'anger' or 'guilt' unless something else comes to mind. Or are you hooked on the 'buzz' or challenge? If so put one of those as a heading. Often a crisis occurs because something in our life needs to be changed or you need to go in a different direction - it can mark a turning point. Yet it is also an opportunity to work through old memories which need to be released, it is overall a time to understand yourself a bit better.

Or you may just wish to explore your beliefs - Here are some usual headings; Relationships, Men, Women, I am/Me, Work, Feelings, Happiness, Change, Money, Life, Food, My health, Sex, Intimacy etc.

Some areas will need to be explored a little further so you know where to start. For example if you want to explore a relationship issue you will need to know what the issue is about. You may be arguing alot but what is the real problem? If you are arguing because your husband is out at work all the time or you have little money, you need to think about how these make you feel. Your husband working a lot may cause you to feel unwanted, therefore you need to work on that feeling of unwantedness, or with money it may bring up fear therefore fear will be your heading. Or if you are unhappy at work, Why? Explore it, how does work make you feel? Bored, inadequate, stressed? If so go with the most appropriate heading. Other areas will be easier to pinpoint, if you have a phobia about spiders you can just put spiders as a heading. The heading alone will probably bring up all the necessary feelings! or if you felt sad or angry this week just go with that. I hope this is clear what it boils down to is this, general issues like relationships, illness, work, family have to be dissected so its no longer a general issue but a personal one to you. So you can distinguish what your personal feelings, reactions or beliefs are about it. If it seems too overwhelming to work it out yourself then start with the general heading say relationships and start there. From the list you will be able to pinpoint what the problem is with the technique I will show you. So, for example, you may find the crux of the matter is a fear of abandonment. From this you will then need to compile a list on abandonment to examine it further. For additional help refer to the list of symptoms described in the previous chapter. With a physical symptom refer to the ailment directory in the appendices at the back of this book.

Hopefully you now have a heading, if not do this exercise with 'happiness' or 'change' as a heading - as you may be resisting both. Now sit quietly and, if you have not already done so, write the heading on the top of a piece of paper. Relax and like we did in Chapter 3 begin to focus on the topic or feeling and list in sequence like a shopping list all your feelings, thoughts, emotions, how it affects you, any physical feelings, how you behave and your beliefs around this area. Everything you are going through or thinking when the problem or issue is present. Make each item on the list one word or as short a description as you can without leaving anything out. You need more than five items every time you do a list. It is essential that you write down every thought which comes to mind, being guided by your unconscious. Your unconscious will be adding to the list too, this is why it is so important to write down everything that comes to mind even if it doesn't make sense, seems irrational, or is the opposite to something else on the list. It is not uncommon to have conflicting thoughts or ideas with issues, or for something different to be going on in your unconscious than in your conscious. Do not delete anything when you have completed the list. The list must reflect your beliefs entirely, the list must not be about what you want to or try to believe, or what someone else believes. Be honest with yourself and write without judgment, after all no one else is going to see the list. Also remember the list may contain references to the past and the present. Keep on writing until nothing more comes or can be added to.

To explain this technique more clearly I am going to use a case study. Ginny came to see me suffering with depression and low self worth, she was drinking daily and attracted emotionally unavailable men into her life. During one of the sessions Ginny talked about feelings of rejection from her current partner and I asked her to write a list.

Rejection
A. Alone

B. Unlovable
C. Worthless
D. Scared
E. Ugly
F. Sad
G. Hurt
H. A Nobody
I. Not Wanted by him

Now with your own list write the alphabet down the side before each individual word or sentence, like in the example. If the list exceeds 26 items continue with AA, AB, AC and so on. Always use letters and not numbers.

The next step with your list is to connect all the items together. Here is Ginny's example;

Rejection

A.	Alone	E
B.	Unlovable	C
C.	Worthless	E
D.	Scared	A
E.	Ugly	B
F.	Sad	A
G.	Hurt	F
H.	A Nobody	C
I.	Not Wanted	E

This means taking the first Item on your list and intuitively sensing what it links with, for Ginny her first item 'Alone' linked or naturally went with 'Ugly'. Her next item 'Unlovable' linked with 'Worthless'. Then the third item 'Worthless' linked with 'Ugly' and the fourth 'Scared' linked with 'Alone' and so on.

Take your list and in sequence link them up. When linking go with intuition let your unconscious show you. Some points to remember are;

A letter cannot link back to itself, so A cannot go back to A.

Each item can only connect to one other item. So if we look at the above example 'Alone' can only go to 'Ugly'. If Ginny felt 'Alone' went to something else too she would need to decide which held the strongest link and go with that. Remember let your unconscious show you.

More than one item can link back to another item. In Ginny's example 'Unlovable' and 'A Nobody' both linked back to 'Worthless'.

Remember there is no right or wrong way to connect each item, the connection you make will be right for you.

Constructing a map from your list

Let me talk you through the linking up of Ginny's list to create a map. This map will show you how each thought and belief on Ginny's list relates to each other, this then allows you to locate the primary and secondary thoughts. The primary thoughts are the core or strongest element of the issue, the secondary thoughts feed into these. It just allows you to break the problem down so you can see how it is structured. This way you can work with and eliminate what is detrimental to the unconscious and yourself in a much more precise way. The primary thoughts are highlighted.

A goes to E - (we start the list with what A went to, which is E)

E goes to B - (then we go with what E goes to, which is B)
Then B goes to C and C goes back to E.
You do not need to write it out as above but take your list and

begin to map it out like below. Here is Ginny's so far;

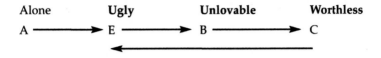

When we look at the list we notice that D, F, G, H, and I are still missing. When I add them in the list looks like this;

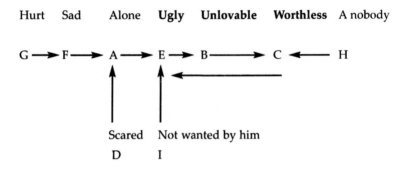

You will see that E, B and C create a loop. This loop is very important because it shows us the primary thoughts or beliefs which create the strongest amount of energy in Ginny's experience of rejection. This is the core of the issue and all lists will have a core. This loop (core) which we will work with when tracing it back to its source is the one part of the whole map which must be eliminated and updated if we are to successfully change the thought process, and resolve the problem. All other thoughts, which are secondary, are feeding into the loop giving the primary thoughts power. This is why when you look at the loop in your map you will instinctively know the emotions or thoughts contained in the loop have the most intensity when you are experiencing the feeling or problem in your day-to-day life. Also the part of the loop which have the most feeding into it, in this case 'Ugly' is the most prevalent to use when looking for the cause because it contains the most potency.

When you have mapped out your list you may not only have one loop but two, or three. These loops and their secondary thoughts feeding in will be a system on their own. They should not be connected to your other loops or systems on your map. For example let me demonstrate this with another list from Ginny.

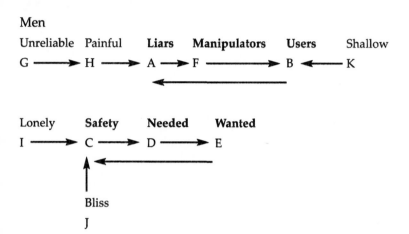

As you can see Ginny has two separate systems to work with here, this can either indicate two past memories that have affected her feelings about men. Or two separate agendas holding a lot of energy coming from the same memory.

Also be aware of some systems which may seem to some positive but are infact negative and restricting. The above list shows a system relating to men as 'Safety - Needed -Wanted'. Clients who have held similar beliefs have said to me, "What's wrong with that?" Well it's ok to want a man in your life but when you're relying on him to feel safe in the world or to make you happy then your viewing life and yourself in a limited way, belief restructuring is all about changing limiting beliefs, creating independence and setting yourself free. If you have any beliefs which you know are not allowing you to be the best you could be, they need to be transformed. Also beliefs which are judgmental need to be restructured, Ginny believed that men were

'Unreliable, Painful, Liars, Manipulators, Users and Shallow'. Some would say to me, "Well that's true!", but is it true for all men? No of course not. What we believe we achieve, if you believe men are this awful then you will attract men who behave this way. So yes some men function at this level (due to their own childhood) but not all men. Ginny learnt to view men in this way due to her experiences with abusive men in her past. Had she had happy and loving experiences with her primary male care givers she would have a completely different thought pattern, a positive one. This would have in turn pulled to her men who fulfilled that positive belief, but instead she attracted takers the unavailable type who danced with her through a roller coaster of emotions. The type who left her depressed and insecure, the way she felt as a child. So if you're attracting the 'wrong type' yourself then this reflects your beliefs. The next time you say, "Look I told you all men are liars look what he's done to me now," realize it's all your creation. When you seek the cause and change the belief system you change your outer reality and create a positive conclusion.

Because our thoughts can conflict it is not unusual for us to have a positive system alongside a negative one. Let me show you with this example;

Friends

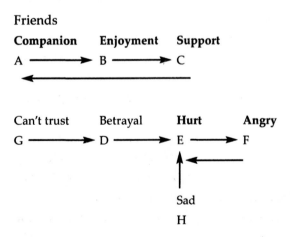

Companion   Enjoyment   Support
A ⟶ B ⟶ C

Can't trust   Betrayal   **Hurt**   **Angry**
G ⟶ D ⟶ E ⟶ F

Sad
H

This list shows conflicting beliefs and thoughts about friends. The positive system has in it contained 'Companion - Enjoyment - Support', this is good it comes from positive experiences about friendship and does not need to be changed. If you have a positive system when you create a map you do not need to do anything about it, it is the negative we need to work on. Some systems will have positive words feeding into it but the loop is negative or detrimental, this is because some systems start off with happy thoughts which can turn sour. Like this one;

Traveling

Freedom	Excitement	Happy	Going fast	**Panic**	**Help**	**Let me out**
A $\longrightarrow$	B $\longrightarrow$	C $\longrightarrow$	D $\longrightarrow$	E $\rightarrow$	F $\rightarrow$	G

When traveling this person was ok until the vehicle went fast then they were thrown into panic. To resolve this we would still need to find the cause and eliminate the negative that has attached to the positive.

Now if you have got to this stage and are thinking, "This is too difficult" or "I can't do this" then it may be a good idea to start with a list on these feelings. You may have beliefs which could sabotage your success with this exercise or other work in the book, this is why it is usually a good idea to think about thoughts which may be detrimental to your progress. Examples are those outlined above or maybe 'I'm a failure", I'm not good enough'. If you find any beliefs of this nature cropping up at this stage work with these. If you feel your not good enough or stupid and firmly believe this you are going to find areas of this work confusing (confusing - another belief which may occur for you to work on) or perplexing and give up. At this stage you may want to look at the 'Overcoming Inner Blocks' exercise too. If you still find your having a problem maybe you could ask a friend to go through it with you, or move onto the next chapter and come back to this section later. Whatever happens don't give up!

Working With The Map - Stage 1

If you read the following example of the therapy I did with Ginny when her map was complete it will give you some idea of the process. That is how to access memories, work through a memory, assist the inner child, deal with others in the memory (if appropriate), restructure beliefs and change thoughts or emotions. Then we shall progress through your list step by step. So for now we are going to look at Ginny's list on 'Rejection'.

Rejection

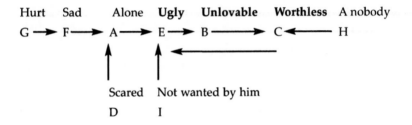

After Ginny relaxed this is how the dialogue went.

ME: "Where did you first learn to believe that rejection meant ugly, unlovable, worthless, where did you first learn to believe that rejection meant ugly, unlovable, worthless?"

(This question I repeated a few times and then I asked Ginny to repeat it in her own mind to herself. So now she is repeating in her thoughts, "Where did I first learn to believe that rejection meant ugly, unlovable, worthless?" I asked her to continually repeat the question so as to saturate the mind with this thought. I asked her to go with the very first thought that came to mind after repeating the question.)

GINNY: "I see my nan in the living room I am there too. I'm holding my baby sister on the sofa"

ME: "Go on.."

GINNY: "My mum is in the kitchen"

Ginny starts crying

ME: "What's happening now?"

GINNY "I've dropped the baby, I've dropped the baby. She was on my knee but she's fallen on the floor. She smacked her head on the hearth"

Pause

ME: "And what's happening now?"

GINNY (still crying) "My nan has grabbed me by the arm, she's screaming at me she's shaking me calling me a stupid girl. My mum runs in and shouts at me as well. My nan slaps me around the face really hard and tells me to get out of sight. My mum does nothing and I run to my room. I have to stay in there for ages............ I want my dad but he has left I feel that no one likes or wants me"

ME: "And those feelings of rejection, ugly, unlovable, worthless, did you feel them at this time?"

GINNY: "Yes most definitely"

ME: "And how old are you at this time?"

GINNY: "I'm only five"

ME: "OK Ginny I want you to once again repeat the question, 'Where did I first learn to believe that rejection meant ugly, unlovable, worthless'. If there is an earlier time, earlier than this time it will come into your mind now. If not this memory will stay with you"

(It is important to locate the first time the beliefs and feelings where formed/experienced. Sometimes you may visit many memories where the beliefs were reinforced before you locate the first time. That's ok just work back with your unconscious ensuring you have the first time before you begin restructuring the beliefs in your unconscious mind.)

GINNY: "I don't sense an earlier time. I'm sure this time where I dropped my sister is the first time"

Working With The Map - Stage 2

ME: "Now Ginny I want you to imagine you your adult self, the person you are today, entering that scene. But I want you to imagine yourself as your most confident self, a strong self, a very loving self and tell me what you see"

(It is important that the adult Ginny now becomes part of the memory. This will help heal the memory and encourage Ginny to rely on herself rather than the men in her life to help her feel better.)

GINNY: "I see myself looking out of the bedroom window, I look really sad. I'm really missing my dad whose in America now"

ME: "What do you the adult want to do?"

GINNY: "I want to go and hold her"

(Ginny enters the room and explains to the child that she is her future self who has come to help and support her at this time.)

ME: "How has the child responded to you?"

GINNY: "She is very happy to see me"

ME: "What is happening now?"

GINNY: "I go to pick her up and hold her close"

ME: "Become your child self again and just experience how it feels to be the child now"

GINNY: "I feel really safe now, there is someone in the world who seems to care about me. Its lovely"

ME: "Now become your adult self and talk to the child. Reassure her that what has happened wasn't her fault and the adults around her have responded unfairly. Tell her that the adults response reflects problems inside of them and is not to do with the child. Let the child know she is special, unique and important no matter what the adults tell her or how they act or what she has learnt to believe"

GINNY: "Hello little Ginny, I'm so happy to be here with you to help you at this time. The adults around you have problems inside themselves which they take out on you. This is unfair and not your fault. Just because mum doesn't help you, daddy left and nanny is cruel doesn't mean there is anything wrong with you my darling. You are special, lovely and unique. You are important and I love and want you"

(At this stage some of Ginny's childhood feelings of rejection and associated feelings could be dissipating as she reassures herself that her identity need not be based on others views of her or behavior toward her. Some inner children need more reassurance or explanation though like in the case of Ginny.)

LITTLE GINNY: "But why do they treat me so bad, why did daddy leave? He's gone to America and I haven't heard from him. I must have something wrong with me, I must be ugly or something no one seems to care"

GINNY: "The adults around you are responding in the only way they know how given their upbringing and beliefs about the parenting. The problem is in them and not in you"

(Sometimes it takes time to reassure the child that the problem is not in them but in situations or people outside their control. Even if a child appears to be behaving badly there are always underlying reasons for the child's behavior. This may need to be explored further to allay guilt and self sabotage.)

Working With The Map - Stage 3

ME: "Now Ginny I want you to take the child away from that situation but before you go do you want to say something to the adults downstairs?"

(Some people are firing on all cylinders wanting to have a go at the adults, this is ok and will be further explored shortly. Some people prefer not to maybe not feeling ready or believing the adults are not worth their time, or it just isn't necessary.)

GINNY: "Yes I want to go and speak to them, I'm very angry at their treatment of the child"

(Ginny checks that the child is ok to witness this, the child is delighted that someone is finally going to stick up for her. Some inner children would rather not watch the adult at this stage and may opt to stay in their bedroom until the adult has finished. It is always important to check with the child as some feel they should be loyal to their parent or carers despite their treatment of them. If you were badly treated as a child or abused and you feel confronting your parents is disloyal, you may well discover as memories are unearthed your attitude changes.)

GINNY: "I'm going downstairs with the little me in my arms. My mum and nan are in the kitchen. I walk in and begin shouting at them I feel so angry"

(Some people want to do this but find it daunting. In this case I ask them to be taller and stronger than they are now, sometimes becoming a giant! Or they could have someone there to back them up like a super hero or imaginary friend. It's important to keep the back up as a fantasy figure unless it is your therapist or counsellor. Relying on your current boyfriend or best friend to help you and your inner child creates dependency in your waking life. Also having super powers is ok like lasers coming from your hands if you feel you may be under attack or the ability to restrain the adult in some magical way.)

ME: "How are they responding to you now?"

GINNY: "My nan did start to shout but I'm louder and bigger than her, she is cowering now. I feel so powerful! I'm telling them the effect they are having on the child and that they should be ashamed of themselves. My mum is saying sorry. Now I turn and take the child out of the house"

ME: "Ask her what she wants to do now? It can be anything, you can go anywhere. What would be a special treat, where would she really like to go?"

GINNY: "We are going to a lovely garden filled with flowers and butterflies. Little Ginny has a new dress, she looks really happy. We play, tell stories and sit together under the tree. Its such a lovely day"

ME: "Now I want you to put that image of you and Little

Ginny somewhere in your mind, a safe place so you can look at it whenever you want over the next few days"

Working With The Map - Stage 4

ME: "Now Ginny I want you to imagine that you can see into your unconscious as if you were looking inward there into the depths of your mind. And there in your unconscious imagine you can see millions and millions of tiny brain cells. Some are strands, some are clumps, all performing their own unique function within the mind. Now imagine that four brain cells are making themselves apparent to you maybe becoming larger or getting closer, just seeing four cells linked together. Focus on the first cell and notice that it has rejection contained within it. This may be written on the cell or you may just know it contains the belief, feelings and the energy of Rejection. Then attached to that cell is a cell containing Ugly, and attached to that a cell containing Unlovable and lastly the cell containing Worthless"

GINNY: "Ok I see them"

ME: "Now imagine your unconscious has two very special tools specifically designed and developed to assist you. These are your beliefs tool, a beliefs creator and a beliefs destroyer. Some people imagine actual tools or gadgets like a hammer or gun or giant pin for the destroyer tool, and some imagine a magic wand, a pair of hands or a balloon pump for the creator. Or some imagine a powerful factory line or computer programme to do the job. So as you relax just let your unconscious select and show you the most appropriate and powerful tools for you"

GINNY: "Um...I see a massive hammer and a magic wand"

ME: "Good now with your massive hammer I want you to destroy those cells which contain Rejection, Ugly, Unlovable and Worthless. Those beliefs which you hold about yourself are untrue, they are inappropriate and out of date. You learnt to believe these beliefs because of the way you were treated. You inadvertently decided that rejection meant you were ugly, unlovable and worthless but these do not speak the truth about you. They are false beliefs and need to be updated, they became imbedded when you were five and they created a pattern for the rest of your life. But we can change that pattern now, we can destroy these decaying beliefs and create new beliefs which reflect who you truly are. Do you feel ready to change this now?"

GINNY: "Yes please!"

ME: "Do you see that the beliefs were inadvertently created and do not speak the truth about you?"

GINNY: "Yes I do. It might take a bit of getting used to but I can see these feelings are about the past and I want to change them"

ME: "Wonderful, now take that hammer and completely obliterate those beliefs. Let me know when they are gone"

Long pause

GINNY: "They've gone now"

ME: "Now in their place, with the power of your beliefs creator tool the magic wand I want you to create some new beliefs, empowering, positive and liberating beliefs, beliefs which will allow you to behave and think in the way that is the most appropriate way for you now, the most balanced and harmonious way. These new beliefs reflecting the person you are becoming as you now change and evolve. So think about what has been destroyed and allow your unconscious to show you the new beliefs to replace these"

GINNY "Ok......................................I see, I am lovable, I am unique and special, I am free"

ME "Good, now allow those new beliefs to take their place in your unconscious mind................and let your imagination take you into the future, maybe next week or a few weeks from now. See yourself somewhere it can be anywhere, somewhere you would expect to see yourself a short way in the future. Imagine yourself doing whatever you are doing with those new beliefs firmly in place. See yourself believing you are lovable, unique, special and free"

GINNY "Mmmm.....I see myself just walking along in town"

ME: "How do you look, what are you thinking, what do you notice about yourself?"

GINNY: "I have a big smile on my face, I am more upright, more confident, I feel attractive"

ME: "Anything else?"

GINNY: "Yes I feel safe in the world. Even though I'm still seeing Steve he isn't affecting me, I'm not allowing him to get to me, I seem quite free really!"

ME: "Great, now just stay with that image for a while knowing that your unconscious is taking care of everything. That future you is the person you are now stepping into. You don't have to be concerned with how this will all occur it will happen without you even trying. And when you are ready come back to the room you are in now"

'Gold Counselling offers insight into the core of the personality. It is a rapid and powerful methodology for uncovering the framework of emotional beliefs in the unconscious mind, facilitating lasting change in the body-mind'

Dr. J. Stanley

Working With Your List & Map (please read through this section first if you want to familiarize yourself with it)

When you have your list linked up and mapped out I want you to prepare to relax. Make yourself comfortable and ensure you won't be disturbed for the next forty minutes or so. Perhaps by turning the phone off or putting a note on the front door. Now look at your map and decide which elements of it you are going to work with. Remember to always work with words which are in the loop, especially those which have others feeding into them. There may be words close the loop which have a lot of energy going into them too, which you may want to include when asking the unconscious for the cause. Like in the example below, 'Depressed' has a lot of energy going into it and is close to the loop therefore I would go with this as well as 'Angry' and 'Hate'. You may need to go with your intuition when deciding which elements to work with, but remember the loop is the core, the driving force, it is powering the problem in your day to day life and must always be worked on - even if you have no idea why those thoughts are there. If you have many words in your loop it is not necessary to go with all of them, concentrate on those that feel strong or have a lot being directed into them.

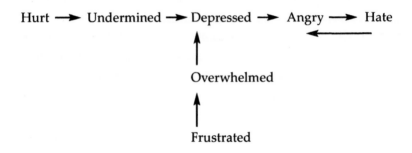

Now with the title of the list highlight those words you will be focusing on.

Working With Your Map - Stage 1

Now when you are comfortable begin to focus on your head and relax the muscles of your scalp................... relax the muscles of your forehead, eyes, cheeks, jaw, mouth and tongue.................. breath in deeply two times and as you exhale feel tension leaving your body.............just relax...................beginning to let go more and more..............allow your breathing to become easy and rhythmic.......... focus on your neck and shoulders and allow any tension to just drain away............. your shoulders becoming all loose and slack as you do...................let them become limp............. feel the relaxation move down your shoulders and into your arms, at the same time relaxing your chest and your upper back...............that's right feel that gentle calmness move through you.............becoming more and more peaceful............. feel the restful relaxation moving down your arms to your hands and fingers, down into your tummy and right the way down your back..................................... all the muscles of your back relaxing......................................letting go of tension in your tummy...............................feel your arms and hands becoming heavy....................breathing away tension with each breath out.................. as you breath out imagine all thoughts, cares and worries are being breathed into a fluffy white cloud................. just breathing away all worries in your life, all things on your mind, any thoughts which are preventing you from relaxing..............let them all go into this cloud and see it becoming gray...........Just seeing or sensing all those day to day issues drifting from your mind into the cloud.................let your mind become quiet and peaceful..................... relax your hips all the way into your thighs and down your legs..........................now let that cloud float away taking all those thoughts and emotions with it..........................your legs becoming heavy now.......................your feet becoming still and relaxed....................your body and mind relaxing into a state of calm relaxation.....feeling so peaceful..........................the cloud disappearing on the horizon.............and you relax more and more...............................

Now looking at your title and words and say to yourself, 'Where did I first learn to believe that ....(title)...................... meant ......(words)........... Where did I first learn to believe that....... (title)............... meant.........(words).............. and repeat over and over. Fill your mind over and over with that thought, allowing yourself to drift back to that very first time.. Now go with the first thought that comes to mind, it is important to go with the very first thought, even if it doesn't make sense. Don't rush the process - allow yourself time, some people see into a blackness for a while and then something comes, for others the process is more instant.

Accessing the memory

You may have a clear image or flashes of pictures, you may just have a thought, an unexpected emotion or a feeling in your body. Whatever happens is right for you so just go with whatever your unconscious shows you. If you have an emotion or feeling in your body allow your unconscious to now show you inside your imagination where that emotion or feeling originates from, let an image come to mind now or you may have a sense of being somewhere..........................Focus on that thought and begin to build a picture....... Sense yourself there and what clothes you are wearing, look down at your feet. Do you have shoes, socks or something else........... Are you indoors or outside?.......... What kind of day is it warm, cold, sunny, rainy?........... Look around you, what do you see?........ Make that image clearer the colors more vivid........... Is there anybody else there or are you alone?............ Where could you be?............. What are you doing?.............. If there are others around what are they doing or saying?........... What do you sense? Allow it to become clear............................. I wonder how old you are?............ How are you feeling?............. I wonder how that would be if you were actually inside the child looking out of the child's eyes? If you are not already experiencing this............................ Now keeping your list of words in mind begin to explore this memory. What happens? What do you say or think? If anyone else is there what are they saying or doing? Let the memory run freely. Even if it feels like your making it up don't worry! Trust your unconscious to show you the right image or memory. Use you imagination if your not sure what happens next, what do you imagine happens next? Where do you imagine you are? Just relax and go with it................

(If after a while you find nothing is happening then come back to the exercise at a later time, or work on another issue. If you feel you are blocking the process in any way then go to the 'Overcoming Inner Blocks' exercise in the Chapter 5 and return to this exercise when you feel ready).

If any emotions come up allow yourself to feel them. Most childhood memories you go back to will have emotion attached, and this is ok. Your unconscious has stored this emotion alongside the memory and it needs to be released. So if you feel like crying don't hold back, if you feel angry or afraid or any other emotion just let that surface. Some emotions can seem overwhelming but they cannot hurt you. As children emotions can be felt intensely even for the smallest indiscretion. Just allow that emotion to flow through you, it is part of the healing process and is essential for your recovery. You may also experience physical sensations, especially if this is the case with a memory recalled like choking, being hit, butterflies in tummy etc. If you happen to evoke a memory where you are choking or suffocating and are encountering the physical sensations too this may feel alarming yet it is an essential part of the process. This is therapy and sometimes you have to persevere. In persevering and seeing it through you will find the results amazing.

So view, experience, become a part of that memory. Be inside your child self and see what happens, take as much time as you need over this.

Now focus on your list of words again. Do they come from this time? Do they' fit' the memory? As you focus on the thoughts and feelings on your list did you feel or think them at this time as a child? If not repeat the process again until the appropriate memory surfaces.

Ok, now just ask your unconscious if this is the first time you learnt to believe ...(title).....meant......(words)..... You may need to repeat the question. If this is not the first time your unconscious will show you or you will sense a new memory when you were younger and you will need to go back to 'Accessing the memory'. If not stay with the current memory.

Some memories you recall you may already have been aware of to whatever degree, but hadn't realized the impact it had on you. Other memories may be completely new, if so it could be a repressed memory. Locating a repressed memory is normally positive proof that you have found the originating cause and should explain why you have been thinking, feeling or behaving in a certain way as an adult. This in turn will alter if not transform the problem altogether (if the problem is only altered but not resolved it just indicates that further work needs to be done in this area).

Working with your map - Stage 2

Now I want you to imagine your adult self is entering the scene, the person that you are today reading these words, walking into that childhood memory. But imagine yourself to be your most confident self, your assured self, your grown up self. As discussed previously if you in anyway feel nervous or worried because any adults there seem intimidating, see yourself as bigger or stronger or to have special powers. Or take a super hero or some fictional character you admire with you, it could even be an animal.. Now notice what you see...............look at the child and sense how they are feeling and what they are experiencing......now you may have come in at the beginning of the memory, some way through or at the end. Just go with your own experience and decide what you want to do............... Do you want to go to the child and pick them up? Does the child need more help than that? (i.e. if the child for example is being abused in some way do you need to pull the abuser away first? If this feels difficult because the abuser is still frightening to you remember to use super powers or enlist the help of two imaginary door men). If you feel unable to pick the child up or even hold their hand do all you can to make them safe or comfortable. This may mean taking away the source of distress, or removing them from it. So if a parent is being critical you may wish to tell them to be quiet, or ask the child to stop listening. If the child is having a near drowning experience pull them out of the water. If the child is being bullied stand in front of the child to shield them. Whatever you do ensure you help/rescue even if it means just hugging the child..........

Whatever ails you as an adult is a signal that your inner child needs help and rescue. Your inner child has waited a long time for someone to come back for them, so don't be surprised if you become very emotional at this stage. Seeing and helping your inner child can be a very moving process and it is not uncommon to cry or feel deep compassion. On the other hand if you feel indifferent, angry or negatively affected by the inner child please see 'Problems with connecting with the inner child' in Chapter 5 when you have completed this exercise.

Rescuing or helping your inner child cannot erase what has happened to you or change the past, but it can soften the blow. Many people feel a new sense of comfort and tremendous healing once they have helped the inner child, even though they know the memory still exists.

In some cases rescuing or helping the inner child may not be called for but rather an observation of events on your part. So say for example you were working on your beliefs about 'Work' you may recall a memory of your father saying 'Work is always hard and boring'. You may realize you took on the belief because you didn't doubt your father's word and now wish to change it. Or you may believe life is a struggle after watching a TV programme and now want to create a new belief. These examples have less intensity attached and are more to do with dealing with thought processes. If you feel this is the case continue this exercise from an observational point if you wish, but never leave your inner child stranded or upset if they need your help.

Now explain to the child that you are their future self and you have come to help them. Tell them you are now here to support them at this time and with any other memories they need to show you. Tell them anything that feels right and comfort the child...................................... Ask the child how they feel about this and notice how they respond to you............................

Sometimes trust needs to develop between you and your inner child, and they may hold back (once again please see 'Problems with connecting with your inner child'). For others the inner child may be desperate to be held by the adult.

Now become your child self and see how it feels to have your adult self in your life, someone who is completely on your side.............

Now become your adult self again and talk to the child. Reassure them that what is happening here is not the child's fault...

Some people have a problem with this, can we really say the child has no responsibility? Yes we can. They cannot be held accountable. When children fight in the home they are reacting to the stress within the adults, when children bully they are feeling powerless outside school, if the child returns to the abuser they are lacking love in their life and so on. There is an underlying reason for everything.

If it helps the inner child, and is appropriate, seek the underlying reason for the inner child's reaction or behavior. Help the inner child understand that what has happened is not their fault................................

Very often it is the inner world of the parents/carers which causes problems for the child, even if for example a child felt daddy loved sister more than her the problem is still in daddy, usually coming from his childhood and has nothing to do with the child's looks, personality, attitude or behavior - even though daddy might say or infer it is. Or taking another example, if your sibling was hurt accidentally whilst in your care please remember children are too young to take responsibility for other children. If something goes wrong the adult in charge is always accountable, even if you got the blame.

The inner child may wish to discuss this, be open to questions and always give reassurance, love and support. Never blame, criticize or berate the inner child. Remember whatever it is, is not their fault. The problem is not inside them but in the situations or people outside their control..............................

Working With Your Map - Stage 3

Now it is time to remove the child from this situation, but before you do you must decide if you wish to speak to whoever else is there before you go, if appropriate, (the child may in fact be alone or the person they are affected by may be absent or even dead or the child may be affected by something that involves nobody but the child themselves). So are you aggrieved or angry in some way? Do you want an explanation for certain actions or behaviors? Would it be helpful to the child if you spoke on their behalf? Or do you have something else to say or express? If not imagine taking your child to a special place somewhere they would love to go, it can be anywhere at all. Or maybe you would like to give them a gift, it can be anything their heart desires. Ask the child if they have any questions, or are confused about anything? Is there anything else they need to share with you? Or you may just want the child to merge with you. To do this see yourself holding the child very close to your body and allow them to merge very gently into a safe place inside of you, you may imagine them becoming smaller. If you have something to express please read on, if not move onto Working With Your Map - Stage 4).

When confronting others involved remember to check this is ok with the inner child and if they want to witness this. If not put them somewhere safe and ask them to wait for you. If they are afraid ask your parent self to take care of the inner child. Your parent self looks just like your adult self and plays a nurturing role. They are substitute carers who help your adult self when needed.

Ok, for this part you may wish to imagine yourself taller, with special powers or a fantasy figure to help. If not that's fine, often just being your adult self is sufficient.

Imagine walking up to the person/s you want to talk to, then with assertiveness and clarity say want you want to say. Express yourself fully. If they keep butting in imagine you have powers to silence them. You may wish to explain why something they did or said affected the child so much, you may get angry and start shouting, you may want answers. If so let the other person/s talk, but do not let them blame or criticize the child, or become abusive to you. Sometimes the person/s will be sorry or say they hadn't realized the affect they had on you...........................

Painful emotions may arise at this time which need to be expressed, so again if you need to cry then do so. If you feel very angry this must be dealt with, keeping anger inside is very damaging and damage to the self is not an option anymore. Some of my clients feel guilty when they discover hateful and angry feelings toward their parents, yet if your parents were inadequate, abusive, neglectful, absent or down right thoughtless you have every right to be angry. If you were in the care of someone who ultimately damaged you at some level, you are entitled to be angry. It does not mean you are going to visit their home today and hurl abuse at them, as expressing your anger privately to yourself or a therapist can be just as effective. But to do this you must accept that your anger has to be released and disposed of safely. If you are experiencing an emotive memory but are feeling nothing, numb, empty or having difficulty getting the emotion up then work with the 'Overcoming Inner Blocks Exercise' and then come back to this area.

Sometimes I find watching a film or reading about someone else's story which runs along the same lines as my problem a good way to get a feeling up. Or often a memory will be recalled and the emotion unexpectedly comes up a few days later. Or if you ask for spiritual help from your higher self or some other source you may find the emotion is unexpectedly evoked by something you see, dream about or experience in your day to day life. Always remember to ask for help, their is an unlimited amount of help available for you in the unseen realms, you just have to ask.

Dealing with anger

Shout, swear, scream, or even hit or hurt the person you are angry with. Some people who have been abused as children may need to go as far as killing or torturing the abuser. This does not mean you are really a killer or a cruel person, it just reflects the intensity of your emotions. Child abuse in any form is degrading and devastating, intense anger is the normal outcome for a child made to feel powerless and humiliated. Sometimes you have to go to extremes with your inner work to let this go. You will not become violent in your waking life after doing these exercises, in fact the opposite is true. All of my clients who have fully dealt with their anger feel more peaceful and happy as a result. You may also find repeating the visualization to shout out, kill or hurt the tormentor is necessary for the emotions to be fully released.

Physical release

When feeling intense anger during this work you may need some kind of physical release too. If so get a pillow and place it on your bed, imagine the problem person or the situation which has made you angry, and with clasped fists hit the pillow over and over, hit it as hard as you can. As you do you may wish to shout or say things to the problem person like, "Get away from me" or "I hate you." Swear, scream (placing the pillow over your face to muffle the sound if you have neighbors), cry, say what you like - it's your call and no one is going to stop you. You can also strangle the pillow or hit it against a wall if this helps. In my office I have a baseball bat, nothing dispels anger more safely and effectively than hitting a pillow or mattress with a bat. My clients find it empowering and releasing. Again you may have to do all these exercises several times to fully release emotional hurt and pain from the past.

When you are done take the child from the situation. Ask them where they would most like to go, it can be anywhere they choose......... Then imagine yourselves there and have fun with the child, or just sit quietly together............. Does the child have any questions? Do they still need reassurance or time to cry? Is there anything else they would like to share with you? Are there any other beliefs of problems that have come as a result of this memory that need to be addressed?....................When you are finished hold the child close and let them merge with you, finding their safe place inside you. Or just allow this image to take its place somewhere in your mind.

Working With Your Map - Stage 4

Ok nearly there just one last thing to do!

Imagine looking into your unconscious mind, just focusing there in depths of your unconscious. Imagine your mind is filled with tiny brain cells, millions and billions of them. See the strands and clumps of cells, all performing their amazing and unique function. Some create positive thoughts and feelings, others create negative ones. Each are responsible for what happens in your life, all that you create and experience. All the negative happenings start here, your thoughts generate your life. This is why it is so important to locate the negative thoughts and change them, in doing this you change your life bit by bit. It's a powerful process and very liberating. So if you're ready see a strand of brain cells making themselves apparent to you now, cells all linked together coming closer getting larger............ Now remember your mapped out list and those words you highlighted in the loop and maybe others feeding into the loop. When we think of Ginny's example she imagined a cell with 'Rejection' contained within it, then attached to that 'Ugly', then 'Unlovable', then 'Worthless'. Don't worry too much about the format so long as you are seeing the words you highlighted or sensing their energy in the cells. So if Ginny didn't visualize the word rejection in or on a cell she may have sensed the energy that rejection created for her in the cell. When you work with your unconscious mind you are working with a sensory organ, so just sensing your experience is normal...........................Ok when you see or sense the cells that represent your mapped out list (the highlighted parts) imagine you have a very special tool, a beliefs destroyer tool. Your unconscious mind will select the most appropriate tool for you. Some imagine actual tools or gadgets like a giant hammer or gun or giant pin. Some see a large factory or computer programme. Just let your unconscious show you the most powerful destroyer tool for you..............................Now utilize the power and energy contained within your beliefs destroyer tool to destroy, obliterate and wipe out those old out of date beliefs. They are inappropriate, old and fossilized. They were create a long time ago when you were young. You didn't have the adult reasoning to question the impact this was going to have upon you or whether the belief was accurate, but you do now. You are in control and you decide what lives there in your unconscious mind and these out of date thoughts, beliefs, and feelings need to go. It is time to update the system in line with the amazing person you are becoming (always ensure you destroy the beliefs and thoughts which were contained in the loop as the loop is the driving force in the whole system. If this is not eliminated the problem will not be either)...

If you have any problems letting go of or destroying the beliefs or thoughts, you may need to go back to the memory and speak some more to the inner child to ascertain why there is resistance. If you the adult are resisting this change, or questioning its benefit see 'Overcoming Inner Blocks'.

Good, now assuming those beliefs have been destroyed let your unconscious show you another tool, your beliefs creator tool. Your unconscious will easily and naturally show you the right one for you. Imagine a tool used for creating, some see a magic wand, or a pair of hands, or a balloon pump. Others a factory production line or computer programme. Let your unconscious show you the right tool for you........................and now with the help of your unconscious mind it is time to fill that vacuum with new beliefs and thoughts. Thoughts and beliefs which are positive, calming, empowering and liberating. Beliefs and thoughts which mean you will feel and behave in a way that is the most balanced way for you, the most harmonious and effective way. You are changing and evolving and your beliefs reflect this.

Your new beliefs may be the opposite to what's been destroyed so 'Aimless' could become 'Purposeful' or 'Worthless' could become 'Lovable' and so on. Or if you believed, "All women betray" it may be more appropriate for you to believe, "I am lovable I attract relationships which reflect this." Ensure the belief is realistic or something you can work toward, saying, "All women are trustworthy" is not essentially realistic. Working on loving yourself and believing you only attract loving women with integrity would be more appropriate. Also remember to keep the new belief positively worded, "I am full of confidence" rather than, "I am not going to be shy anymore." And in the present tense, "My life is filled with happiness" rather than, "Soon I will be happy or happiness is coming."

Don't worry if the belief seems out of reach like "I am a success!" anyone who has made a success of their life began it with a thought. New beliefs are like seedlings they have to be planted, then watered, given light and encouraged. So as you make those small steps which reflect your beliefs the plants in your garden will soon begin to grow.

Now with your beliefs in place let them easily and naturally become a part of your unconscious taking their unique place there. Your unconscious will place them appropriately and they will begin their own unique function. Your unconscious mind has taken in all that has been said and knows exactly what needs to be done. You don't have to be concerned how these changes will occur since they have already begun, these changes will take place without you having to do anything at all....................now let your imagination take you into the future, maybe next week or a few weeks, or some months. See yourself, you can be anywhere but it is somewhere where you are acting out on these new beliefs, feelings and behaviors. Remember your new beliefs and see yourself at a future date thinking, feeling and behaving in a way which shows these new beliefs working for you. So if you believe you are a non-smoker, see yourself at a party and not smoking. See yourself relaxed and unaffected by the others smoking around you. Or if you believe you are eliminating sugar from your life see yourself on holiday as your new trim and slim self..

And now return back to the room you are in as your present day self.

Well done!!

The more you use this technique the easier it becomes. In fact it becomes so simple you can use it anywhere, so long as you have a little bit of time to relax and do the work. And the more you do it the more you will want to do it as you enjoy the results of this amazing inner change process. This is part of your journey to freedom and can be utilized any time you have a problem, inappropriate belief, issue, upset, crisis, a pattern, an illness or anything that occurs to make you feel uncomfortable or out of balance. When I began doing the Gold technique I was writing and working on lists all the time. Issue after issue was transpiring, and the more I did the more I needed to do, it kind of had a snow ball effect. Then as time moved on and I healed the past I found I was doing less inner change work, and had more time to devote to creating the life I'd always dreamed of. Now I do lists about two or three times a month, relying on my uncon-scious to pull something to me to work on. Like the other day when these feelings emerged 'Uptight, restless, fed up, achieving nothing, frustrated, hands tied, restricted, want to break free, treading water, tired, fatigued, angry'. These came when I wasn't able to spend much time in the week writing and I was frustrated by problems purchasing a holiday home in Devon, UK. Yet they were really about my helplessness as a child when my dad walked out.

You may have much to work on, or you may be wondering what to do next. If so just let life run its course. Just reading this book and working on the exercises outlined has suggested to your unconscious and spirit that you are ready to change, and because you are ready life will bring lessons and circumstances to you to facilitate that change. You may get inner hunches, feelings, messages, synchronicities occurring, external happenings, flashbacks, dreams etc. The messages and signposts are everywhere. At the beginning they are usually pointing to inner child work, after a while they will point you in the direction of your life purpose. Nothing is too small either. One day I was feeling gloomy and thought, "Tut, its just one of those days must be 'cos its raining," then I decided to write a list. It was small list, "Sad, restless, down, bored, gloomy" which linked back to a Sunday afternoon laying on my bed when I was little. I only needed to visit the child and give her a hug and let her tell me what was wrong for my spirits to lift. It only took five minutes but it made such a difference.

The above work which we have done together is outlined below in a much simpler format. This can be used when you just need a reminder of how the process takes shape and saves you working through the above more detailed outline when it is no longer necessary.

Create a list from your chosen topic, link the list and map it out.

Decide which words in and around the loop your are going to work with, then:

Stage 1

Relax and repeat where/when did I first learn to believe.....................

Allow the memory (along with the emotion if appropriate) to surface.

Experience the memory as your child self.

Ask the unconscious if this is the first time. If an earlier memory surfaces work with that.

Stage 2

Enter the scene as your adult self, enlisting help if required.

Rescue, help and/or hug the child. Tell the child who you are and that what is happening is not their fault.

Stage 3

Talk to other persons present (optional).

Express emotions. Do physical release exercises to as described above if necessary.

Take the child from the situation. Go to a special place where you can spend time together. (Again this is optional, sometimes the child will be happy to stay where they are).

Stage 4

Imagine the cells you are working on in your unconscious mind.

Use your destroyer to eliminate them.

Use your creator tool to create new positive thoughts and beliefs, and let those new thoughts take their place in your mind.

See yourself in a future scenario with the new beliefs/ thoughts in place.

Return to the room you are in.

Giving beliefs back

At Stage 3 there is also the option of giving the beliefs back. If you decide to do this at any time you need not carry on with Stage four, as the process will complete itself here. Here is an example:

Terry learnt to believe that flying was dangerous, but this was his dads belief. On revisiting the memory he witnessed his dad panicking, pacing the floor and generally behaving like a terrified child leading up to their flight abroad. Terry learnt that flying was a frightening experience, but the belief was never his. At Stage three of the above process before taking the child away Terry imagined a huge wooden banner around his neck. Engraved on the banner were the words; 'Flying - scary, restless, danger, panic, help, thoughts racing'. After learning that the beliefs really belonged to his dad Terry imagined the heavy banner that had weighed him down for so long being lifted from his body. The banner was then placed around his dad's neck, it was put back in it's rightful place - it belonged to his dad. Terry then imagined a sash around his body and saw embroidered on it words stating new positive beliefs about flying. This technique can be used at anytime you realize the belief you've held on to for so long actually belongs to another person.

Similarly if someone abused, criticized or deliberately hurt you and made you feel bad about yourself the negative thoughts you took on from this really belong to them. For example Penny was both emotionally and physically abused by her dad and as a result she learnt to believe she was, 'worthless, no good, unlovable'. In this visualization I asked Penny to imagine she was wearing a t-shirt that was too large for her. On the t-shirt she saw the beliefs, 'worthless, no good, unlovable'. Now anyone who abuses, hurts, neglects or criticizes a child is probably harboring beliefs like this. If they didn't believe this about themselves they wouldn't behave like this toward others. So in light of this I asked Penny to imagine the over sized t-shirt being lifted from her body and being put on her dad, and there was nothing he could do about it he had to wear the t-shirt. Penny could then see that the beliefs, 'worthless, no good, unlovable' fitted her dad perfectly given his treatment of her. It allowed Penny to see that the problem was inside her dad and not about her. Penny then imagined herself in a pretty dress with new positive beliefs about herself embroidered there. Only do this exercise if you feel the beliefs fit another person.

Sometimes individuals feel guilty at giving beliefs or negative statements back as it can often look as though you are giving the person something they didn't have before, but this is not the case. The truth is they already hold these beliefs, it is already a part of their psyche. It helps nobody if both of you hold the beliefs, all you're doing is reinforcing the negativity in the world. Remember we create our own reality and it is not your fault if your parents or carers harbor problems which were later taken on by you, they are responsible for their problems and they are also responsible for themselves. Once you give a belief back it is in their hands to do something about it although in reality most parents and carers are not interested in discovering what holds them back, but that doesn't mean you have to carry the baggage they never learnt to resolve. It doesn't have to be your problem anymore.

7

'You are not responsible for what was done to you as a
defenceless child, but you are responsible for taking positive
steps to do something about it now!'
Susan Forward

In this chapter when I refer to parents I also mean carers or those
responsible for your long-term (and short term if you were
fostered) care.

Who Is Responsible For Your Childhood?

When we think back to chapter one and remember the section
about denial and rationalization, we see here the largest blocks to
grasping who was responsible for your childhood. So many
people either deny that what their parents did was in any way
alarming, or rationalize why they did it. This is especially true if
you see your parents as ill, inadequate or with many problems of
their own. Yes maybe it was hard for your parents, maybe they
were poor, maybe they were mentally ill, maybe they didn't mean
it. The point is whether they meant it or not, are sorry or not, you
have still been affected if not damaged at some level - and they are
responsible for this. They were your parents and they had a duty
to take care of you. If you were abused, if you were hit, if you
were criticized, if you were neglected or abandoned - they are
responsible. This doesn't mean they can't be understood and
perhaps forgiven in time, maybe they can but for now you have to
understand where the responsibility lies. When you clearly see
that your parents were adults and accountable (no matter what
problems or misfortunes stalked them) and you were a helpless
child, you will finally be able to let your pain, grief, or anger
emerge. While you are still saying, "But it wasn't their fault" or
jumping to their defence you are not allowing the inflamed
material from your past to surface. This is because when it does

you feel guilty and tell yourself you're over reacting or not being tolerant or are even ungrateful. Yet this has really nothing to do with it, not putting liability where it really belongs is a way of avoiding internal work. This means we say, "Ok you did nothing wrong which means my problems are not to do with you, so if they do not stem from the past then there is no cause, that's good because I do not want to find the cause which may have something to do with you. Mmmm, hold on I don't want it to be about you so I'm going to keep in this cycle of denial and meanwhile I could try pills, support groups, or some other super-ficial treatment that way I can pretend to be getting better and you don't have to be answerable, yes that sounds good I'll do that." Most of society is not having this inward conversation consciously, but outwardly it is being acted upon. Sadly most of society say, "It wasn't about my parents, it wasn't about my past, I was born like it" or "It's to do with something else." This narrow mindedness is what keeps mankind afflicted so don't let it keep you afflicted. Don't become the sacrificial lamb that keeps everyone 'safe' and 'happy'. While families act like this nothing gets resolved, when nothing gets resolved no one grows, nothing changes, stagnation set's in, every day's the same, it's a wasted life. You deserve so much more than this.

So let's look at it this way, your parents intention is irrelevant. Whether they intended to hurt you or not matters very little. You may know they did not intend to get it wrong or you may know they did, what matters here is that it happened. You were affected, this is what matters now. And because you were affected you have to resolve it, and to resolve it you have to know that your parents were accountable and you have let go of denial. It starts here. This does not mean your relationship with your parents has to suffer (unless they are still treating you like a child or are mistreating you in some way, then things have to change), but it means you have to gain a new perspective.

If you were hurt, abused, damaged or affected by someone

other than your parents, then that person and your parents are responsible. Your parents were responsible for your care every day (even if they were absent from your life). So if a teacher was able to persecute you, a relative was able to abuse you or a foster parent was able to criticize you that person is accountable, and so are mum and dad. This is because they should have been looking out for you, should have been there for you to talk to, should have been there to make sure you were ok. Even if their work took them to India, or they were crippled, or left the family home, were alcoholic or just too busy - they were responsible for you. We create our own reality and so we are responsible if we can't be there for our children. Even if it sounds a bit harsh or too much to expect we have to bypass that for a moment. I know life is life and things happen, people get taken away, things go wrong, everyone suffers at some point, but the point here is your inner child has no awareness of what life is really like. They don't know how difficult it is to be a single parent, to be broke, to be angry, to feel helpless or hopeless as an adult. They don't understand that mum won't let dad visit, or mum has to be at the hospital day and night to look after baby brother, or dad feels worthless and needs to have affairs. Your inner child has anger, pain or hurt and these feelings have to be acknowledged and released. This means just for a while you must get unreasonable. You must throw reason out the window and say things like, "I don't care if you died mummy you left me alone," "It doesn't matter if you were depressed Daddy you still hurt me," "I know mummy moved away and you couldn't find us, but I'm still angry with you," "I know you had to go out to work but my child minder still abused me," "I know you didn't know that Daddy touched me but I still hate you for not protecting me," "I know you thought the teacher's harshness was for my own good but I am so angry at your limited attitude" and so on. This way of viewing things helps your inner child immensely because their thinking is linear. They think mum and dad should have been there for them even if you were adopted, fostered or your parents had a seemingly reasonable excuse for not taking care of them. This matters not to the child who expects and has always expected their parents to be the ones to give guardianship to them. Any lack of guardianship, for whatever reason, is a betrayal to the child. When the child has worked through this 'unfaithfulness' then you the adult can encourage them to see the reality of the situation, if appropriate (what I mean by appropriate is helping the child to understand when a parent didn't intentionally mean to hurt them, not always if a parent did intend it, as stated before no child is ever expected to condone an adult who deliberately harmed them), but this can only happen when the child has dispelled their animosity and is ready to see things in a new light.

'The greatest grief's are those we cause ourselves'
Sophocles

Self Blame

As touched upon throughout the book we seem to be accustomed to self-blame. This also prevents us from seeing that our parents are amenable. It also means you can blame yourself and avoid inner work. If you're saying, "I'm bad," "It's because of me," "I should have behaved better" etc. It's like saying, "There's no way to solve it because I'm defective." This message has been internalized by your child because often children do get the blame or blame themselves, and it is being used by you to avoid the real issues. The real issue is you must understand who is responsible, acknowledge it, accept it and free your inner child from a guilt and self- condemnation. To do this you need to speak to your inner child, or remember the following list by Susan Forward when doing an inner journey. She states;

You were not responsible for:

1. the way they neglected and ignored you

2. the way they made you feel unloved or unlovable
3. their cruel and thoughtless teasing
4. the bad names they called you
5. their unhappiness
6. their problems
7. their choice not to do anything about their problems
8. their drinking
9. what they did when they were drinking
10. their hitting you
11. their molesting you

and I shall add some more;

13. their divorce
14. their leaving you
15. their death
16. their inadequacies
17. their moods
18. their unfaithfulness to their partner
19. their poverty
20. their being held back or lack of freedom
21. their need to adopt or foster you
22. their inability to show you affection

Please include anything else you have felt responsible for.

Then Susan advises you repeat the exercise but precede everything on the list with 'My parents were responsible for.......'

So Are You Responsible For Anything?

It would be very tempting, especially if you are very angry with your parents, to assign everything to the people in your past and put your feet up, but it doesn't work like that! Why? Because nothing will change. We have to remember that blaming others is dis-empowering, so its ok to understand who is responsible when you were a child but when you're an adult your problems then become your responsibility. In some ways it may seem unfair that someone else caused your troubles but now you are responsible for sorting them out, but that's the way it is. If you keep blaming your parents and do nothing about your issues they won't go away, because although they caused them, they can't make them better - only you can do that. It is up to you to shape up your life, you are 100 per cent responsible for your happiness. No one can give that to you. As talked on earlier you create your reality and what you focus upon becomes your reality, so if you walk about blaming others, feeling angry with others and accusing others you just get more of the same, and that same thing is feelings of helplessness and disempowerment. The only way you are going to overcome your childhood distress and your current agenda's is to take complete responsibility for them as they stand now. That means to take responsibility for your health, your depression, your fears, your anger, your thoughts, your hang-ups, your addictions and so on. Your carers were responsible then, but it's up to you to get better now.

This does not mean you won't have days where you want to blame your parents, teacher or whomever else. Sometimes the only way to truly get anger or grief up is to be in a state of condemnation, to accuse, admonish and tear into. This is a normal part of healing. You may even find it difficult to let go of this state, and find recrimination a necessary place to be. All the time I was angry about my past, I was blaming my parents. They went hand in hand. It wasn't until I had truly resolved the anger then I could let go of blame. This process for many probably feels inescapable, yet there has to come a time when we put it to rest. We have to see that blaming and accusing others of how our life is running will only hurt us, not the other person. So let it be an issue if it helps, get angry, write letters, shout at the imaginary parent in the chair telling how they've messed up, bring it up and let it out. But always remember at the end of the day the resolution to your problems is down to you. If you don't reach this juncture then you may well continue to create the same problems, negativity and disablement. The only way to take control in your life is to take full responsibility now. This means saying, "Yes I was hurt, neglected, abused, abandoned or something else as a child but that was then, now I wish to attract happiness, fulfilment and peace, blaming others sabotages this and keeps me in a state of victim consciousness. I do not want this state, so I take care of myself, I learn from the past and I realize only I can heal myself, I refuse to give my power to others any longer."

Confronting Parents/Carers

Before addressing this section I'd like to say that I'm aware that some of you reading this may have only minor problems to deal with and for the most part your parents may have acted responsibly and lovingly, and your childhood was good. When I talk about confrontation I am focusing more on parents who were continually inadequate, absent, cold, controlling, abusive, humiliating, alcoholic, neglectful etc. This does not mean you may not want to talk to your parents about some things that happened to you, even if it seems small. Even small things can have a big effect. In this case your parents will probably continue to act lovingly and support your concerns, in fact they would be more concerned if you hadn't mentioned it. If this is your parents approach then your very fortunate and the following steps may not apply. If you were not so fortunate then please read on. Also recognize any possibility of denial if you are thinking of skipping this section, as mentioned earlier we often 'forget' how awful our parents were and wear rose tinted specs to avoid the pain and pretend our parents cherished us.

So you may understand that only you can heal your current state, and you also understand that your parents/carers are accountable for your childhood. If the healing process is to develop many of us need to confront our parents/carers directly, telling them what happened and how it affected us, then and now. This is to say, "Look you were responsible for me and I need you to know what happened and how it made me feel, and how it still makes me feel." Now at this stage of the therapy many people say, "I couldn't possibly confront my parents!." At first it is a daunting prospect. Some people will feel no need to confront, which is fine, my only caution is if you're taking problems out on your partner, friends or children or your constantly talking about the wrong doings of you're parents, then you may harbor a desire or need to talk directly to your mum and dad. Also if you're saying things like, "I wish I could tell them what I'm going through," or "I wish they knew what it was like for me as a child," then confrontation is going to be good for your progress. I only encourage clients to confront their parents if it is going to help the client them self, and for most confrontation is key to letting go and moving on. It can also create dramatic and positive changes. These changes include;

Self-empowerment - especially when you relationship with your parents is imbalanced, like parents who continue to control, intimidate or criticize.

Increased self-respect - especially if you've never been able to stand up to your parents.

Change in perspective - which means you stop blaming or being angry with your partner, children, dog etc.

The laying out of new rules - especially good if your parents are interfering or treat you like a child.

Feeling liberated after facing your fears and telling them the truth - especially if they are in denial or have minimized what happened.

There are many more positive outcomes to confrontation and everyone's experience of it is unique in it's own way. Yet some confrontations may not always bring the results, in the long term, you had hoped for. We shall look at this in more detail shortly.

Once you make the decision that confronting your parents is inevitable for your recovery and progress it is very important to do it when you are ready. This readiness may not come for a while, you may start with, "Nope sorry can't do that!," which becomes, "I think it will help but I'm scared" then, "Right lets do it I can't wait any longer."   Confrontation for many is scary and others are afraid of upsetting or hurting their parents (even though some of these parents showed no distress when hurting them as children). Much of these feelings are the reverberations of the inner child and this is why confrontation is best when you have done much inner work and have a well-established adult self. This means your time helping your inner child has allowed you to grow and become your resourceful, balanced and strong grown-up self. You only really get to this place when your inner child is no longer in charge and you have found, and grounded, your grown up presence. At this time you will feel more confident, self assured, and not held back by your childhood fears and feelings of inadequacy. You will also be able to see who was responsible for your problems as a child and will no longer be blaming yourself. When you are at this place (or at it most of the time) you are in a good position to confront. This is because confrontation requires you to be strong and focused. It requires that you are able to handle your parents rejection, lack of apology or responsibility. You are able to cope with their denial, saying they "Can't remember," or determination to blame you as a child. Some parents get angry, cry, go into 'poor me' mode or manipulate you by saying things like, "Why are you bringing this up now, can't you see I'm stressed," or "Your gonna make your mother ill bringing up the past, its just so selfish." Most parents will do anything to defend themselves and make you feel bad, especially if they are inadequate parents anyway. They are not going to change their ways just because you are ready to. This is why you must not expect too much, and you should expect them to react defensively and negatively. Of course on the rare the occasion parents may say they are sorry, or want to know more, or want to help. Some parents may think about things after the confrontation and realize they were wrong, and try to make amends. Which leaves you in the position to decide what to do.

When confronting parents it is essential to have realistic expectations and to understand your reasons for doing it, and these reasons are listed above. It is also important to remember that your confrontation is successful because you had the courage to go through with it, even if you didn't get out of it what you had hoped.

So what are your options when considering this encounter? Well you can either arrange a meeting with your parents or you could write them a letter.

> 'Fortune favors the brave'
> Terence Phormio

Arranging a Meeting

Meetings should be conducted in a private not a public place. Your own home, rather than the home of your parents may give you added strength. If they cannot travel to you perhaps you could hire a hotel room local to them for a few hours. If you are in therapy your therapist may be happy to facilitate the meeting and give you support, although its unlikely your parents will attend if they know they are going to be confronted about past events with your therapist looking on. In this case you don't have to tell them, remember this is for you and your progress is more important than your parents pride. Whatever the case your therapist will (or should) always act professionally and with courtesy toward your parents. She/he is there to make sure you are heard, not to do the confrontation for you.

Before the confrontation it is always a good idea to practice what you are going to say, and the points you want to bring up. Your confrontation will probably not go exactly as rehearsed but what you prepared will still be in the back of your mind, and you don't want to leave realizing you had forgotten something important. You could always take your notes with you to refer to if this helps. Then you need to decide if you are going to see your parents together, assuming they are both alive and its practical, or separately. This depends on you, your parents and your situation. For example, if your mother still does not know your father abused you may want to speak with her alone. If it helps you could always see them separately then arrange another meeting to see them together. Be warned though parents often collude and will enlist denial to maintain the equilibrium they feel safe with. They may also concoct some kind of verbal assault or prepare to make you feel responsible, so seeing them together in the first instance is often favored as they will have little opportunity for these time wasting and diversional tactics.

The meeting itself

It is very normal to feel very nervous before meeting your parents. This is why it is essential to be in a relatively stable place before the confrontation, otherwise those old feelings of helplessness, guilt, fear etc will take over. This is because questioning your parents actions goes against the grain of society, considering we are supposed to respect our parents even if they didn't respect us. Well times have changed and nowadays you have every right to say, "Why?." The fear may also comes from your innate reluctance to hurt your parents, cause them distress or stand up to them. This is further exacerbated when your parents treat you as though you are betraying them, which they probably will. They may become overwhelmed, talk down to you, say you have no respect, try to make you feel guilty, or insult you. They may become angry, shout or throw things about (if you feel there is a threat of assault then do not go ahead with the meeting, instead you might want to try the letter writing alternative -as below). It is always best to expect the worst from your parents, after all if they were always so concerned for you and not themselves, always listened, always supported you, respected and cared for you neither of you would be in this position. This is why rehearsing for all eventualities is indispensable and being at a good place mentally is crucial. If you can remain calm and focused while your parents' cry, shout, collapse or blame you, you will experience a moment to be proud of. As Susan Forward says, "What's important here is not their reaction but your response."

Before the meeting begins it is important you have your parents agreement to hear you out. This means they do not interrupt you until you've said your piece. After this they can have their say. If they continue to interrupt, won't listen or become too abusive tell them you'll have to leave the room. If this happens you can always reschedule or write them a letter instead.

From *Toxic Parents* I have condensed some typical reactions (with ways you can respond) that come up during a confrontation:

'It never happened' - Parents will use denial or poor memory to avoid their own feelings of inadequacy or anxiety. They'll insist that your allegations never happened, or that your exaggerating, or your father could never have done such a thing. Alcoholics reinforce this by drink-induced memory lapses. Your response: 'Just because you don't remember or were not aware of it doesn't mean it didn't happen'.

'It was your fault' -These parents are almost never willing to take responsibility for their destructive behavior. Instead they'll blame you. They will pull up a list of how difficult or bad you were as a child, and how you created the problems. In variation to this they may blame your current circumstances by saying, 'Why are you attacking us when your real problem is you can't hold a job, control your child, keep a husband etc'. This may even come disguised as sympathy.

Your response: 'You can keep trying to make this my fault, but I am not going to accept the responsibility for what you did to me when I was a child'

'I said I was sorry' - Parents may promise to change, to become more loving, to be more supportive, but that's often just a carrot on a stick. Once the dust settles, the weight of the old habits takes over. Some parents may acknowledge what you say but do little about it. The line most often used is, 'I've said I'm sorry, what more do you want?'

Your response: 'I appreciate your apology but that's just the beginning. If you're truly sorry you'll be available to me when I need you and you'll work through this with me to make a better relationship'.

'We did the best we could' -Those parents who either were inadequate or were silent partners to abuse will frequently deal with confrontation in the same passive, ineffectual ways as they've traditionally used to deal with problems. These parents will remind you how tough they had it and how hard they struggled. In some senses you may feel compassion for them, but you must not put their needs ahead of your own. Your response: 'I understand that you had a hard time, and I'm sure you didn't hurt me on purpose, but I now need you to understand that the way you dealt with your problems really did hurt me'

'Look what we did for you' -Many parents will attempt to counter your assertions by recalling the wonderful times you had as a child and the loving moments you and they shared. By focusing on the good they can avoid the dark side of their behavior. They'll say things like, 'This is the thanks we get' or 'Nothing was ever enough for you.'

Your response: 'I appreciate those things very much, but they didn't make up for the beatings (constant criticism, violence, insults, alcoholism etc)".

'How can you do this to me?' - Some parents act like martyrs. They'll collapse into tears and express shock and disbelief at your 'cruelty'. They'll act as if your confrontation has victimized them. Of course it may be sad for parents to face their own short-comings, to realize they have caused their children significant pain. But their sadness can also be manipulative and controlling. It is their way of using guilt to try to make you back down. Your response: 'I'm sorry you're upset. I'm sorry you're hurt. But I'm not willing to give up on this. I've been hurting for a long time too'.

It may be your confrontation is about someone else hurting or affecting you and your parents were not there. In this case you need to assess how your parents lack of input impacted you. For example, if you were abused and they didn't know, this doesn't mean you should be any less angry with them. Or you may have been bullied but felt you couldn't confide in them. Whatever the issue if the problem was bad enough to disturb you and they were not available emotionally or physically to hear you, or to pick up on the signs that you were in distress you have a right to be angry. This is very important and should not be disregarded just because they didn't know, if you're angry about it and angry with them they need to know now. This is also true for victims of sexual abuse who were threatened with imprisonment or violence if they told their parents. Of course the parents are not directly responsible for this, but they are responsible for their child's safety and whereabouts at all times. This means you may understand your parent's position as an adult, but your inner child may have felt let down and unprotected. If so, this is what you need to verbalize to your parents. So if your parents say, "We didn't know" your response could be, "I understand that and I realize you were not directly involved, but I still need you to know how it affected me and how angry I have been that you did not realize I needed help and how you failed to protect me."

Not all confrontations have to be difficult, in fact many are calm. What you have to remember is the confrontation is not a time for you to argue with or punish your parents, or an opportunity to get something back from them. It is a time to tell the truth about what they or someone else did, how you felt about it, how it affected you in the long term, and how you want things to be now. For extra assistance meditate for a few seconds before the meeting and ask your higher self to be with you.

'I was angry with my foe: I told it not, my wrath did grow'
William Blake

Writing a letter

Letter writing is good because it allows you to write to anyone, so long as you have their contact details, who hurt or troubled you as a child. It is also a good way to let your parents know what happened to you, and how it has affected you, without direct confrontation. Most of my clients are only interested in writing to parents and not others like abusers or teachers as they are afraid of repercussions, or having contact with someone they'd rather not see again. With this you have to use your own discretion. So for this section I shall be directing the letter writing to parents only.

When you sit down and draft your letter you need to make sure to cover all aspects, that is; to outline what they did or didn't do for you, to tell them about others who hurt you in childhood (if you want to say at this stage), how all of this felt for you as a child, how it affected you growing up, how you feel now, and how you want things to be from now on. This is a helpful structure to work with but you can tailor it to your own needs, or add other areas that come up. You may find you write the letter many times before it feels right to send it, and if you find yourself getting heated or angry whilst writing return to the letter a few days letter, as you may find you want to re-word some of it. Remember letters are to be written primarily by your adult self, so maintaining a clear and assertive stance is a good way to show your parents that you are serious. Also you may want to write a separate letter to each parent as you may have differing issues with them. Here is a letter by Marian to her mum;

Dear Mum,

This letter may come as a shock to you as we seem to always get along, the truth is I don't feel like that underneath and I want you to know what is really going on. I'm tired of being false just to please you. I'm tired of being false to protect you. It is affecting me too much and I have learnt lately that it is ok to put myself first.

I want to tell you about my childhood, and how it has affected me. Now your always saying don't bring up the past but I need to talk about this. Talking about it is the only way I am going to recover from it.

When I was little you spent far too much time away from home, I later learnt you weren't at work but at the pub. Because of this I had to be looked after by Auntie Lucial and Uncle Jeff. It wasn't a very nice environment, Auntie Lucial was ok but Jeff hit me a lot and sometimes got weird. Whenever I went to them after school he made a point of peering through the crack of the door to watch me undress, he was so creepy. Then he would fly into a rage with Lucial and whack me. I always felt so uncomfortable there, I hated it. I felt scared and alone and I seemed to wait hours for you to pick me up. Then when you did you didn't look yourself, always swaying and laughing and pretending you were pleased to see me. If you missed me that much why didn't you ever pick me up from school and spend time with me. Anyway when we got home you just slouched in front of the tele and didn't even ask me about my day, you showed no interest whatsoever. How could you have done that to me? Didn't you love me? Then the weekends were awful with you dragging me around to pubs or me watching you get drunk at home. What a life! I felt so alone, so unwanted, so worthless. I always wished I hadn't been born, I hated my life and I hated you. I used to watch my friends having fun with their mums, their mums were always there. I felt so embarrassed, you didn't even come to our plays. Since then life hasn't been good, I always seem to end up with drinkers who neglect me like you did. I feel so bad about myself and find it hard to hold down a job because I'm so tired all the time, and depressed. I hate taking the anti-depressants but I'm afraid I will go down hill if I don't keep taking them. My whole life is a mess, everything. I have no money, no friends, no decent man and no decent job. I wish I could stop eating as I hate being overweight.

I'm finally getting help now and am beginning to realize just what an effect my childhood has had on me, no wonder I'm in such a mess!

I want you to be sorry for what you've done to me, I would like you to say sorry too. I want you to see just how damaging this has all been and how much you've hurt me. You have to take responsibility for neglecting me and leaving me at Uncle Jeff's. I am your daughter remember.

When I see you I don't want you to remind me of how fat I'm getting, or how awful I look. I don't want you to criticize my clothes or make me feel like a failure. All of this serves to make you feel better, because deep down you harbor so much guilt. I'm not having it anymore. I want you to think about why I comfort eat, why I'm poor and why I have no confidence, because it all links back to my past. It all links back to your treatment of me. It is not me who is failing, it is you who has failed. You failed me mum and I want you to realize that and start treating me with respect. If you can't do this then I'm not sure how the relationship can continue.

Please reply

Marian

Marian never did get a reply, instead her mum sent Marian's sister round to tell her what a fuss she was making. Marian tried to have a meeting with her mum but she never showed up, and when they spoke on the phone her mum always hung up (one of the problems if you're thinking about confronting by phone). Marian wrote other letters to her mum but she never replied. It seemed whatever Marian did she couldn't get her mum to acknowledge what she had done, or even to say sorry. Because Marian's mum was unwilling to help or change Marian decided to stop contact with her, this is because the whole episode was affecting her ability to progress. In the end she just had to let go of any hope of recompense.

Prepare for change

Once the confrontation is over there will be a gap until you talk to your parents again, or a gap from them reading your letter and contacting you. In this time your parents will have time to think and so will you. They may come to the conclusion they need to change if they fear losing you, or they may get angry and not bow down for a while or they may not bow down at all. You on the other hand would have gone through a major shift, and this may bring feelings of relief, strength, euphoria, satisfaction or anxiety and confusion. Either way you have made progress and are redefining yourself. You have stood your ground and have said things that you've needed to say for a long time, you have told the truth. The truth is what ultimately sets us free. It is important that your parents know what happened to you, how you felt and how it has and how it is still affecting you. There is nothing wrong with this, why should you carry it all? Let them take responsibility for your past and realize for yourself that it wasn't about you but about them. One of the biggest hurdles my clients face is acknowledging that their parents failed, not them. It is time to look at this situation clearly and to stand up and say, "This wasn't fair". To also understand that you are a person with feelings, and your childhood affected you! You weren't a child who was never phased, or never needed to cry, or just got on with it -even if your parents wanted to believe it. So it's ok to take a stand and say, "What about me?". Any anxiety or confusion will probably be based on your fear of rejection or disapproval from your parents, so it's important to remain focused on why you needed to confront and to remember that it's all part of your growth and transition into adulthood. So whatever the outcome it will be best for you. And once the dust has settled you will probably find talking to your parents becomes a much more open and honest business as you feel more empowered (even if they are not pleased with it).

Sometimes the impact of a confrontation can have implications for your parent's relationship, although most will collude and justify each other's actions. This happened to Paula who told her mother about the abuse she suffered as a child. The abuser was her dad and they were still married. After this revelation Paula's mother asked her dad to leave and they went through a period of separation. Paula felt guilty about this and had to realize if her parents broke up it was her fathers (and mothers) responsibility, all she did was tell the truth. In living a lie she had to spend time in her parents company pretending everything was ok, and she couldn't do this anymore, it just didn't fit the healthy and well person she was becoming. In time Paula's parents did get back together. Now Paula sees her mum by herself but has mixed feelings about it, she can't understand why her mum went back to the man who abused her own child. I'm sure in time Paula will work out what to do.

> Truth is the cry of all, but the game of few'
> Bishop George Berkeley

Other family members/friends and entrenchment

After bringing the truth to light you may get mixed reactions from siblings or those close to your parents. Brothers or sisters could have potentially different reactions. Some siblings may have been with you throughout your journey sharing a similar path, or for some it may be new news and they may still support you. Some may even confirm your memories. Some may not remember your childhood so clearly and feel bemused or confused by it all. Others may be in complete denial and feel angry at your accusations. Those in denial come in two forms, those who remember and those who don't. The latter who remember but deny it are either too afraid to face it or are entrenched in the parental relationship. That is they are too emotionally involved, or are too dependent upon, or are gaining something else from the relationship to risk giving it up. They don't see that their emotional health is being compromised by this involvement they are still acting like children in a detrimental kinship. As some parents get older, especially the more unhealthy ones, they can begin to realize that their impending fragility, or the potential loss of their spouse, requires support. That is they may recognize that their survival or care is most likely guaranteed if they befriend or make amends with their children. I know it sounds shallow but we are talking about the kind of parents who have continually, intentionally or not, hurt their children. These parents' motives are always self-centered, but it is from this narcissistic self-absorption that entrenchment can occur. These parents begin to become the parents they never were, always being there for the child (who is now an adult) showing support and being concerned. Entrenchment can also come out of a need to control or through guilt about past actions, as egotistic parents fear not being needed or being abandoned themselves, or they have a deep dissatisfaction with their own lives.

Some adults choose to be entrenched with their parents and constantly seek their approval and in doing this put their parents needs first, others can be entrenched because they continually react to their parents and become angry or have strong negative feelings. If your parents have any control over you then your still entrenched. Remember healthy balanced parents won't want to have control over you, although you may still have concerns over their wishes for you. This is normal and a part of family bonding and closeness. It is when you are putting your needs above your parents, feel it's up to you to placate them or make them proud, worry your parents wouldn't survive without you, avoid telling them things for fear of disapproval, fear standing up to them, fear hurting them, feeling guilt as if you have always been wrong, or feeling you have to honor them, then your relationship is entrenched and imbalanced (don't worry if you are still doing any of this to some degree becoming 'un-entrenched' takes time and you are working at it, even if you still get sucked in). So any sibling who argues your case, even though you know you both had a rough childhood, may in some way be entrenched (or in denial) and you have to accept that they may or may not overcome this. Either way your health cannot be jeopardized and if your siblings do react negatively to your confrontation, or the whole family goes into turmoil you have to remember; you are facing and speaking the truth which makes you the most healthy member of your family. Plus no-one has the right to shout, hurl abuse or insult you just because you are doing what you know is right and is best for you, you cannot bury your feelings or needs anymore just to keep the rest of the family happy. And remember just because other family members don't remember or it didn't happen to them doesn't mean it didn't happen!

Only confront if you think it will aid your growth, and help.

Most of us are uncertain about confronting at first but if you feel you can't hold onto the information any longer, or feel its only right to tell your parents the truth, or you feel you are becoming affected through hiding your feelings, then confronting would be a good idea for you. It is something you need to think about, and needs to be addressed when you are prepared for any outcome, such as other family members rejecting you or in the rare instance your parents cutting you out of their life. Either way confronting can be highly rewarding, so long as you keep your perspective clear.

Dealing with elderly, sick, disabled or deceased parents.

If your parents are elderly, sick or disabled you may be more reluctant to confront them about past issues. Everyone's situation is unique, and just because they're old, frail, ill or wheelchair bound doesn't mean a confrontation cannot take place. Obviously in these situations an air of caution is recommended, as you don't want to cause more harm to a parent, even if you're angry that they harmed you. So I always say you have to assess it yourself, do you think your parent will come to more harm if you talk openly and honestly about your feelings? If you do and are worried about causing deterioration then you may have to write a confrontation letter that you don't send, or imagine your confronting your parent with role-play. That is to pretend your parent is in the room and you talk to them, or talk to their photo. Some find this approach very helpful but if it is not enough then you may have to reconsider talking to your parent. Confrontation is a strong word, if you were to approach it as 'talking about your childhood' in a mature yet softer way would this help? Sometimes we think a parent is weak or unable to handle things and then can be pleasantly surprised by their response. One of my clients spoke to her elderly dying father about his treatment of her as a child, because of his imminent need to face his own mortality he had become a much calmer and appreciative person. Their discussion allowed him to say sorry and put closure on what had plagued him for years before he past away. My client felt liberated by finally being able to tell him the truth before he died. Some parents may still react negatively, but their general poor health does not worsen. In fact in most cases if you confront your parent quietly, but still saying what you need to, it doesn't have a detrimental affect whatsoever. So although you may be unsure please don't allow yourself to repress feelings if they truly need to be expressed, in the end your parents are still responsible for what happened to you as a child and you cannot keep putting their needs above yours.

Confronting a parent who you care for and live with may mean you have to move on from that if feelings become too fraught or if resentments are high after a confrontation. This does not mean a confrontation should not happen, or should be avoided. This situation is a little more complicated though and you may need to find out what assistance your parent is entitled to if things turn sour and you have to leave. Many people experience a great sense of guilt if they fall out with the parent they are a carer to, but it is not your fault. If your parent decides to be angry or hostile toward you with no sense of remorse for your past then that is their choice, it is not your responsibility to take care of them or to try and placate them for their benefit. You are only responsible for yourself. If you are looking after your parent because; you feel obliged, they expect it, out of guilt, out of fear, you don't want to upset them, you don't want to let them down, you think you should make their lives better etc, then you need to re-evaluate your life. You were not put on the earth to take care of your parents unless it fills you with joy. If it fills you with joy and does not come from a need to get something from your parents or obligation etc, then that's great! If you are filled with resentment or guilt and long for other things, then you must follow your heart. You must do what is best for you, you must stop putting yourself second and ignoring your needs. Plus if your parent hurt, abused or damaged you in anyway as a child they do not deserve your care now, unless they are truly sorry and want to make amends and their self-reproach is genuine. Yet then it is, of course, still up to you. When people undergo therapy it means working through a process of growing up, this usually results in the ability to detach from parents. This doesn't mean you don't care about them, but if they've hurt or detrimentally affected you leading your own life without their direct involvement becomes natural, needed and welcome.

If your parent is deceased then role-playing, or talking to your parents spirit (that is to talk to them if you believe their presence is in the room), or confronting a photo may be required. Some people write a letter then burn it, as you watch the smoke filtering up you can imagine your parent is somehow receiving the message. The most effective technique though is to confront your parents' grave, if you can get to it. It may seem strange but writing a letter and reading it aloud, or just talking from your heart to your parents grave can be extremely powerful!

A happy future with your parents?

Your future relationship with your parents is now up to you following the confrontation and their reaction to it. Or if you didn't confront them you still need to think about what's best for you. If your parents still treat you with little respect, have no regard for what you've said, are still abusive and are unwilling to change then you may decide to keep your distance or cut off contact all together. This may sound harsh but if your interactions are difficult, painful or jeopardize your emotional health then you may need to take drastic action. In this case Susan Forward suggests a separation period of three months, "This means no meetings, no phone calls, no letters. I call this 'detox' time because it gives all involved a chance to get some of the poison out of their system," she writes, "and to evaluate how much the relationship means to them." You may even find after this trial period your parent's behavior improves, if not then permanent separation may be the only way for your well being. This, of course, is not an easy choice, it is a painful choice were you will naturally need to be supported, probably by a counsellor, through a grieving process. Once over this, which will take time, your new found freedom will bring unprecedented rewards, like those described by women who rebuild their lives once they leave their abusive husbands.

Of course permanent separation from your parents is the last resort, unless you were sexually abused by one of them most people opt for the superficial but cordial approach, especially if your parents want to be cordial to you but don't necessarily want to give you anything more, or are unwilling to change. Sometimes a compromise is called for. Its like saying, "Well you know all this stuff now but you don't really want to help, that's ok because I'm just better for telling it to you. I don't want to go back to how things used to be but it would be a shame to break off contact. So it would suit me to see you on occasion and stick to neutral topics. This also means treating me as an adult and letting me run my own life without your opinion on it" these new rules will have to be voiced to your parents. What's important is not to expose yourself to pain or degradation anymore from your parents, so it's okay to stay in contact so long as your emotional health is not compromised.

You may be one of the fortunate few whose parents react in a positive way. That is they want to listen, to understand and to help. Even a small inclination of this is positive and can be worked upon. Some parents may still be distressed or confused, but are genuinely sorry and want to make some amends. This may take time as you talk through your feelings, and discuss issues over time. It's like your re-assessing your relationship and setting new rules, new ways of communicating and fresh boundaries. They can also learn how to discuss their feelings and how things were for them when you were a child, not to make excuses but to talk it through. It can be an overall growing experience, which can be of great benefit to you and your family. Some families have even gone into family therapy following a member confronting, to aid communication and share feelings. This is quite unusual though, and many parents say they want to begin a new or appear remorseful, but soon settle back into old ways of behaving and acting.

'Forgiveness does not ask that you forget something happened'
Burt Hotchkiss

Forgiveness - Yes or No?

One thing I always stress and that is you don't have to forgive to find peace, create the life you want, be happy, be wealthy or find freedom. It is not a precursor to health, and sometimes it is used as a way to avoid inner work. Often people say to me, "I've forgiven my parents, there is no need for me to get angry about this," to then find they are still feeling depressed or anxious. Forgiveness, if you choose it, is best left to a time when you feel well consistently. That is the majority of your emotional work is done, you've got angry, raged, cried, grieved, faced the pain, worked through issues, addressed beliefs, overcome problems, healed your inner child and so on, in other words when your through your 'therapy'. Now therapy can take many years, as you find you can reach even higher levels and discover even more about yourself through analysis. You are a complex and amazing creature, healing takes time - lots of time. As you heal one issue another will transpire, this is normal and it just means you are now ready for the next concern. Life, or your unconscious, will not throw everything at you at once although it may feel as though it does! As time goes on the problems become less intense and you feel your true self emerging. It is at this time you are ready to think about forgiveness. In the meantime lets just clarify what we mean by forgiveness.

In a religious and spiritual context forgiveness means to

absolve others who have hurt us, no matter what they've done. Now this concept is ok for Jesus, The Dalai Lama and Buddha but will it work for you? People who can see the bigger picture, show mercy, know they have forgiven (in fact believe there is nothing to forgive) and feel at peace with it are very enlightened beings. They have reached a stage of growth, spiritually, mentally, and emotionally, which allows for this. Until you have reached this level you may choose to address things in a different way, just until you're ready. Enlightenment often comes some time after 'therapy' and is achieved through meditation and connecting to the All That Is, God, Goddess or the Oneness. It is when your true 'spiritual' journey begins, and you will be guided to this. This does not mean you cannot forgive at this stage, but it should not be at the expense of your emotional well being.

Forgiveness is not saying, "Ok you hurt me but now you're off the hook" it means "Ok you hurt me and I won't forget what you did, you are still responsible for that, but now I am ready to stop hurting about it, stop talking about it, stop blaming you and move on." Forgiveness is really about moving on, it is not saying, "Ok it doesn't matter I'm over it now" because it does matter. It was a problem for you as a child and may have had crippling effects as an adult, so it does matter, but you are now ready to move forward with your life. You are ready to say, "I forgive you but you are still responsible for that time in my life." You are also saying, "I'm at peace about this" and this statement is the only way you'll know if you are ready to forgive. Are you at peace about the way your mum criticized you? The way your dad abandoned you? The way your mum hit you? The way your uncle abused you? Until you are without question at peace about the past you are not ready to forgive. You must honor yourself, you must put yourself first, you must slow down and not allow denial and the need to get through it quickly to sabotage your future happiness. Forgiving too early and then avoiding the inner work is a form of denial it's like saying "I've forgiven mum and dad now, so that means I'm ok" - are you? This for many is the easy way out and means they don't have to suffer any pain, fear, anger etc although they are still left with problems like negative beliefs and childhood conflicts. So don't put forgiveness first, put it last or until you're ready. It won't speed things up, in fact it could hamper your progress if you forgive but still feel angry, aggrieved, stressed, numb, panicky etc.

Forgiveness can be full of empty promises too if you believe it will bring you peace and everyone will love each other. The only way you can achieve peace and harmony for yourself and others is for you to work on yourself and for them to work on them self. So the best thing to do is to keep on working on yourself and let everyone else get on with their stuff. You may find the only way to create peace is to move away from others who are not peaceful, as often forgiveness means, "I let this go, but to maintain my inner composure I must let you go."

On occasion you may find yourself 'unforgiving' as family problems re-erupt or your problems spiral again, and this is ok. It's best to 'un-forgive' and go back to it later, rather than hold onto something which is not serving you or allowing you to acknowledge your true feelings.

In conclusion I still maintain that you do not have to forgive to feel well (although it can help with long term inner peace). Forgiveness is a personal issue and comes from a place of the healed, and cannot come from a place of pain unless the pain is denied.

Giving Up The Need For Revenge.

So we may have to put forgiveness on the shelf for another day, but what about the need for revenge? Letting go of the need for revenge is not forgiveness, it is something you need to do to help yourself and it needs to be addressed as soon as possible. Again when I say as soon as possible I am not asking you to compromise, so in your own time is imperative. In other words you have to be ready, but you also need to let it go as soon as you are ready and not hold onto it. The need for revenge is laced with anger, fear and hurt, a very powerful combination. You may have fantasies about revenging your parents which is all a part of the process. If your parents hurt you and you day dream about hurting them, this is ok. It's therapy in action so long as you are learning and growing from it. That is if you wake up in the morning wanting to burn your parents house down, you take action inside yourself instead. You ask your inner child to show you why they feel angry and work through the issues. Burning your parents house down will only get you into trouble, it may make you feel better, of course, but its not the right action to take for you. You may feel your parents deserve an arson attack, but do you deserve the repercussions? In my experience revenge always hurts the person who wanted the revenge, and it's not worth it. So revenge fantasies must be played out in your mind, during therapy, when writing letters, with your inner child, whilst bashing a pillow or smashing plates, and not actualized. It is a signal that shows you are still angry and should be used as a way to heal, not to hurt. When the anger work is done your need for revenge should diminish.

Naturally we all want to revenge those who hurt children, paedophiles, rapists, abductors, murderers, these kind of damaged humans send a shiver down any 'normal' person's spine, maybe not a shiver of fear but a shiver of rage and disgust. We could look at this in two ways, we could say it was their childhood which made them like that, which is true but cannot absolve them from responsibility as an adult. Or we could say their lack of inner peace, childhood pain, internal rage, feelings of low self-worth and subconscious guilt will always come back on them in the end (I'm not talking about Karma here but erupting childhood damage). Like my father who developed diabetes, suffered from strokes, had his leg amputated and died from a heart attack alone in hospital, probably with bed sores (a life end which in some way reflected his upbringing). Now, I had 'let go' of what my dad did before this happened but if I had still been full of rage and seeking revenge, this outcome would have probably pleased me. So, if someone seriously hurt you as a child, imagine how awful their life is going to turn out because of their internal program. It cannot be any other way, unless they've had therapy of course, if not, they will suffer, they will hurt, they will be having a bad time much of the time. They will keep recreating their terrible childhood, they will have bad dreams, they will have to deal with horrendous emotions, usually fear (unless their emotionless in which case they'll never know love or joy etc), things will go wrong for them, they will be lonely even if they live with others, life will not be good even if they act as if it is. If this helps to satisfy your need for revenge then take it as truth. The inner always manifests the outer.

8

'I saw grief drinking a cup of sorrow and called out, "It tastes sweet, does it not?" "You've caught me", grief answered, "and you've ruined my business, how can I sell sorrow when you know its a blessing?"

Grief

If your childhood was particularly traumatic, painful or difficult then grief is a natural process you will need to bear. The grief is about the loss of your childhood. If anger is the stem and denial the diminishing flower, then grief is the fruit. It is the natural result of awakening. This is because you're gradually emerging from the slumber of denial and looking head-on at the reality of your childhood. This reality can be shocking, enraging and very sad. As children we adopt denial or repression to deal with our pain, as adults we use these defense mechanisms to cope, but when we really want to change and address our problems these defenses have to fall away, what we are left with is the realization of what really happened. When this kicks in the grief for what we have lost can be overwhelming. Of course, the nature of your own childhood will determine how much grief you will need to endure, although the process cannot be measured and everyone is affected differently by their past. Grief is very intense, just as intense as the loss of a loved one but this time you may be grieving for the loss of innocence, happiness, carefreeness, nurturing, love, protection, trust, care, concern, validation, feeling special, being cherished, cuddles, warmth, a loving home, safety, good feelings, spontaneity, good parents, a good education and so on.

As you work with your inner child what you need to grieve over will come to light, you will suddenly or gradually have a strong realization of how things should have been, what you truly deserved in infancy. When this happens you may feel angry and intensely sad all at the same time, when the anger subsides the tears will flow. Sometimes you may have periods of crying, or it may last for a few days. Sometimes it seems never ending or so painful you will never recover, but you will recover and it will end. You need to give yourself time to understand how much you lost and then come to the stage of acceptance. This process must not be rushed, and getting any support you can during this time will be very helpful. Even if it's just to talk about how you feel. Once you have moved through this you are going to feel much stronger, and more able to let go of the past. Grieving is essential to letting go and moving on, and when the work is done you will have a clearer focus on what you want for the future. You will feel a change in yourself for the better, it will feel as though you have moved through a terrible storm but now the landscape is calm and the sun is shining on you. Grief is akin to cleansing, and after any cleansing comes rebirth and revival. You may find your life restructuring itself to be in line with the new you, which is really your true self. This is the person you really are before your mind and body got messed up by your parents, or others. Your true self is infinite, unlimited, wise, balanced, joyous, peaceful and very happy. Your true self will emerge as you support yourself and your inner child through your bereavement, anguish and sorrow. It is a crucial step in the course of healing.

The heartache may be interchangeable between you and your child self. At times you may visualize yourself holding the child as he/she expresses their pain, or you may find its you the adult who needs to cry. For the most part it will be both of you, so if you go through a period of acute anger or crying don't forget to see how your inner child is too. They may well be in need of a hug.

Loving Yourself
Even if our childhood was basically good most of us come away with a reluctance to love ourselves. This may be because society tells us it is arrogant to show self love, or even conceited. Or we

may have had the message from our parents that we our unlovable, useless, less than, not good enough or a failure. Yet if the inner creates the outer loving yourself is as essential as feeding yourself. If you in anyway doubt, dislike or criticize yourself it will be reflected back at you in your outer reality. Any form of poverty, poor housing, lack of support, stress, materialism, rejection from a loved one, poor pay, loneliness etc is a sign of not loving yourself. Those who truly love themselves, that is take care of them self and appreciate their worth (not those who think their 'it' as this comes from low self esteem) create happy and fulfilled lives. Loving yourself is the key to creating the life of your dreams. Many people appear to have the life of their dreams, but if there is no self-love or self value there will be much missing under this facade of success. You can have it all, but to make it happen you must first learn to love yourself. That is to say "No" to your parent's cruel words, to understand the abuse was not about you or to know that the past was not your fault, as well as many other past circumstances which may have eroded your self esteem and prevented you from seeing yourself as wonderful. As noted before, 'All negative thoughts are an illusion, all positive thoughts speak the truth'. If its one thing that brings us down it is our negative thinking, that internal voice of the ego which tells us we can't, we shouldn't, it's impossible, if only, but.., its difficult, ought to, should, must etc. So the steps to loving yourself are:

Hush your Ego's negativity

The ego has two negative outlets, one is negative feelings and the other is negative thoughts. The negative feelings we most often experience are fear, depression, guilt, anger, resentment, frustration, grief, dissatisfaction and jealousy. Most of these feelings are used as a shield for protection. For example, fear can stop you attaining success so you won't make a fool of yourself, depression can prevent you from going out and being with others so you won't get hurt, anger is used to hide fear, resentment pushes down guilt and so on. These protective feelings reveal the depth of your unresolved childhood conflicts and can only be settled by taking them back into the past. As you continue to heal yourself you will then find negative thinking much easier to deal with. When you feel good you don't usually have negative thoughts, your thoughts are generally joyous and carefree. Negative feelings and thoughts go hand in hand, so the better you feel the less of a hold these pessimistic thoughts will have over you. Negative thoughts are also protective, if you expect little of yourself you won't be disappointed. All negative thoughts have their roots in the past, these thoughts are what people have told you or what you have decided due to other's behaviors. This means you could think, "I'm useless, nobody likes me" because your parents said it, or you could think it because dad left and you decided it was your fault. Its important to locate the source of negative thoughts, Gold Counselling (TM) as outlined in chapter 6 is especially good for this, and its also important to remember that negative thoughts do not speak the truth about you even if your convinced they do. Address your beliefs and then change your thinking. Each time you become aware of a negative thought decide you're not going to think like that any longer, and put a positive thought in its place. In The Secret by Rhonda Byrne she states, "Your life right now is a reflection of your past thoughts. That includes all the great things, and all the things you consider not so great. Since you attract to you what you think about most, it is easy to see what your dominant thoughts have been on every subject of your life, because that is what you have experienced". Don't worry if you find you have a stream of negative thoughts because every good thought can cancel out a hundred bad ones, and because manifestation takes time you can change your future reality before those gloomy thoughts have an impact!

Fear is the most common negative thought as we seem to be good at expecting the worst, if we're not sure of an outcome our ego kindly tells how awful its all going to be. If our new love doesn't call back we assume their feelings have changed, if we can't find our child in the supermarket we panic about abduction, if we can't pay the bills we live in terror of losing our home. The ego loves to dramatize. To deal with this let your fear bubble to the surface, visualize that unimaginable outcome. If you have the flu see yourself painfully dying, see your funeral and your family in tears, really wallow in it your ego will love it! Then imagine putting it all into a bubble and let it float away, then see the outcome you want - not the one you dread.

Be kind to yourself

Personal growth is a journey, and on this journey you have to learn to be patient with yourself and you have to accept mistakes. This means recognize your imperfections and let go of getting it right all the time. You must learn to be kind to yourself, even if no-one ever has been. You deserve kindness, consideration, love and happiness. The first person to give it is you, to yourself. As you do you will find the outside world will do the same. So slow down, wait for results, go with the flow, know you are guided protected and loved. All too often we are taught that mistakes and failures are bad, but they're not. Mistakes and failures are learning curves which allow us to reach another level, they always come to serve never to hinder. So if you've been made redundant, had an accident, or suffered a crisis it is for the best. You may not see the good at first but you will in time. So don't berate yourself see yourself as a channel of learning, you have come here to learn, grow and have fun. Life is meant to be an adventure, not a mess. And treat yourself, buy some new clothes, go to the cinema, buy some jewelry etc. Learn to give to yourself and life will too. If you haven't much money take time out to rest, or start a course, or be with friends. Do things that make you feel good, it's ok to pamper yourself, you deserve it. Also learn to relax, just sitting and quietening the mind for ten minutes a day can be extremely beneficial. There are also many wonderful meditation courses available which you can do at home if you prefer.

Those who come from a dysfunctional family have often learnt to be self-reliant and don't expect support, so if you need some extra help ask friends or join a group who share similar problems. If there isn't one locally you could always set one up at home, this is a great way to find companionship and strength. The group is not to focus on the negative but to support each other and share experiences as you work on dispelling your problems.

Being kind to yourself also means saying 'no' sometimes, and especially saying no to obligations that feel like a burden. Being helpful to others is all part of human kindness but its when you are being of service at your own expense you are not being kind to yourself, you are being a people pleaser. You are abusing yourself to be liked and accepted. So you now need to take steps to stop, you need to learn to put you first. Putting you first is about self-respect and it is crucial when you are learning to love yourself. So if you are doing something which feels like a burden, is detrimental to your life or feels heavy find a way to let it go. It is not selfish or uncaring to want to make your life better, it is your God given right! When I first started to say 'no' to things that felt heavy and too much I was pleasantly surprised by the response of others (although not everyone will be pleased with your change in attitude) I found people saying, "That's ok, don't worry, I understand your tired etc" I thought, "Is it ok, really? Oh thank you!." Its like I finally began to see that some people are very understanding, and really didn't want to burden me. I'd been so busy trying to do my best to be liked that others thought I was perfectly happy with helping everyone out. Now I help when it feels good for me, I have the time or I just sincerely want to help, without needing something back or to be liked.

Forgive yourself

Begin to think about all those things you reprimand yourself about. Those areas you feel you failed at, didn't do, made mistakes about, mis-judged, got wrong, hurt others because of, hurt yourself through, were weak about, couldn't resist doing, things backfired because of, or regrets. Places and times you wish you could go back to and make it all right. You may have many remorseful memories, or there may be that one issue that still haunts you. If you asked a good psychotherapist to investigate your claims of guilt or failure-ism, they would ascertain within minutes that it was not your fault and it was linked to your childhood thinking, which is mainly unconscious. It doesn't matter what you've done no matter how awful, your behavior, feelings, and thinking at that time were being controlled by a force much stronger than your will. That force is your unconscious mind, and residing there in your unconscious is your inner child. So any pain you have created for yourself or for others is the creation of your inner child. That part who feels inadequate, angry, fearful, anxious, sad, lonely, worthless, resentful, guilty, paranoid, judgmental, jealous and more. The hurt inner child will always create drama, trauma, pain and hurt because this is a reflection of its inner world, what is within is without. Eckhart Tolle calls this aspect the 'pain-body', he writes. "Many acts of violence are committed by 'normal' people who temporarily turn into maniacs. All over the world at court proceedings you hear the defence lawyers say, 'This is totally out of character' and the accused, 'I don't know what came over me'. To my knowledge so far, no defence lawyer has said to the judge, 'This is a case of diminished responsibility. My client's pain-body was activated, and he did not know what he was doing. In fact, he didn't do it. His pain body did.'"

If you perpetrated a crime, were the victim of a crime, investigated the crime or were in any way involved in the crime you some how created it. Each player played his part, and the more painful your part the more relation it has to your pain body. Your inner child. This doesn't mean we are not responsible, but we can get reasonable with ourselves. The easiest way to do this is to understand ourselves, to show compassion for our human-ness. All adults are at the mercy of their unconscious, if we don't look into this part and heal our inner wounds we will create situations which produce guilt, fear, struggle, anger, remorse, unworthiness and anything else which reflects our childhood turmoil. This is why when we do things we later can't fathom we say, "But I really don't know why I did it, I'm so sorry." And because so much of society is 'unconscious' they are also ready to blame, condemn and judge with little insight into the unconscious forces at hand. If after a court hearing the judge sent everyone into therapy, most of the prisons would be empty!

So think about self-forgiveness, even on small things. Really look at the situation and from past exercises in this book begin to understand why you behaved this way, felt this way, or thought this way. Once you truly understand self forgiving becomes easy, and the same is true for forgiving others. If we all took a magic pill that allowed us to see the bigger picture in every ones situation it could allow for world-wide mercy and eventually - after healing -peace. So to procure your own inner peace know your story and know yourself, once you do this you will see you have nothing to blame yourself for - you are in fact innocent. This doesn't mean you can go out tomorrow steal a million pound and say its because I wasn't nurtured! As you become more conscious you are alerted to become more responsible, so if you feel the urge to do something hurtful to you or others but you know its driven by an unconscious impulse then getting help is the next step, rather than acting on the impulse. Of course if you are overcome by your unconscious treat this as a learning curve and affirm to yourself that you are now taking steps to resolve the problem and heal yourself.

'If someone wishes for good health, one must first ask oneself
if he is ready to do away with the reasons for his illness. Only
then is it possible to help him'
Hippocrates

Take care of your body

Another step to loving yourself is to be aware of what your
putting into your body. This awareness increases as your inner
child heals and your body begins to show you the effect of the
negative and unwholesome substances you are taking in. Through
the years of healing I worked through a laxative and alcohol
addiction, as I began to move through the pain and distorted body
image and develop my feelings of self love I was able to cut these
substances down and let them go. As mentioned before alcohol
(and drugs) is an emotional pain killer, so when you resolve the
pain you can begin to work on the addiction. Your body will help
with this too, as I became more peaceful my body tolerated
alcohol less and less. This meant even a small amount of drink
would produce headaches, dehydration and irritability the next
day, its like my body was urging me to stop, in fact forcing me to
stop. The consequences of such a small amount of liquid didn't
seem worth it, so it wasn't long before I quit.

A part of me still sought comfort so chocolate became a
problem. It was more of an issue at night when I felt least safe,
living in a bungalow as a single mum seemed to plague my
dreams as I had nightmares of myself and my child being
attacked. I'd then wake up in a panic and head for the chocolate
bars. Sometimes I'd eat two or three before I felt safe again, the
feeling of dread and fear was so overwhelming. It took time for
me to understand it as most incidences of waking in terror and
chocolate bingeing were hazy becoming lost in my night time
trance state. I resolved to fathom it though and one night just
before the sweetie binge I wrote down my feelings, crying and
with shaking hands I scribbled, 'unsafe, vulnerable, open to

attack, frightened, unprotected' and as I linked up the list the three primary feelings were unsafe, vulnerable, open to attack. I closed my eyes and sensed myself in a dark room, I was very, very small, a baby. The room was so dark I couldn't discern any shapes, I felt scared, hungry and alone. I began to cry but no one came, I think my mum was asleep. I cried for a long time then I noticed the slither of light around my door. The door opened and someone came in, it was my dad. He picked me up, "Just shut up" he screamed. Then he took off my clothes and proceeded to smack my back and bum several times. His smacks stung and the pain was awful. Then he put me in the cot undressed, walked out and slammed the door. I laid in the darkness in shock and disbelief, tears streaming down my face. As I sat by the table as an adult recalling this memory I still felt the pain on my bare back and buttocks, as well as the shock and fear I felt as a baby - it was all making sense. After this incident I never felt safe in my cot as a baby at night and I longed to cry out to my mum to protect me all night every night. I craved my mother's warmth and breast milk, I just wanted to be with her all the time it was the only time I felt safe. It dawned on me as an adult that chocolate represented the rich sweetness of my mother's milk, it was the only thing that could calm me down when my fears of attack as an adult surfaced night after night. In my childhood memory I rewound the scene and entered the room as my dad was picking up the baby me. I hit him with an invisible ray and he was paralyzed, I took my frightened child self from him. As the paralysis wore off he came at me and I hit him with my giant all powerful fist, and he fell to the ground unconscious. I reassured my baby self, held her close and told her she was safe. We left the room and I returned to the kitchen I was in as the adult with a vivid image of me still holding the baby Michelle. She looked very content. After this my fears evaporated and I gained control of my chocolate indulgence, which then meant I began to lose weight.

So always look to understand the reasons you need drink,

drugs, certain foods, cigarettes etc, to help you get off them. They are serving you for a reason, they are protecting you, but this fictitious protection carries a price. The sooner you unravel your psyche, let go of this false security the sooner you can begin to take care of your body.

Simplify your life

If your life is cluttered with busyness, friends, family, chores, social occasions, children's activities, work or shopping etc. Then you may want to stop and re-evaluate. Any kind of busyness, or having to keep busy is linked to avoidance of feelings or acknowledging a situation. If you were to completely stop for one week what issues would come up for you? If you had time to think what would you need to face? Your empty marriage, your unfulfilled life, your depression, your past abuse, your loneliness, your low self worth, your weight problem, your fear of intimacy, your anger, your feelings toward your parents, your fear of not being important? What would it be? Having to keep busy denotes a problem at a deeper level, for those at peace do not have cluttered lives. Clutter is created for a reason, and as you heal those reasons may become more evident, or you may need to stop and take time to understand what it is your avoiding. To do this schedule time to yourself this week, even if its only for an hour. Then in that hour do nothing, just sit. Do not watch TV, smoke, eat or drink. Just hang up the phone and sit in complete silence. As you do you will begin to feel restless, your ego will say 'this is boring!', ignore it. The feeling you experience isn't boredom, its discomfort. This discomfort preceeds an insight or a feeling. Let it come, you have something to learn.

Another way to simplify your life is to release clutter from your home, work place, car, even handbag or wallet. Clutter holds negative energy, and a cluttered home means a cluttered head. If you want help to remove a blockage or proceed more easily with your healing then de-clutter your environment. That means get rid of anything you don't use, need or value. You'd be surprised how much clutter you have around you, and how much better you begin to feel when you release it. But start small, don't exhaust yourself. Maybe one day do the kitchen cupboards, and after a few days do the lounge. Pace yourself, and take your time. As you unshackle yourself from this stuff you may find your personal growth takes a leap, as de-cluttering is a catalyst for change. As you clear your environment your head will mirror the action, and you may find insights, ideas, feelings or childhood memories begin to appear as your mind clears itself of clutter too.

An important thing to remember is not to refill your home, work place etc with clutter once you have cleared it. Often clutter can build up so having regular clutter clearance days are helpful, but what you really have to be aware of is your shopping habits. How many times do you go out shopping and come back with something you don't really need? To keep yourself clutter free when shopping say, "Do I really want this?, Do I really need it? Will it just add clutter to my home in time?." Also ask yourself, "Am I shopping to avoid an issue or feeling I need to face?."

Have fun and nourish your soul

In the busyness of life many of us forget to have fun and to nourish our soul. Having fun means doing things that bring us joy, like taking up a dance class, being with friends, going on holiday, playing with your children, painting, taking up a sport. Anything in fact that you really enjoy and feel enthusiastic about. These same activities may also nourish your soul, although for many nourishing the soul means attuning to things that bring you peace and joy at a deeper level - experiences that are deeply resonating, allow your heart to expand and make you feel connected. For me its the wild coastline of the west country in the UK, the sunlit pine forests with vibrant waterfalls and the expansive views of the Exmoor hills and valleys. These places make me feel alive and energized as if filled up to the brim with the beauty of spirit and life, my heart beats faster as I take in, with excitement, the awe of all the beauty around me. It truly nourishes my soul. Nature is most people's chosen favorite for nourishing the soul as it calls to our wild and free self, the expansive part of our conscious which knows no limits and is eternal, just being on a beach, walking through a forest, or being in a garden can fill them with warmth and joy. Many experience this delight when listening to certain music, reading poetry, being creative, visiting a sacred place, reading a book, being with certain people, meditating or just sitting in solitude and quietness. Nourishing your soul allows you to feel awesome in a way that nothing else can.

So are you having enough fun? What do you enjoy doing? What is fun for you? What gets you excited and enthusiastic? Or what helps you relax and unwind? Are you nourishing your soul? What makes you feel expansive and full of joy? What fills you up with peace and happiness? If you don't know what do you think it would be? What do you feel drawn to when you need replenishment?

All too often in our society we seek solace from the TV, drink, food, negative conversations, feeling sorry for ourselves, shopping, clubbing, busyness or doing anything else which distracts us but actually does nothing to maintain our joy and well being. As you grow and change, and commit to this, you are going to find your old ways of coping become less and less interesting or necessary and your soul will begin to show you what you really need and what can bring you infinitely more bliss than a superficial soap opera or a bottle of wine. So begin now to think about how you can bring more fun and play into your life, and how you can nurture your deepest being.

Take responsibility

When you become truly responsible for yourself, your life and your feelings you become empowered. Blaming others is dis-empowering, and you become a victim. If you want to feel better, work out your patterns, understand your creations, follow your dreams you have to be responsible for all of it. This way you get to be in charge and call the shots, at first it may seem scary but it is very liberating! After inner child work and grief you are in a much better position to take responsibility and create the life you want, not the one ordained by your past. So use every situation to grow and go higher, not to blame yourself or others for creating the situation or illness but to learn from it. Understand that every bad feeling, horrible situation, ache or pain is a message telling you to learn something and grow. When you adopt this approach, and see that everyone in your life has just come to play a part in your production you take responsibility and your life becomes unlimited. Responsibility is the ability to respond, that is you have a choice. You can respond and say I've created this, what can I learn? Or you can un-respond and say this is not my fault I'm doing nothing about it. When you begin to take care of yourself properly you have to understand a fundamental universal law and that is you create your own reality. And as you heal, let go of the past, and begin to nurture yourself you are going to find your reality improving, as the inner you creates your outer world, but this furtherance will only be enhanced by self responsibility and self awareness.

'In every moment the universe is whispering to you.
There are messages for you carried on the wind.
There is wisdom for you in the morning songs of the birds outside your window and in the soft murmurs of an ebbing sea.
Even ordinary everyday events in your life carry communications from the realm of spirit'
Denise Linn

Understand the messages
Signs and symbols as well as synchronicities are everywhere.

Getting literature on what these signs mean is invaluable. For the last two days a small sparrow has been knocking on my consulting room window, I opened my window to see if he wanted to come in but he just sat on the frame continuing to tap. Because the tapping went on from morning to dusk for two days I guessed the sparrow had a message for me, but what? It took me a while to decipher it. I thought it has to do with my consulting room, the place I see clients. A few days before the tapping began I decided not to see clients after the summer and to begin work on another book, following this I cancelled all my advertising. Yesterday when I was seeing a female client the tapping became louder, the bird began to flap about by the window as if the need to communicate was becoming more urgent. At this time I was thinking how I'd miss seeing clients whilst writing. Then the penny dropped! What if I wasn't supposed to stop seeing clients, was that the message? With this in mind I decided to cut down on my advertising, rather than stop it, and see less people. That way I could do both. I felt much better after this realization! Of course it is debatable as to whether the sparrow knew he was trying to communicate with me but Native American shamans believe spirit communicates with us through animals as well as many other things. All occurrences have meaning and significance, every event is connected to another event. I'm sure you have your own stories of how synchronicities have shaped your life.

Messages also come to help us heal, and this is why accidents, crisis and trauma occur. They are just signals to help you discover more about your hidden dimensions. When you begin to see that spirit is always trying to communicate with you the communication becomes much easier, and looking to spirit for direction becomes a natural part of life. The signs become more evident as you tune into them, like a blocked sink, a flea infestation, a broken glass, or road blocks. Or they come in your dreams, as insights, via nature, through some ones comments or even something you watch on TV. A friend of mine was avoiding some inner work she needed to do on the death of her father, but every time she turned on the TV she saw programmes on death and bereavement. One of the programmes she felt compelled to watch and spent the next week in tears, but it was just what she needed to do. Spirit is always ready to help us with our healing.

Give your problems to spirit

When you have a problem which you've tried to resolve through inner child healing, parts therapy etc but have not come up with a solution or have not found peace with it, then it is time to give it up to spirit. This is especially helpful if your in conflict about a decision you need to make or are not sure how to acquire something you need. Like Terry who didn't know how to manifest the money to pay for a course he really wanted to start, he worked through it with his rational mind but because this part has limited solutions it was not proving helpful. Terry listened to a tape I recommended by Denise Linn called 'Golden Sphere of Spirit' which guides you to a sacred grove with a spring fed pool, in the pool are golden spheres. As you take out each sphere you imagine placing your problems in them, then you watch as they float higher and higher into the sky. Here the angels and guides work on them to help resolve the concern. After just a few days Terry had a letter from the housing benefit agency saying they had been underpaying his rent and he was due some back pay, problem solved!! Brenda also found the technique helpful when she couldn't locate the cause of her asthma saying, "I just meditated asking spirit for guidance, a few days later I read an article about a girl's father who died when she was eight. She said she had suffered with asthma and a chest rash ever since. At that moment the memories of my own father's death when I was five began to surface. I finally began to realize that my asthma was about my unresolved grief, it was amazing!."

You have to trust that there is a solution to every problem, and that every childhood trauma can be healed. Its also about having faith that the universe wants to give you clarity on a problem and it also wants you to heal and become free of what holds you back, all you have to do is ask.

'What lies behind us, and what lies before us are tiny matters, compared to what lies within us'
Ralph Waldo Emerson

Follow your dreams

"As we grow up, our Hard Time society 'teaches' us that fairies are just make-believe, that it is childish to believe in miracles, that grown-ups know all there is to know, that we must not be so foolish and gullible - and we learn to put aside our magical selves, and let go of our dreams. Bit by bit, the world of magic fades away, until all that is left is a misty memory which occasionally draws a nostalgic sigh from a tired and harassed adult" Gill Edwards.

To live in this reality is a shame because in truth dreams do come true, we just have to believe we can make them happen. We all have a purpose and that purpose lies in what makes our heart sing, what we would still do even if we didn't get paid for it. Our life's work. We all have unique skills and we all have something to offer which no one else can. Each one of us has a talent or a way of doing things which makes us inimitable, and special. We have come to find out what that talent is and to make our wonderful contribution to the world. Think of something you have always wanted to do but you don't have the time, money or confidence. For some its running a boating club in Australia, for others it may be setting up a business in printing, child care or healing. For others it may be becoming a parent or missionary. It isn't about what your parents want or what you think you should do its about what feels right for you, and you know or will be given direction if you ask spirit what that is.

Following your dreams is also about attaining those things that will make you even happier and fulfilled. It may be acquiring wealth, having a soul mate, traveling, losing weight, a beautiful home, being stress free or at peace, being able to drive, going on a jungle trek or healing from an illness. Everyone's dreams are varied and tailored to them, and each dream is possible no matter how big or small. All you have to do is think what your dreams are. On a piece of paper write a list of what you'd really like, how you would like to see your life and yourself in a few years from now. And don't put limits on the list, even if it feels silly or unobtainable. They are only out of reach because you don't believe you can have them, but the truth is you can. So imagine your most perfect life, and leave nothing out! Following your list you may want to think about what is stopping you from taking those necessary steps toward those dreams. Is it your lack of confidence, lack of faith, feeling not good enough, or something else? Working on your dreams means working through blocks and healing your inner child. It is a journey of self discovery and changing attitudes. It means ignoring the skeptics and those who expect differently from you, its about believing in yourself and following your heart. Its knowing that miracles can happen and will when you begin to follow your bliss. A great motivator in following your dreams is the DVD of *The Secret* by Rhonda Byrne, newly released and selling rapidly, this powerful film will eliminate any doubts you have about getting what you want. I highly recommend it.

My deepest fondest wishes to you

When I get to the end of a book I've enjoyed, found helpful or interesting I close it with a sense of loss. Now as the author coming to the end of this book also fills me with a sense of loss too, as I have enjoyed writing it and talking to you! I too hope you have found the information helpful, enlightening and easy to digest, as the subject of psychotherapy is by no means light but it can be satisfying. So well done on your journey so far, and may the techniques and teachings in this book give you invaluable help in your travels. Personal growth is an ongoing voyage which takes courage, wisdom and motivation, so great work so far. May the rest of your travels be healing, joyful and liberating and may you have everything you have ever wished for in time. In my meditations I shall be sending you love and light to help illuminate your path, and remember your guides are with you every step of the way too. Love and Joy, Michelle.

'People are like stained glass windows. They sparkle and shine when the sun is out, but when the darkness sets in, their true beauty is revealed only if there is a light from within'
Elisabeth Kubler-Ross

'Who would attempt to fly with the tiny wings of a sparrow when the mighty power of an eagle has been given to him?'
The little book of Miracles

APPENDIXES I

Directory Of Common Physical Ailments And Their Emotional Link.

All physical ailments and illness are linked to thought and emotions which will have their roots in childhood. To begin to understand what that link might be we have to know what our body is trying to tell us, and the list below gives some indications. If an explanation does not 'fit' with your particular problem then you need to go with your own intuition or ask your higher self for answers.

Abscess - Anger brought on by feeling powerless and frustrated. Often linked to feeling suppressed anger with someone from your past.

Acne - Created to keep others away due to low self esteem and general self dislike. Fear of losing control, conflicts over sexuality and intimacy. Repression of childhood hurts.

Agoraphobia - Fear of death or emotional instability rendering you powerless (related to a fear of change). Most cases were dependent on their mothers feeling responsible for their happiness.

Aids - Inability to accept sex gender with a refusal to love themselves for who they are. On a cycle of guilt and disappointment which leads to self punishment.

Allergies - Internal conflict related to your love for someone, it may be that you cannot tolerate them any longer or fear becoming dependent on them. The same also relates to situations. Allergies in children are a cry for attention when the parents are in conflict.

Food allergies state you resist pleasures in life, and animal allergies mean you feel easily attacked by others. Allergies also occur when you need attention and concern from others. Also seeing the world as a threat.

Alzheimer's disease (also Dementia) - The need to escape from present reality, often afflicting those who have taken care of everything and have felt others haven't cared enough for them. This illness takes away the responsibility allowing them to now be cared for, deep down they seek love and nurturing.

Anemia - Losing your love of life. Feeling discouraged and hopeless.

Angina - Fear of grief or upsetting experiences. Feel trapped and overwhelmed by concerns.

Appendicitis - Insecurity and dependence on others resulting in repressed anger and feeling trapped. You are literally bursting to let your feelings out but are afraid.

Asthma - You want to take on too much not allowing for personal limitation. You want to appear strong to gain love. Repressed grief.

Back pain - Lower back (base of spine) fear of losing your freedom when helping others. Lower back (waist region) feeling unsupported because you feel you should do everything yourself to acquire things. Upper back (from waist to neck) emotional insecurity needing others to do things for you to feel loved and safe. Feeling someone is on your back all the time. Suppressed hurt and self pity. Perfectionism and taking life too seriously.

Bad breath - Tremendous internal pain. Thoughts of hatred,

vengeance or anger directed toward those who have hurt you. These thoughts shame you and you try to ignore them.

Baldness - The need to control others, believe you are correct and have little regard for others opinions. You want and love to be obeyed.

Bedwetting (persistent) - Underlying emotional stress usually related to a fear displeasing father or a father figure. The child (or adult) has very high expectations of themselves due to parents (mainly father's) messages.

Blood disorders - 'Blood relative' (or those you see as family) problems and conflicts. Worry and anger issues. Not being true to yourself and enjoying life. Poor self image and self regard.

Bone disorders and breaks - Fear of not being able to support yourself or others. You only feel worthy when others are dependent on you, but fear letting them down. Indicates a fear of authority. Also wanting to break free or postponing an event.

Breast problems - Too motherly over others needs, or worries over taking care of your own children. You expect too much of yourself. Your mothering is related to how you were mothered, there are conflicts here to be healed.

Bronchitis - Family issues, quarrels or crisis. You may need to branch out and find independence from your family but feel guilty.

Burns - Guilt and self punishment. Repressed anger.

Cancer- Tremendous emotional hurts from childhood usually relating to rejection or humiliation. Repressed anger, hurt, guilt, grief and revengeful feelings toward your parents are festering inside causing the cancer. Feeling hopeless or helpless, lack of meaning or purpose.

Cellulite - Blocked creativity due to a lack of self confidence and self worth. You may have many inspired ideas but fear expressing them. The need to control others and prevent them from expressing their own unique self.

Cold Sore - Judgmental toward the opposite sex or partner. Cold sores allow you to avoid intimacy, maybe due to anger.

Common cold - Wanting to keep someone away from you who you dislike, or feel walked over by. You may be mentally congested as you want to walk before you can run and try to do too much. Your belief system (which is false) may be telling you colds can be caught if you've been around someone with one. Self pity, suppressed tears, need for a break, confusion and uncertainty. Releasing of toxins.

Constipation - Lack of trust. Inability in expressing oneself due to fear of rejection or displeasing others, or harboring negative feelings about a past happenings and not letting go. Problems with letting go of money or material things.

Convulsions (and Epilepsy) - Anger, self-loathing and hatred toward the self which result in a desire to self harm, unable to love themselves.

Cysts - Unresolved issues regarding sadness or grief.

Cystitis - Frustrations over emotional problems and waiting for others to make it better resulting in unexpressed anger often, but not always, toward partner.

Depression - Unresolved emotional wounds usually relating to the opposite sex parent. These issues are related to rejection, hurt, or humiliation which left you feeling unworthy, alone and afraid. Need to grieve or express rage.

Diabetes - A deep desire to be loved which means you give alot to other's, and want a lot for yourself. You are doing too much to attain things instead of going with the flow, and feel responsible for other's happiness.

Diarrhea - Rejection of ideas or situations which cause you emotional uneasiness. Also poor self image, over-sensitivity, rejection, guilt, fear are all feelings related to diarrhea. Not allowing yourself to be nourished.

Dizziness - When experienced means you are avoiding a situation which is triggering an unresolved childhood memory or emotion.

Ear disorders - Poor hearing indicates difficulty in hearing about other's needs, or not wanting to take advice. Inflammation or infection, internal anger.

Eczema - Poor self confidence resulting in uncertainty and fear, especially about the future.

Eye problems - Fear of losing someone or something so you close your eyes to it.

Fainting - Feeling powerless or distressed in a situation which has been occurring for some time.

Fever - Suppressed anger or hurt.

Flu - Reaching a crisis emotionally and physically because you feel prevented from doing what you want and being who you are. Life is making you feel suffocated.

Foot problems - Feeling stuck or treading water because of fear. Also concerns over losing your job, or needing to slow down in life.

Glands (also Laryngitis) - Swollen glands indicate an inability to communicate your feelings to another causing anger within.

Gout - Suppressed desire to control and inflexibility.

Hay fever - Indicates a suppressed childhood hurt which occurred in the spring.

Headache - Conflict or indecision. Self criticism or trying too hard to understand something.

Heartburn - Not allowing yourself something or someone you have a burning desire for.

Heart problems - Loss of heart in a situation. Blocking the joy of life. Overwhelming emotions. Taking life too seriously. Exhaustion from trying to please others

Hemorrhage - Preventing pleasure in your life and suffering in silence.

Hemorrhoids - Festering stress and fear.

Hernia - Feeling trapped in a situation.

High blood pressure - Anger toward family or partner. Focusing on unresolved past emotional pain. Pressure to make others happy.

Incontinence - Feeling childlike and not equal when with a certain someone. Feeling out of control. The need to let go of emotions.

Infection - Allowing yourself to be invaded by the thoughts and feelings of others which is consuming you.

Inflammation - Internal conflict. Repressed anger.

Kidney problems - Over-emotional and highly sensitive in relation to others and wanting to help creating imbalance. Feelings of powerlessness in a situation. Also high expectations of others.

Liver disorders - Repressed anger, sadness and pain.

Low blood pressure - Regularly feeling you cannot achieve what you want. You listen to your ego's negativity and give up before you even start. Feeling powerless to change anything.

Lung disorders - Underlying deep sadness and feeling suffocated in a situation. Suppressed tears and feeling unworthy of life.

Meningitis - Unable to face a situation which has emotionally shaken you.

Menstrual cramps - Underlying rejection of the female role due to your own mother's life. Rejecting your own femaleness and resenting men.

Migraine - Not being true to yourself due to the influence of others. Conflict and suppressed resentment.

Nausea - Sick of your life situation, a particular situation or someone around you. Or fear of someone or something going on around you.

Neck pain - Inflexibility or lack of control in a situation.

Nose bleed - The need to express emotion, usually tears.

Edema - Conflict between the head and heart, and holding onto emotions. Needing protection. Holding onto the past.

Rheumatoid arthritis - Anger towards others who haven't figured out your needs because you don't communicate them. Self-denigration, bitterness and resentment.

Shingles - Repressed anger and bitterness regarding a situation around you.

Shoulder pain - Too many obligations, feeling burdened, putting others before yourself.

Sinusitis - Repressed anger, tears and grief.

Skin problems - Over sensitivity, worry about how others see you and are self critical, related to underlying shame. Also fear of intimacy and unresolved rejection issues. Boils - anger. Dry - cutting off emotions. Weepy - need to cry.

Snoring - Not able to express yourself or be heard during waking hours.

Sore throat - Pain in swallowing signifies the inability to swallow a situation, person, trauma or upset. Resistance to change. Also guilt about leading your own life and repressed anger.

Stiffness - Inflexibility , stuck in mind-set.

Stomach Ache - Upper region, worry too much over other's welfare. Lower region, worrying too much over a situation

Stroke - Refusing to trust in the flow of life, lacking in spiritual faith.

Teeth problems - Tooth ache or decay on the right indicates unresolved issues with your father, the left your mother. Bruxism (teeth grinding) signals suppressed anger.

Tonsillitis - Being controlling or judging others, or feeling angry and frustrated in a situation.

Ulcer Stomach - Feeling powerless and intimidated by others. Deep seated fears.

Varicose Veins - Taking on too much with a desire to be free.

Venereal Diseases - Underlying shame regarding wanting and having sex.

Virus - Negative thoughts which cause you to feel resentful. Not being your true self.

Vomiting - Being sick of someone. Inability to take on new experiences or ideas.

APPENDIXES II

Sexual abuse is when an adult involves a child in any activity from which the adult expects to derive sexual arousal. This may take the form of touching, inappropriate kissing, penetration, oral sex, using sex toys or aids on a child, prostitution and participating in pornography. As well as being flashed at (exhibitionism), being sexual or having sex or masturbating in front of a child, showing x-rated films or material to a child, taking photographs for sexual reasons, improper use of sexual language or 'flirting' with a child.

According to statistics published by the NSPCC 86 per cent of sexual abuse crimes are committed by relatives or someone known to the child. This could be anyone who has access to the child, like a relative, babysitter, teacher, neighbor or friend. The most common abuser though is the father. The abuser could easily be a policeman, clergyman, counsellor, doctor, shop assistant or anyone in a position of trust. Despite the myth that children are only abused by the drop-outs, alcoholics, criminals etc.

Frequently child abusers look for a child who needs time and attention. So often clients I have seen who have been sexually abused report a lack of attention and validation at home, they are needy for love and affection. They become a prime target for paedophiles because in the first stages of abuse 'trust' is gained. This means the abuser is nice to them, shows an interest and wants to spend time with them. For a child who is deprived of recognition this attention is very attractive. Then the abuser will begin sexual interactions with the child, which may start off as fondling or touching. The abuser will pacify the child by saying, "Lets play a secret game" or "Isn't this fun." The abuse will then progress to other forms of sexual stimulation for the abuser. If the abuser is the father then building up trust may not be required, and they may coerce the child into sexual activity by touching at first or by actively forcing themselves on the child.

Most abusers are men or women with little control or power over their own life, they may feel awkward and inadequate with the opposite sex or peers. Their inadequacies mean they exploit children to feel powerful and in control. They have low self-esteem and are emotionally immature. Many may have an authoritarian background but lack control over their behavior and emotions in their personal life.

The reason sexual abusers are able to continue the abuse is due to their ability to manipulate and intimidate the child into keeping it a secret. The offender will do anything to keep the abuse concealed, one because they want to continue the abuse, and two because they want to avoid the degrading consequences of being found out. Even if they feel justified in what they are doing (in some cases bizarrely telling themselves they are helping the child) they are still aware that child abuse is a crime and sickening to society. This could lead to family and outside rejection, as well as arrest and prosecution. So most abusers tell children anything to keep them quiet (like you'll go to prison, shame the family) despite the long-term psychological damage. Due to this it is estimated that 90 per cent of child sexual abuse goes undetected.

The consequences of childhood sexual abuse can be both devastating and life long, if appropriate help is not sought. Many adults who have been abused as children still feel ashamed, and in some way to blame for the abuse. They spend their whole lives living with what feels like an internal monster, which has to be pacified, repressed and kept locked in their unconscious mind. The symptoms of abuse though may still be evident and what follows is a resume of the problems that can occur: Fatigue, depression, anxiety, panic attacks, inability to concentrate, become bored or restless easily, perfectionism, irrational fears, frequent illness, fear of rape, lack of trust in others, mind in a muddle, relationship problems, change jobs frequently, poor body image, poor self image, over eating and weight gain, malnutrition, poor confidence and self esteem, self destructive behaviors i.e. drugs, fast driving, drinking, taking risks, money problems, treats self badly, hates self, feeling contaminated and ugly, feeling overwhelmed, enter into destructive abusive relationships, desire same sex relationships, eating disorders, sexual problems, insomnia, self mutilation, morbid jealousy, insecurity and self sabotage.

Sexual abuse can be catastrophic, not only because it is such an abhorrent violation against a child, but also because it encompasses physical and emotional abuse too. When a child is being sexually assaulted, they are being physically abused. Some of these children even have to endure extremes of physical abuse too as noted earlier, and for others the physical abuse can be sexually deviant in nature. They may spend years with the fear of being found out, suffer shame and guilt, feel terrified of being abandoned, feel humiliated and out of control, powerless, hopeless and inadequate, feel different to others, dirty and damaged. So it's not surprising that many sexual abuse sufferers also endure much of the emotional abuse that was covered in the previous section. Parents who run a household where the children are being sexually molested are usually inadequate and socially inept adults. Even if they are not perpetrating or have any awareness of the abuse mothers who don't know attract an abusive husband for a reason - usually to mirror their own poor self image and inner problems.

FURTHER READING

Psychotherapy/Self help

Forward. S., Toxic Parents (Bantam, NY, 1989)

Hay. L., The Power is Within You (Hay House, California, 1991)

Jenson. J., Reclaiming Your Life (Penguin Books, NY, 1995)

Parks.P., Rescuing The Inner Child (Souvenir Press, London, 1990)

Parker. J., Raising Happy Children (Hodder & Stoughton, London, 1999)

Peiffer. V., Positive Thinking (HarperCollins, London, 1989)

Philips. G., Gold Counselling (Anglo American Book Company, Wales, 1997)

Proto. L., Be Your Own Best Friend (Piatkus, London, 1993)

Reinhold. R., How To Survive In Spite of Your Parents (William Heinemann, London, 1990)

Taylor. C.L., The Inner Child Workbook (G.P.Putnam's Son's, NY,1991)

Virtue. D., Losing Your Pounds Of Pain (Hay House, California, 1994)

Metaphysics/Spiritual

Ackroyd. E., A Dictionary Of Dream Symbols (Blandford, London, 1993)

Bourbeau. L., Your Body's Telling You: Love yourself! (Les Editions, Canada, 1997)

Byrne. R., The Secret (Simon & Schuster, London, 2006)

Edwards. G., Living Magically (Piatkus, London, 1996)

Edwards. G., Stepping Into The Magic (Piatkus, London 1993)

Edwards G., Pure Bliss (Piatkus, London, 1999)

Linn. D., Signposts (Random House, London, 1996)

Millman. Dan., The Life You Were Born To Live (H.J. Kramer, California, 1993)

Sams. J., Medicine Cards (St. Martin's Press, NY, 1988)

Scott-Peck. M., The Road Less Travelled (Random house, London, 1986)

Tolle. E., A New Earth (Penguin Books, London, 2005)

RESOURCES

For Gold Counsellors in your area contact:

The Institute of Analytical and Creative Thinking (TIACT)
PO Box 115
London N12 9PS
Tel: 0845 257 8358
www.tiact.com

For a current information regarding 'Keys To Freedom'
Workshops, One to One therapy please log onto:
www.keystofreedom.co.uk

Or write to:
Keys To Freedom
P.O BOX 10050
Chelmsford
CM1 9HL

BOOKS

O is a symbol of the world, of oneness and unity. In different cultures it also means the "eye", symbolizing knowledge and insight. We aim to publish books that are accessible, constructive and that challenge accepted opinion, both that of academia and the "moral majority".

Our books are available in all good English language bookstores worldwide. If you don't see the book on the shelves ask the bookstore to order it for you, quoting the ISBN number and title. Alternatively you can order online (all major online retail sites carry our titles) or contact the distributor in the relevant country, listed on the copyright page.

See our website **www.o-books.net** for a full list of over 400 titles, growing by 100 a year.

And tune in to myspiritradio.com for our book review radio show, hosted by June-Elleni Laine, where you can listen to the authors discussing their books.

MySpiritRadio